Left Tuscany

If you were to pick one country that by its very nature embodied ingenuity, art and beauty, Italy would surely be it. Welcome to the country that ruled the world two millennia ago, with an empire that at its zenith reached all the way from Britain to Babylon, leaving roads, modern-day law, mileage and the Latin alphabet in its legacy. *Benvenuti* to the cultured land that gave us the piano and the violin, opera and ballet, and the celestial, exquisitely wrought visions of Michelangelo, Raphael, Giotto, da Vinci and Botticelli that cavort across gallery walls and church ceilings in Rome, Florence and Venice – each one a petal on the blooming flower of the Renaissance.

The art splayed flamboyantly across every town and city is wondrous, but even it cannot measure up to the ravishing allure of the country itself, which sweeps you up in its romantic embrace. Italy's love of indulgence shows in its obsession with *mangiare* (eating). And who can blame it? Parmesan and Parma ham, soft-centred Neapolitan pizza and fresh-fruit gelato, espresso and cappuccino, pasta in a zillion different guises, the lingering ricotta-filled sweetness of Sicilian *cannoli* and the mouth-puckering tartness of *limoncello* – every bite is a revelation, every meal an exuberant, three-hour-long feast. Just you wait.

This book is not your typical guidebook. Rather than describe hotels or restaurants, we want to introduce you to the personality and, dare we say, the very heart of Italian culture and landscape. Which means this book is broken up not into regions or sights, but into five chapters divided by the themes that season Italian life, for visitors and locals alike:

→ **Bravo Italia:** The Italian Icons You Already Love

→ **Tradizione:** Treasured Heritage, Hill Towns & Harvests

→ **Viva Italia:** Modern Life & the Italian Way

→ **Che Sorpresa!** Underrated & Unexpected Experiences

→ **Dolce Vita:** Indulging in Italy's Sweet Life

By leading you on a page-by-page scavenger hunt in this book, we want to show you how, whether you're cruising through the vine-ribboned countryside of Chianti in Tuscany, clambering in the Dolomites, or bustling for the freshest produce at a crowded Sicilian market, Italy will amaze, enlighten and enthrall like nowhere else on Earth. And everyone is welcome to take a generous bite out of it.

...and with that,
welcome to **Italy**

Contents

4

Landscapes & Journeys

Exploring postcard-worthy vistas

Above **Amalfi Coast Road**

Italy is *amore a prima vista* (love at first sight). We're not talking a mere flirtation, but a fully blown, red-hot love affair that grips you from the first instant you clap eyes on its landscapes, which inspire towards the lyrical and profound. Like a scalding-hot espresso shot, such intense beauty is a jolt to the system. The country's insanely lovely spread of deep-cut, vine-blanketed valleys, silver-green olive groves, wild mountains, hillsides frothed with pines and cypress trees, hissing volcanoes, powder-white beaches and medieval hill towns more than justify its nickname of the *bel paese* ('beautiful country').

This is true whether you are swinging along the nail-biting hairpin bends of the Amalfi Coast between ragged mountains and a sea of stained-glass blue, marvelling at the cliff-clinging villages of Cinque Terre, discovering your favourite Roman neighbourhood, or lounging on a cove on Sardinia's Costa Smeralda. Try as we might, we can never convey on paper the romance of a peachy Sorrento sunset, the way the sea spreads out like a blue silk cloth in Capri at the hour when cicadas strike up their tentative drone, or the citrus-sharp perfume wafting from lemon houses on Lake Garda.

Travel here isn't about spectating – this is a country made for embracing life to

Above Matera

its fullest by slow touring, socialising or striking out on foot. Tick off medieval hill towns like rosary beads in Tuscany. Listen for the Duomo's out-of-tune chime sitting on piazza steps in Renaissance Venice, Florence and Lucca in the golden light of evening. Hole up for a day or two in a prehistoric *sassi* cave in Matera. Hike a heart-pumping *via ferrata* (iron road) in the pink-spired Dolomites, an off-the-radar trail in the wild Appenines of Abruzzo, or a path skirting a volatile volcano in the Aeolians. And let yourself fall for Italy time and time again.

Experiences

Food & Drink

An experience to savour

So you probably know that good food is the way to an Italian's heart, but we're not talking fancy-pants cooking: just quality ingredients, a pinch of know-how, a sprinkling of herbs, a dollop of love and generosity that knows no bounds. Carlo Petrini launched the Slow Food movement here in 1986, and today the Italian kitchen still hinges on the Holy Trinity of simplicity, seasonality and sustainability. Primary ingredients are given their chance to shine: be it a San Marzano tomato grown in volcanic soil below Mt Vesuvius, freshly caught seafood hitting a chilli-spiked grill in Naples, or a pungent, richly aromatic *tartufo bianco* (white truffle) unearthed in damp autumn woods near Alba.

The importance the Italians afford to *mangiare bene* (eating well) goes way beyond the need to satisfy appetites. The world grinds to a halt for *pranzo* (lunch), the latest political scandal is resolved with the barista over *un caffè*, a stroll in the *centro storico* detours via the gelateria, the pre-dinner *aperitivo* is a fine excuse to meet friends and gorge on a free buffet. Eating alone? Unheard of. As the proverb goes, *chi mangia da solo si strozza* (he who eats alone chokes).

Delis and markets brim with temptation: silky buffalo mozzarella from Campania, nutty Parmigiano cheese, wafer-thin Parma ham, syrupy balsamic from Emilia

Romagna, ricotta-oozing cannoli from Sicily and Turin chocolate. Not to mention velvety red Barolo, Amarone and Montepulciano wines from the vines of Piedmont, Veneto and Tuscany. Scoff *marinara* pizza, topped with tomato, garlic and oregano, hot and chewy from a wood-fired oven in Naples, crispy *panelle* (chickpea fritters) on Palermo's backstreets, or a humbly delicious meal of *fave e cicoria* (fava beans and chicory) in *cucina povera* country, Puglia. Just remember, flattery will win you new friends and second helpings.

Experiences

Arts, History & Design

Masterpieces: ancient and new

Whether you're talking the immeasurable riches of the Roman Empire, da Vinci's Renaissance masterpieces, Vivaldi's *Four Seasons*, Gucci's tailoring or the va-va-voom of a classic Vespa, Italy has always aimed for the high bar in the arts and design. This is a country that where beauty and culture filter through every layer of society, and the things it makes (and has always made) are darned gorgeous, revealing an attention to detail bordering on the obsessive.

Historically speaking, Italy is like a giant pop-up book where you can wander through the epochs of the past. Where else can hold a candle to the wonders of ancient Rome, the compelling ruins of cart-rutted Pompeii in the shadow of a still-smoking Mt Vesuvius, the Greek temples and Roman theatres of Sicily and the baroque exuberance of Reggia di Caserta palace?

As you unzip the boot, you'll find epic art and architecture that leaves you speechless everywhere: the soaring dome of the Vatican's St Peter's Basilica, epitome of Renaissance splendour, Michelangelo's frescoes waltzing across the Sistine Chapel, Caravaggios demanding attention in Rome's Galleria, da Vinci's *Last Supper* in Milan and the baroque feast that is Lecce in Puglia.

Beyond the canvas, Italy has inspired far beyond its borders with its artistic brilliance – from the poetic genius of Dante's *Divine Comedy* to masterworks by Rossini and Puccini staged at La Scala and the marionette magic of the nose-growing Pinocchio (courtesy of Tuscan-born Carlo Collodi) and Sicily's *opera dei pupi*.

While you'll still find time-honoured artisanship – be it a Neapolitan workshop preserving nativity traditions, graceful Murano glass in Venice or hand-crafted violins in Cremona, Italy also knows how to innovate. And whether it's the latest Gaggia espresso machine or Ferrari, couture Armani or Naples' commuter art stations, it does so in its own daring, inimitable style.

People & Culture

The Italian way of life

Above **Battle of the Oranges festival**

Italians are every inch as riveting as the country they inhabit. As passionate, fashionable, hot-headed and fast-talking as Europeans get, they aspire to a life coveted by millions. Strong espresso, capsule wardrobes, mutual admiration and a burning love of football are things that make an Italian's heart beat quicker. That, of course, and *la famiglia* (the family), sheltered by the warm, protective wing of Mamma, who is inevitably a brilliant cook – and don't you dare disagree.

Italians are a sociable lot, and the further south you go the louder and more gregarious they become. But all believe that conversation is far too important to be cut short by tardiness. When they go to the deli, they factor in time for discussing the merits of a particular pecorino, when they pause for *un caffè*, they expect to chat with the barista, when they head out for the ritual *passeggiata* (evening walk) over the piazza or along the seafront promenade, they idle over gossip and gelato. Life's too short to rush and a little daily decadence goes a long way. There should always be time to sip a negroni under the arcades with *amici* (friends). The exception to the rule? When they are tear-arsing around in a car or on a Vespa. Then they are always in a hurry: even if the light is red and overtaking is blatantly *proibito* (prohibited).

Barely a week goes by without a holy feast or festival to sweep you up in its fervour. For a glimpse into the Italian mind, join them to party. Roam small-town piazzas full of beauty and banter. Hole up for the night in an ancient cave in Matera. Ride with Italy's last cowboys in the Maremma. Listen to the songs of the gondoliers echoing through Venice's canals. And know that Italy is a cultural one-off.

Impressions

Italy has inspired centuries of artists, poets and playwrights: from Dante's Inferno to Shakespeare's tragic Julius Caesar. Directors have captured its beauty and hedonism time and again on the silver screen.

Above **Assassination of Julius Caesar**

"The Creator made Italy from designs by Michaelangelo."
Mark Twain

"Italy will never be a normal country. Because Italy is Italy. If we were a normal country, we wouldn't have Rome. We wouldn't have Florence. We wouldn't have the marvel that is Venice."
Matteo Renzi *(interview with Time, 2014)*

"Italians know that what matters is style, not fashion. Italian style does not have social or age boundaries."
Stefano Gabbana *(Interview magazine, 2011)*

"Italy and the spring and first love all together should suffice to make the gloomiest person happy."
Bertrand Russell *(The Autobiography of Bertrand Russell, 1970)*

"Travelling is the ruin of all happiness! There's no looking at a building after seeing Italy."
Fanny Burney

"I find it beautiful when we're in Italy that everybody sits down at the table together. My mother-in-law is like: It doesn't matter what's going on in the house, who is fighting, who is upset, who has appointments, you sit down at that table at one o'clock."
Debi Mazar *(interview with Sari Lehrer, 2009)*

"Love and understand the Italians, for the people are more marvellous than the land."
EM Forster *(Where Angels Fear to Tread, 1905)*

"If you stop for lunch elsewhere in the world, you tend to eat a sandwich, and a bad one. Italy is unique for the style of life. I think everyone envies it a bit."
Lapo Elkann *(interview with Vogue, 2013)*

Movies

Ladri di Biciclette (Bicycle Thieves; 1948)

La Dolce Vita (The Sweet Life; 1961)

Il Gattopardo (The Leopard; 1963)

Cinema Paradiso (1988)

Il Postino (The Postman; 1994)

La Vita è Bella (Life Is Beautiful; 1998)

Le Conseguenze dell'Amore (The Consequences of Love; 2004)

Che Bella Giornata (What a Beautiful Day; 2011)

La Grande Bellezza (The Great Beauty; 2013)

Books

Divine Comedy (Dante Alighieri; c 1307–21)

Christ Stopped at Eboli (Carlo Levi; 1945)

The Italians (Luigi Barzini; 1964)

The Name of the Rose (Umberto Eco; 1980)

The Silent Duchess (Dacia Maraini; 1992)

Gomorrah (Roberto Saviano; 2006)

The Secrets of Rome (Corrado Augias; 2007)

The Italians (John Hooper; 2014)

The Tragedy of Julius Caesar (William Shakespeare; c 1599)

A Day in Italy

For an Italian, a wake-up call might be the clang of the Duomo bell or the clatter of a stovetop *caffettiera* (espresso-maker). They're in a hurry, so it's the usual quick breakfast: a stand-up *cornetto* (croissant) and *caffè* (coffee) at their favourite corner bar. But there's time for the once-over in the mirror (appearances matter and socks should match, after all) and a stop for a quick chat with the neighbour before dashing off. Tardiness should never mean rudeness. Hopping on their Vespa or in their car, they curse the lack of parking and almost crash before finally nabbing a space and arriving at work.

Then they might glance at last night's football scores in *La Gazzetta dello Sport*, check the Corriere della Sera for news and chat with colleagues about the latest *molto cool* (very cool) bar before work truly begins. Finally: it's 12.59pm and Italy grinds to a halt for a lengthy lunch. Italians might wish their colleagues *buon pranzo* (a good lunch) and enjoy a lavish meal with a glass of wine, but no dessert because they're watching their *figura* (figure). It's almost 3pm but there's time for a swift espresso and a natter with the barista before heading back to the office.

At 6pm sharp, many will down tools to meet friends for a happy-hour *aperitivo* (pre-dinner drink) at a hot new café, nibbling snacks with their *spritz*. As dusk falls, it's time for a *passeggiata* (late-afternoon or early-evening stroll) as the piazza lights up. By 9pm, they might be back home, watching TV and checking Facebook on the sofa while devouring a bowl of pasta. They're dreaming about a holiday in the Caribbean, but it will be Calabria again without a pay rise. Around midnight, they drift off to the beeping of scooters or the backbeat of cicadas.

Experiences by Region

Northern Italy

Above **Palazzo Ducale**, Venice

Sophisticated cities and snowy slopes

Above **Duomo**, Milan

Northern Italy has a pinch of everything that shapes the Italian dream and more besides. The wild, ragged Alps and the pink-granite Dolomites that pucker up on the country's northernmost fringes give way to fertile foothills, pedigreed vines, highly cultured towns with exuberant art and architecture and vivacious cities that set the style barometer.

In this wealthy and wise chunk of Italy, culture thrives. And in Venice it reaches its zenith. Floating on a lagoon, this city of merging light and water appears like a mirage and is particularly poetic by moonlight. Beyond the Grand Canal of gently rowing gondoliers, it enthralls art lovers with the unfathomable intricacy of Basilica di San Marco's golden mosaics, the lavish Palazzo Ducale, and Galleria dell'Accademia's wondrous works by Tintoretto, Titian and co. In narrow backstreets adorned with fresco painter's colours, you'll find artisan studios where master craftsmen still ply ancient trades and chatter-filled *bacari* (bars).

Fast-paced, forward-thinking Milan, one of the world's fashion HQs, is a catwalk for couture and snappily dressed locals. But it too has cultural cachet, with its Gothic Duomo, a sublime vision in pink marble, the cutting-edge Museo del Novecento bearing Renzo Piano's hallmark, opera at lauded La Scala, and da Vinci's *The Last Supper* captivating all who admire it in the convent of Santa Maria delle Grazie.

But it doesn't stop there. Northern Italy bows to the artistic brilliance of Ravenna, erstwhile seat of the Roman Empire, with its eight Unesco World Heritage Sites and Byzantine basilicas glittering with hand-cut mosaics. Not to mention the uplifting walled city of Bergamo and erudite Bologna with its 11th-century university. Padau amazes with its Giotto frescoes, Vicenza with Palladio's Renaissance play of light and shadow on Piazza dei Signori, and Verona with its balconied streets where Romeo wooed Juliet. Lesser-known still are Cremona, home to 100 violin-making workshops, Aquileia with its rich Roman past, and elegant Trieste on the Adriatic and Slovenian border.

"Even Italians grow wide-eyed at the mention of Slow Food capital Piedmont, a gastronomic wonderland"

Northern Italy swings effortlessly between the urban and the outdoors. One look at the Alps that pop up spectacularly in the Valle d'Aosta has skiers itching to slalom in the shadow of Mont Blanc, Matterhorn and glacier-encrusted Monte Rosa. The vast wilderness of Parco Nazionale del Gran Paradiso thrills hikers with mile after soul-stirring mile of hiking trails and distant glimpses of Alpine ibex in the Graian Alps. East of here, the Dolomites work their own magic, with heart-pumping *via ferrate* (iron roads) twisting high into their rosy pinnacles, and quaint, German-speaking hamlets topped by castles in the Alto Adige.

More gentle and refined pursuits await on the shores of lakes Como, Garda, Maggiore, Iseo and Orta, where graceful villas and botanical gardens dip into startlingly turquoise waters. Anyone craving a little romance will find it in spades on the cliff-flanked Riviera – notably Cinque Terre, with its quintet of higgledy-piggledy hamlets painted in ice-cream shades and interwoven with walking trails.

If all that art and fresh air has piqued your appetite, the north will feed you beyond your wildest dreams. Even Italians grow wide-eyed at the mention of Slow Food capital Piedmont, a gastronomic wonderland, with Alba white truffles, cult-status Barolo and Barbaresco wines and chocolate in opulent Turin cafes. Emilia Romagna gives you Bologna, 'la Grassa' (the fat one), famous for its *mortadella* (pork sausage) and *ragù* meat sauce served over silky strands of tagliatelle. Detour to Modena for aged balsamic vinegar, Parma for Parmesan cheese and *prosciutto di Parma*, Milan for *risotto alla Milanese* (with saffron and bone marrow), and Venice for *cicheti* tapas with local prosecco or robust Amarone reds. Food is never an afterthought in Italy, but in the north it's often the main event.

Right **Villa Balbianello**, Lake Como

Central Italy

Above **Umbria**

Wine-rich hills, Renaissance heroes and medieval towns

Above **Pantheon**, Rome

Italy's midriff is wholeheartedly Italian, rammed with ancient Roman sites, Renaissance treasures and alley-woven, high-spirited towns that gather around stately piazzas where the *duomo* chimes, *trattorias* do a brisk trade, Vespas screech narrowly past each other on cobbled backstreets and café terraces crank into action at *aperitivo* hour. Almost every aspect of daily life here has 'Made in Italy' stamped all over it.

There's an undeniable poetry to the way the landscapes unravel as your journey leads you through Italy's heart. The most romanticised stretch of this central belt is Tuscany, where the countryside rolls elegantly on through the vine-laced Chianti country, past medieval hamlets perched like eyries on hillsides and oak and chestnut woods. In the Val d'Orcia, breeze-bent cornfields bleed into poppy fields prettier than anything Monet could ever paint. Neighbouring Umbria and Le Marche to the east might play second fiddle in terms of visitors, but they are every bit as lovely: olives, vineyards, meadows and hills plumed with cypress trees ripple south to the snow-dusted Apennines and east to the Adriatic.

Edging south, Lazio in Rome's backyard offers respite from the big city, with its sandy coastline, volcanic lakes, Etruscan tombs and hilltop monasteries. Bordering it to the east, Abruzzo and Molise are the Italy the world forgot. Shaken recently by earthquakes and seemingly immune to time and trends, this off-the-radar corner of the country is one of its last true wildernesses, with mountain trails where you'll encounter more goats than people, ramshackle farmhouses and wheezing trains.

No amount of hyperbole can capture the sheer elation you'll feel when in Rome, a capital to usurp them all, with its operatic streets, matchless portfolio of museums and basilicas, and haunting ruins winging you back 2000 years to when it was an unrivalled superpower. Rome bombards you with architectural and artistic splendour: the great gladiatorial arena of the Colosseum, the Pantheon, Michelangelo's Sistine Chapel and Galleria Borghese's Caravaggio collection for starters. Its cultural rival, Florence, is an effusive love letter to the

"History is put on a pedestal all over the region"

Renaissance, crowned by Brunelleschi's miraculous Duomo and home to the Uffizi Gallery where da Vinci and Botticelli shine.

But Central Italy is not a two-city wonder; history is put on a pedestal all over the region: from Pisa's ludicrous Leaning Tower to Perugia's *palazzo*-lined *centro storico* and Perugino art treasures and Siena's compelling Gothic centre, host of the hell-for-leather Il Palio bareback horserace in summer.

Stray beyond the cities and you won't regret it. Slow tour Tuscany to hill towns like San Gimignano, where the 14 towers of the walled town rise up like a medieval Manhattan, or Umbria to volcano-topped Orvieto and its glorious wedding cake of a cathedral, or saintly Assisi, where St Francis was born. In Lazio, you'll be floored by the Roman ruins of Ostia Antica and Tivoli, and the Etruscan necropoles in Cerveteri and Tarquinia.

Enticing outdoor escapades reach from hiking in the Parco Nazionale d'Abruzzo, Lazio e Molise, where rare Marsican bears hang out in the shadow of 2912m Corno Grande, to diving and sea kayaking off Elba, and coastal walks in Le Marche's beach-laced Parco del Conero.

As for the food, you're in for a belt-busting feast. Central Italy is more driven towards the *terra* (land) than the *mare* (sea). Tuscany swings with the seasons in farm-to-table dishes heavy on slow-roasted pork, chestnuts, porcini mushrooms, pecorino and extra-virgin olive oil – all washed down with gutsy Brunello and Chianti red wines. Rome does some of the country's best pizza, cracking *spaghetti alla carbonara* and nose-to-tail grub. Umbria has the country's finest *norcinerie* (butcher shops), brimming with *salumi*, wild boar delicacies and black truffles.

Historically, artistically, culturally and gastronomically speaking, this central chunk of the country is, quite simply, Italy in a nutshell.

Left Corno Grande, Parco Nazionale d'Abruzzo, Lazio e Molise

Southern Italy

Above **Mt Vesuvius**, Campania

Beautifully sun-bleached, ancient and complex

Above **Sardinia**

If you could squeeze the very essence out of Italy as easily as you can turn lemons into *limoncello*, the zesty, pithy bit would be the south. Presided over by ever-smouldering volcanoes, the southern cities brim with dilapidated beauty, speeding scooters, boisterous greetings and loveable chaos. This is as loud, unadulterated and passionate as Italy gets. Sunbaked towns are lined with sherbet-bright houses where bloomers hang out to dry in rosemary-scented breezes. Cliff-straddling resorts perch over coves strung out like pearls and a sea of pure sapphire. The interior is cloaked in citrus orchards, olive groves and pine woods that are thrumming with cicadas. In between, Greco-Roman ruins provide an insight into the ancient world of frisky emperors and bodacious goddesses.

Toss aside your fixed itinerary for a moment, as the best way to get familiar with Campania, 'the boot' of Puglia, Basilicata and Calabria, and the islands – Sicily, Sardinia and the Aeolians – is to tune into their laid-back groove, listening to the waves and peering up to skies that never seem to have known dust or cloud. Welcome to the *Mezzogiorno* (Southern Italy)!

Once overlooked entirely as the down-and-out, dangerous cousin of Rome, Naples has spruced up its act of late and is now charged with a raw energy and theatrical edge. Back alleys of crumbling beauty lead to bountiful markets, baroque chapels, crowded piazzas and scruffy bars with cocky baristas. Culture? You bet. The showstopper in the Unesco-listed *centro storico* is the Museo Archeologico Nazionale, with its haul of Roman treasures looted from Pompeii. But maybe you came for opera at the Teatro di San Carlo where Verdi was once musical director, a tour of the city's subterranean ruins, or, let's face it, the food. All Italians go into raptures about Neapolitan cooking. Pizza was born here and it's still legendary: giant, wood-fired discs topped with tomatoes, mozzarella, basil and a drizzle of olive oil. Then there's the spaghetti, perhaps spiked with hot pepper or served *alle vongole* (with clams).

Spreading out around Naples, Campania beguiles with its coastline and

"White heat rises from vineyards and silvery olive groves, mountains, forests and small fishing villages."

archaeological sites. Horizon-hogging Mt Vesuvius has blown its top more than 30 times and eerie Pompeii is a stark reminder of its malign forces, as is fossilised Herculaneum which suffered a similar fate. Further south, Paestum hides some of the best-preserved ancient Greek temples in existence. Beyond the history wow factor, the region romances with the ravishing Amalfi Coast – cliff-hugging Sorrento and flower-wreathed Ravello – and the chic island escapes of Capri and Ischia, with their clear waters for summer dreaming.

The boot is formed of Puglia, Basilicata and Calabria, a region made for slow touring because *fa tropo caldo* (it's too hot) to rush. White heat rises from vineyards and silvery olive groves, mountains, forests and small fishing villages. Beyond bolshie ports like Brindisi and Bari, there is the coastline of Promontorio del Gargano, bathed in pearly light; Matera, European Capital of Culture 2019, with its compelling *sassi* (cave dwellings) and 7000-year

history; baroque stunner Lecce; and the Valle d'Itria's beehive-like *trulli* houses. The region's earthy authenticity is reflected in its *cucina povera* (peasant cooking), using staples like durum wheat, tomatoes, artichokes, fava beans and whatever fish is going fresh.

Calabria's toe kicks Sicily into the Tyrrhenian sea. The island is spiced up with its own distinct identity, fabulous coastlines, terrifically preserved Greek temples and stratovolcano Mt Etna huffing and puffing away in the east. Gritty-but-pretty Palermo triumphs in food and culture, with its opera house, Arab-Norman churches, street food (try *panelle* – chickpea fritters – for starters) and cafes selling decadent *cannoli* (pastry tubes oozing sweet ricotta).

Sicily's island neighbours are the Aeolian Islands, where lava-spitting Stromboli rises in a perfect pyramid above a cobalt sea, and Sardinia, where you can flop with celebrities on some of the loveliest beaches on Earth.

Right **Amalfi Coast**

Bravo Italy

The Italian Icons You Already Love

Long before you set foot on Italian soil and unzip the length of its boot, the *bel paese* (beautiful country) will have already fired your imagination in more ways than one. The ruins of ancient Rome and the gladiatorial clout of the Colosseum – such history! The cliff-hugging towns of Cinque Terre, the hills of Chianti wine country, the sea views on the Amalfi Coast – such landscapes! Uproarious crowds at a football match – such passion! Pizza delivered from a wood-fired oven in a gloriously dishevelled Naples backstreet – such food!

We could reel off the icons till kingdom come but they'd never do Italy justice. No matter how many books you've read, maps you've thumbed or movies you've watched, when you see, smell, feel and taste Italy for real – that's *amore*.

The country packs in Unesco World Heritage Sites (47, for the record) and does signature sights like nowhere else on Earth. You might well gasp out loud when you first clap eyes on the Colosseum, toss a lucky coin into the Trevi Fountain in Rome, or see Florence open up like a pop-up book around you from the medieval arches of the Ponte Vecchio. And gasps are, frankly, to be expected the moment that you ponder Michelangelo's finger-touching *The Creation of Adam* fresco in the Vatican's resplendently Renaissance Sistine Chapel. Or get lost in the detail of da Vinci's *Last Supper* in Milan.

From that first properly frothy cappuccino to that last, lingering gelato on the steps of the Duomo, as vintage Vespas splutter on by into the higgledy-piggledy heart of a *centro storico*, Italy's eye for detail in daily life elevates the ordinary to the irresistible. Bravo indeed.

Mangiare Bene

When the magic words 'tutti a tavola' (everyone to the table) are uttered, you won't see an Italian for dust. Food is the national obsession and eating here goes way beyond tasty home cooking and a sociable setting. You never really know Italians until you share a bowl of pasta and glass of vino with them. So seize every opportunity to do just that.

Aah... *mangiare!* Bar the quick espresso and *cornetto* (croissant) that often constitutes breakfast, it has to be said that Italians spend a disproportionate amount of time eating – or thinking about eating. And who can blame them? The food in Italy is, after all, the edible incarnation of Italian good-living, ripe with the bounty of the land, rich with the sharp, clean flavours of the sea, fragrant with palate-awakening wild herbs and citrus, and liberally doused in thick, green, peppery olive oil. It is an honest, generous cuisine totally in sync with the epicurean nature of its people. Indeed, nothing gives an Italian greater pleasure than for guests to praise their cooking by going for second helpings.

The Mediterranean diet, first promoted by American scientist Ancel Keys, who studied the dietary patterns of Campania in the 1950s and found them to boost health and longevity, is the very essence of Italian cooking. We're talking lots of fresh fruit and vegetables, whole grains and legumes, oily fish for omega-3 fats, liberal quantities of extra virgin olive oil, and the occasional glass of red wine high in antioxidants. The Italian diet is not one of denial – it's the fine juggling act of having a lot of what's good for you and a little of what you fancy. And it's also about ensuring that everything is made with fresh, high-quality ingredients, whether it's a multicourse dinner in a posh restaurant or pizza *al taglio* (by the slice). *Mangiare bene* (eating well) is considered a right for the many, not a privilege for the few.

Processed food has no place in a country that's been tanking up on super foods since long before they became fashionable. Many Italians can still trace their ingredients from farm to fork, or indeed from their own vegetable patch to plate. Chefs, too, take pride in sourcing and orchestrating menus that sing with local flavours – be it delicate shavings of pungent, aromatic *tartufi bianchi* (white truffles) in Alba, Piedmont, glistening swordfish from Sicily's waters or *salumi* from Italy's pork capital, Norcia in Umbria.

Before you can even begin to delve into the nuances of the country's regional specialities, however, it's important to understand the foundations upon which Italy's food empire rests. On paper, it is beautifully simple, with recipes that are quite straightforward and involve minimal ingredients. But there is a real art involved in nailing the basics.

There is, perhaps, no finer example of this than *salsa di pomodoro* (tomato sauce), without which Italian food would be unimaginable. For this, the San Marzano plum tomatoes that thrive in the volcanic soil near Vesuvius are plucked ripe and fresh, then blanched, skinned and reduced to make a silky passata. Toss in garlic, chopped onions, a pinch of sea salt and a few sprigs of basil and you'll

never think of tomato sauce in the same way again. It is this sauce that forms the base of an excellent Neapolitan pizza or *spaghetti al pomodoro*.

But the plum tomato is a king with a court. Let's not forget the fleshy, orangey-red Cuor di Bue (ox heart) variety that are great in salads and never taste the same outside of Italy. Or the tangily sweet Principe Borghese tomatoes, which are vine ripened and sun dried. Others are partial to the Pachino variety, another protected tomato, this time hailing from southeast Sicily, where the climate is so mild they grow year-round. They are either *ciliegini* or *datterini*, shaped like cherries or dates.

So you see something as simple as a tomato really isn't so simple in Italy. And that's also true of that other most famous and revered of Italian staples: pasta. On liberating Naples, Guiseppe Garibaldi swore that it would be *maccheroni* that would unite the country. Sophia Loren credited it for her curves: 'Everything you see I owe to spaghetti.' Indeed, a love of pasta is deeply ingrained in the Italian psyche. Whether it's light, silk-smooth ribbons of fettucine and pappardelle, made with just plain flour (Tipo 00) and egg, or dry pasta made with semolina flour and water – both have their place in the Italian kitchen. The former pairs well with the creamy sauces and meaty *ragù* recipes of the north, while the latter goes brilliantly with the tangier tomato-based, olive oil-laced dishes of the south.

Beyond this simple divide awaits a world of complexity – you could literally map Italy out in pasta, the *primo* (first course) of choice. Travel your taste buds with Liguria's *pasta com pesto* with parmesan, basil and pine nuts, Puglia's

strascinati con la mollica (pasta with breadcrumbs and anchovies) and Lombardy's *tortellini di zucca* (pumpkin-stuffed pasta). Over on Sicily, try *pasta alla Norma* (with basil, eggplant, ricotta and tomato), or on Sardinia, *culurgiones* (a local take on ravioli, filled with potato, pecorino, garlic, mint and nutmeg). And this is just tip-of-the-iceberg stuff.

What does Italy put on its pasta and pizza besides tomato sauce? Fabulous *formaggio*, of course. While you'll be familiar with PDO cheeses like nutty, crumbly *parmigiano reggiano* (Parma, Reggio Emilia, Modena, Bologna and Mantua), washed-rind, blue-veined Gorgonzola (Lombardy and Piedmont) and luscious, creamy *mozzarella di bufala* (buffalo mozzarella), there are literally hundreds of regional varieties to nibble on – from pungent, unpasteurised cow's milk Asiago, hailing from the north, to sheep's milk Fiore Sardo (Sardinian Pecorino).

Naturally, the regional riffs on Italian food are endless. Serious food lovers will adore northern regions such as Emilia-Romagna, home to some of the country's tastiest exports, among them wafer-thin Parma ham and earthy dishes like *stinco di maiale al forno con porcini* (roasted pork shanks with porcini mushrooms). Its rival foodie regions include Piedmont, birthplace of the Slow Food Movement. Here you can gorge yourself silly on white truffles, hazelnuts, peaches and pedigreed Barolo and Barbaresco red wines in Alba or nibble nougat and drink Lavazza coffee in Turin.

Moving on south you hit Tuscany, which tastes every bit as good as it looks (go for the porcini, chestnuts, truffles, pecorino, gutsy Brunello and Chianti reds, the

Florentine-style T-bone steak...). Though lesser known, its eastern neighbour, Umbria, has some treasures up its sleeve – there's Norcia with its black truffles and *salumi* (cured meats) and hill town Torgiano with its olives and fine Rubesco reds.

Unzip the boot a little further and you'll hit Rome: spaghetti heaven. A detour into the Testacio neighbourhood is great for nose-to-tail treats like *trippa alla romana* (tripe cooked with potatoes, tomato, mint and pecorino). Just south, in the full-on frenzy of Naples, the Vespas are surely on a mission to seek out the city's best pizza margherita. But the Neapolitans have a sweet tooth, too, as reflected in their fondness for a *sfogliatella*, a shell-shaped ricotta pastry, and zingy *limoncello* (lemon liqueur) that is liquid summer. The heel of the boot, Puglia, stays true to rural tradition with *cucina povera* (peasant cooking), including hearty vegetable casseroles and *agnello* (lamb) slow cooked until meltingly tender. You might want to save a little room for dessert in Sicily – the *cannoli* (pastry shells filled with sweet ricotta) are quite special.

Let's face it, one trip will never suffice to get a proper taste of Italy – and why on Earth would you want it to?

To read about:
Slow Food see page 98
Harvest Time see page 128

Left Stored wheels of parmigiano cheese.
Polesine Parmense, Emilia-Romagna

The Perfect Pizza

A derivation of the flat breads of ancient Greece and Egypt, pizza was already a common street snack by the time Naples' 16th-century Spanish occupiers introduced the tomato to Italy. The New World topping cemented pizza's popularity and in 1738 Naples' first pizzeria opened its doors on Port'Alba, where it still stands. Soon after, the city's pizzaioli began to enjoy minor celebrity status.

Naples

Campania's no-nonsense attitude to food – keep it simple, keep it local and keep it coming – remains deeply rooted in the traditions of the poor. This is especially true in its predilection for pizza, a mainstay of *cucina povera* and one of the foundations on which Naples' gastronomic reputation stands.

Naples has other delights: *sfogliatella*, that divine oyster of puff pastry stuffed with sweet ricotta and candied fruit; *gatto di patate*, a kind of potato cake; and *trippa Napoletana* (tripe), but pizza seems to define this pulsating, noisome, chaotic, irrepressible city. Maybe it's the combination of simplicity (there are only five ingredients in a pizza base – flour, water, yeast, salt and olive oil) and complexity – the intensity and balance of the toppings. The vivid raucousness of the flavours knitted together by the integrity of the base. Or perhaps it's because, like the sociable Neapolitans themselves, it's immensely sociable food – also one which can be consumed at speed, even on the move. And it makes use of ingredients provided by the rich agricultural land around the city.

To this day, the city's most famous dough-kneader remains Raffaelle Esposito, the 19th-century inventor of the classic pizza margherita. As the city's top *pizzaiolo*, Esposito was summoned to fire up a treat for a peckish king Umberto I and his wife, Queen Margherita, on a royal visit in 1889. Determined to impress the Italian royals, Esposito based his creation of tomato, mozzarella and basil on the red, white and green flag of the newly unified Italy. The resulting topping met with the queen's approval and was subsequently named in her honour.

More than one hundred years later, pizza purists claim that you really cannot top Esposito's classic combination when it's made by a true Neapolitan *pizzaiolo*. Not everyone is in accordance, though, and Italians are often split between those who go for the thicker Neapolitan version and those who favour the thin-crust Roman variant.

Rome

Remarkably, pizza was only introduced to Rome post-WWII, by southern immigrants. It caught on. The gloriously simple pizza is a favourite casual (and cheap) Roman meal, with Rome's signature wafer-thin bases, covered in fresh, bubbling toppings, slapped down on tables by waiters on a mission. Pizzerias often only open in the evening, as their wood-fired ovens take a while to get going.

Most Romans will precede their pizza with a starter of bruschetta or *fritti* (mixed fried foods, such as zucchini flowers, potato, olives etc) and wash it all down with beer – only craft beer in the case of the city's trendiest new pizzerias. Pizza menus are traditionally divided into *pizza rosso* ('red' pizza, meaning with tomato sauce) and *pizza bianco* ('white' pizza with no tomato sauce, traditionally simply sprinkled with rosemary, salt and olive oil, but available with a variety of optional toppings today).

In Search of Authenticity

There are two, and only two, classic pizzas: marinara (tomato, oregano, garlic and olive oil) and margherita (tomato, mozzarella, basil and vegetable oil). But the trouble with Italian food is this: pizza is a subject that is likely to provoke debate even among normally mild-mannered folk. Just as one cook assures you of one thing, the next throws up their arms in dismay, and exclaims that pizza/pasta/*ragù*/etc made that way is only fit for dogs.

However you taste it, tomatoes are the backbone of a pizza topping. According to Neapolitan lore, these should be San Marzano tomatoes, a tricky customer that needs a lot of looking after but is

suited to the Campanian sunlight and air, and to canning. San Marzanos have thin skins, thick flesh, few seeds and a deep, intense flavour. Some pizzerias will use fresh *pomodorini,* cherry tomatoes, in season, but virtually all pizzerias turn to the canned San Marzano. If you're looking for super-San Marzanos, however, then the unpeeled tomatoes of Sabatino Abagnale, under the label Il Miracolo di San Gennaro (the Miracle of San Gennaro), grown in the rich, minerally soil near Sant'Antonio Abate, south of Naples, are the ones to look out for. Technically speaking, because these are canned with their skins on, they cannot be marketed as San Marzano tomatoes under strict local rules, although they are the traditional variety grown from old seed stock, in the traditional way.

It stands to reason that the mozzarella cheese on a perfect pizza can, of course, only be from the buffalo. Or can it? *Mozzarella di bufala,* with its high fat and liquid content, can soften the crust too much when it melts, and many prefer *fior di latte,* mozzarella made with cow's milk. This being Italy, and Naples in particular, the preference is not for any old *fior di latte,* but *fior di latte* from Agerola on Monti Lattari above Positano, south of Naples. Here Salvatore De Gennaro allows the cheese to ferment slowly for 12 hours to produce a high level of acidity. The initial cheesemaking processes start during the day and the cheese is finished at midnight, ready to go out to Naples' pizzerias.

The Making of a Perfect Pizza

The margherita is a serious test of a *pizzaiolo* because it takes nerve and judgement to get the precise balance between the elements exactly right. Enzo Coccia, pizza aficionado and proprietor of Pizzeria La Notizia (on a hill above Naples' heaving Spaccanapoli), flattens out the *pagnotta,* a little bun of pasta dough that will become a pizza. Actually, to describe Enzo as a mere aficionado is a bit of an understatement. The man lives, breathes, cooks and eats pizza. He's a pizza missionary, a pizza priest. Enzo begins to stretch the *pagnotta,* with deft little workings of the fingers, working it into a rough circle. Then he starts slapping it to the correct size, making sure it is elastic enough and has plenty of air. His dough rises for 10 hours.

Then there's the expert splash of tomato passata, dabs of *fior di latte,* a shower of torn basil leaves, a sprinkling of vegetable oil (it has a higher burning point than olive oil). The floppy uncooked pizza is slipped on a wooden paddle then onto the floor of the beehive-shaped pizza oven. It's warm in there, 485°C (905°F). After 45 seconds or so the pizza is rotated 45 degrees with a deft flick of the paddle. After one minute 15 seconds, it's ready, its edges curled, black-edged bubbles here and there. The fillings are molten and bubbling, but not singed. The outer layer is delicate and crisp. There is a faintly sour, yeasty, savoury tang from the thin sponge beneath. The tomato is fruity, with a hint of Bovril. The blobs of *fior di latte* have oozed and spread, but not too much. Each mouthful gets a soft, unctuous benediction of mild cheese, heightened by the breath of basil. It has balance, depth, deliciousness. It's a marvel, a delight that keeps you interested, coming back for more.

Regulation Pizza

According to the official Associazione Verace Pizza Napoletana (Real Neapolitan Pizza Association), genuine Neapolitan pizza dough must be made using highly refined type 00 wheat flour (a small dash of type 0 flour is permitted), compressed or natural yeast, salt and water with a pH level between six and seven.

While a low-speed mixer can be used for kneading the dough, only hands can be used to form the *disco di pasta* (pizza base), which should not be thicker than 3mm. The pizza itself should be cooked at 485°C (905°F) in a double-domed, wood-fired oven using oak, ash, beech or maple timber.

To read about:
Coffee see page 186
Gelati see page 272

From Fiats to Ferraris

From economical sedans to extravagant sports cars, Italian automobiles span a broad spectrum of budgets and tastes. But, in a country obsessed with motor sport and speed wrapped in a luxury coating, the real attraction lies less with family-orientated Fiats and more with racy Lamborghinis, Maseratis and Ferraris.

What makes Italian cars special is their power and style. No one buys a Maserati for its boot space or economical petrol consumption. They buy it because it looks spectacular, goes seriously fast, and makes the owner feel confident, opulent and cool.

The speed translates to the racing track. Home to legendary autodromes at Monza and Imola, Italy has hosted more Formula One Grand Prix races than any other nation. When the cars line up on the starting grid, engines revving, the noise eruption is loud enough to drown out rock band AC/DC at their most deafening. The crowd isn't muted either. Italian motor racing fans, popularly known as *tifosi*, are famously fanatical, especially when it comes to cheering for Ferrari, Italy's number one team and the distinguished producers of a record 16 world-champion

drivers, including Michael Schumacher. To join in the motoring madness, pack a picnic and some fold-up chairs and head to Monza, 27km northeast of Milan, in early September where general admission tickets for the Grand Prix sell for between €50 and €100.

Back on the road, the conundrum for car lovers with non-billionaire salaries is that Italy's best cars are prohibitively expensive to 99.9% of the population. The solution? Pay a visit to the thin wedge of land between Modena and Bologna – aka 'Motor Valley' – where the world's finest luxury cars are constructed. Here, serious aficionados can appreciate the true beauty of Italian auto-design vicariously by touring four engrossing automotive museums, two devoted to Ferrari – including the Museo Enzo Ferrari in Modena – and two to Lamborghini.

Lest we forget, for every Lamborghini there are literally hundreds of Fiats. Never write off these diminutive, durable and much-loved cars, which were first produced in Turin in 1899. Classic Fiats such as the Topolini and the Cinquecento are as emblematic of Italy as the red, white and green flag. Their HQ city, Turin, hosts the finest all-round motor museum in the country, the recently expanded Museo Nazionale dell'Automobile which tells the definitive history of Italy's auto-obsession from Enrico Bernardi's three-wheeled quasi-tricycle through to Schumacher's Ferrari.

To read about:
Vespas see page 84
Targa Florio see page 248

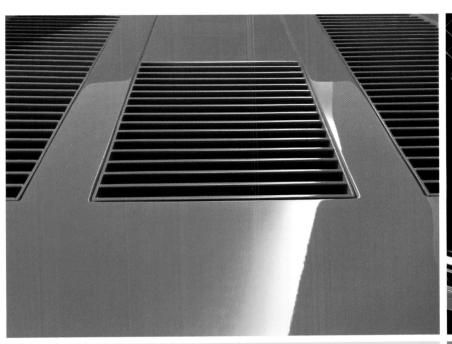

Football: Italy's Other Religion

Calcio (football) reigns supreme in Italian sport. There are no other contenders. Indeed, some people have suggested that Italians engage in two impassioned acts of worship on Sundays: the first at the chiesa (church), and the second at the San Siro, Allianz or Stadio Olimpico, the revered temples of AC Milan, Juventus and AS Roma.

For proof of the passion, just visit a newsstand. One of the best-selling newspapers in Italy is *La Gazzetta dello Sport*, a sports tabloid published daily and dedicated almost entirely to football. The game and its associated drama has long been a favourite topic for journalistic gossip, after-dinner discussion and political debate. Some even claim that the health of Italy's collective psyche is indelibly linked to how the national team, the beloved Azzurri (the blues), is performing on the world stage.

The English may have invented football, the Germans draw larger attendances and the Spanish generate big bucks with the likes of Barcelona and Real Madrid, but nowhere is football's emotion as intense as it is in Italy. It is a fervour that has produced to-die-for home-grown players such as Franco Baresi, Paolo Maldini and Alessandro del Piero, and propelled the Azzurri to victory in four World Cups, more than any other team except Brazil.

Football was introduced to Italy by the British at the tail-end of the 19th century. Not surprisingly, it didn't take long for locals to stamp their characteristic panache on the 'beautiful game'. By the late 1930s, over a dozen teams were competing in an annual league known as Serie A, and the national side had taken home two out of three FIFA World Cups. Almost without realising it, the Italians had elevated football into a tactical art where elegant attacking skill was backed up by a ruthless watertight defence.

By the 1960s, Italian coaches such as Helenio Herrera had pioneered *catenaccio*, a tight man-marking system that employed the use of an extra free defender known as the *libero* or 'sweeper'. The system was used to great effect by Internazionale (aka Inter Milan) as it rose to become the finest European team of the era.

Internazionale are one of the 'seven sisters' of Italian football. Their closest geographic rivals are AC Milan with whom they share a stadium, the San Siro (officially known as Stadio Giuseppe Meazza), the largest of its kind in Italy where up to 80,000 people crammed in to watch the 1934 and 1990 World Cups, as well as the 2016 Champions League Final. Other teams worth making an Italian football pilgrimage for are AS Roma and Lazio (both based in Rome), Napoli from the southern bastion of Naples, and Fiorentina from Florence. But, in terms of fan-base and legacy, all potential opposition is blown away by the mighty Vecchia Signora (Old Lady) from Turin, better known to the world and history as Juventus.

With 33 Italian league titles, and nine European crowns to its name, Juventus is one of the most successful teams in history. Iconic players who have donned the legendary *bianconeri* (black and white) shirt include such international greats as Zinedane Zidane, Paolo Rossi, Michel Platini and Paul Pogba. With a popularity that extends far beyond Italy, Juventus is said to have one of the largest fan-bases in the world – an estimated 70 million – and you'll spot the black and white striped jerseys on everyone from market traders in Nigeria to tuk-tuk drivers in downtown Bangkok.

Juventus' biggest rivals are its fellow citizens from Torino FC. Traditionally,

Above San Siro stadium, Milan

Torino counts on a far greater number of fans in Turin itself, while Juventus' massive haul is drawn from around the world. Hotly contested matches between the two clubs are known as the Derby della Mole.

In style-conscious Italy, it isn't just the football matches that are important, it's also the way they are played. Well-coiffured and self-aware Italian players prowl the field like Milanese models strutting the catwalk. In a nation that spawned Michelangelo, beauty is everything. There is no hoofing the ball in the air à la British Premier League. Instead, it is manoeuvred skilfully across the playing surface waiting for that all-important moment of divine inspiration which lights up many Italian games. Ironically, the genius is countered by another distinctly Italian football trait: guile. Serie A games are renowned for their fake play-acting and theatrical attempts to curry favour with the referee and it isn't always pretty.

The guile went a stretch too far in 2006 when Juventus and four other Italian clubs were implicated in a match-fixing scandal known as Calciopoli that shook Italian football to its foundations.

Scandals aside, football in Italy remains a great cultural leveller. You'll see plenty of flag-waving in the streets and squares of tourist cities on big game days when the result can – for better or worse – affect the public mood. Bank on far better service in Naples if local heroes Napoli have just won 4-0, but don't expect too much sleep in Rome on nights when Lazio are playing local rivals, AS Roma.

In July 2006, an estimated 715 million people watched as Italy won the World Cup against France. In bars and businesses across the nation, life practically

Seeing a Game

Going to a football match in Italy, particularly to see a big team like Juventus or Internazionale, is a quintessential Italian experience as culturally immersive as eating pizza in Naples or taking a gondola in Venice. Tickets for games usually go on sale 10 to 14 days beforehand and can be purchased online, in club shops or at the stadium. The cheapest seats behind the goal generally cost around €30. Children are half-price. The best cities to see games are Turin, Milan and Rome, all of which support two Serie A teams. The season runs from mid-August to late May.

stopped for 120 minutes and only ecstatically restarted when native Roman Fabio Grosso slotted in the winning penalty. For unbiased observers watching from the sidelines, this highly charged moment seemed to epitomise the passion, emotion, energy and excitement of Italian football, a game of style and skill that, for all its associated baggage, is as closely reflective of the Italian personality as Puccini or pizza.

To read about:
Car Racing see page 248
Horseback Riding see page 250

Give Me Five!

With its collection of five rainbow-bright villages pasted precariously to the clifftops, looking as though the slightest puff of wind would make them topple into the Ligurian Sea, Cinque Terre is postcard-perfect stuff. Set amid some of the most dramatic coastal scenery on the planet, these five ingeniously constructed fishing villages can bolster the most jaded of spirits.

A Unesco World Heritage Site since 1997, Cinque Terre's five villages date from the early medieval period and while much of this fetching vernacular architecture remains, its really unique draw is the steeply terraced cliffs bisected by a complicated system of fields and gardens that have been hacked, chiselled, shaped and layered over the course of nearly two millennia. The extensive *muretti* (low stone walls) can be compared to the Great Wall of China in their grandeur and scope.

For the sinful medieval inhabitants of these villages, penance involved a lengthy and arduous hike up the vertiginous cliffside to the local village sanctuary to appeal for forgiveness. You can scale the same trails today, through terraced vineyards and hillsides smothered in *macchia* (shrubbery). They may give your glutes a good workout, but as the heavenly views unfurl, it's hard to think of a more benign punishment.

Farmers and winemakers here are the mountaineers of the food world, toiling up and down the contours and sometimes taking away their harvest by boat – the easiest way. Hikers are sustained by the plentiful seafood, dishes derived from locally grown ingredients such as lemons, olives and basil – and of course the Sciacchetrà wine that the region is famous for.

Manarola

Bequeathed with more grapevines than any other Cinque Terre village, Manarola is famous for its sweet Sciacchetrà wine. It's also awash with priceless medieval relics, supporting claims that it is the oldest of the five. The spirited locals here speak an esoteric local dialect known as Manarolese.

Monterosso al Mare

The most accessible village by car and the only Cinque Terre settlement to sport a proper stretch of beach, the westernmost Monterosso is the least quintessential of the quintet. The village, known for its lemon trees and anchovies, is delightful. Split in two, its new and old halves are linked by an underground tunnel burrowed beneath the blustery San Cristoforo promontory.

Right **Manarola**, Cinque Terre

Corniglia

Corniglia is the 'quiet' middle village that sits atop a 100m-high rocky promontory surrounded by vineyards. The only Cinque Terre settlement with no direct sea access, steep steps lead down to a rocky cove. Narrow alleys and colourfully painted four-storey houses characterise the timeless streetscape. To reach the village proper from the railway station you must first tackle the Lardarina, a 377-step brick stairway (or jump on a shuttle bus).

Riomaggiore

Cinque Terre's easternmost village, Riomaggiore is the largest of the five and acts as its unofficial HQ. Its peeling pastel buildings march down a steep ravine to a tiny harbour – the region's favourite postcard view – and glow romantically at sunset. If you are driving, the hills between here and La Spezia are spectacular to explore.

Vernazza

Vernazza's small harbour – the only secure landing point on the Cinque Terre coast – guards what is perhaps the quaintest, and steepest, of the five villages. Lined with little cafes, a main cobbled street (Via Roma) links seaside Piazza Marconi with the train station. Side streets lead to the village's trademark Genoa-style *caruggi* (narrow lanes), where sea views pop at every turn.

Village-to-Village Hikes

The Sentiero Azzurro (Blue Trail), a 12km old mule-path that once linked all five oceanside villages by foot, is the Cinque Terre's blue-riband hike, narrow and precipitous. The trail dates back to the early days of the Republic of Genoa in the 12th and 13th centuries and, until the opening of the railway line in 1874, it was the only practical means of getting from village to village.

Since the 2011 floods, many of Cinque Terre's walking paths, including sections of the Sentiero Azurro, have been in a delicate state and prone to periodic or permanent closure. However, Cinque Terre has a whole network of spectacular trails and you can hike from village to village along any of 30 numbered paths. Check ahead on the internet for up-to-date trail information.

To read about:

Hill Towns see page 116
Amalfi Coast see page 286

Rome's Ancient Wonders

In a city of extraordinary beauty, Rome's ancient heart stands out. It's here you'll find the great icons of the city's past: the Colosseum, the Palatino, the forums, and the historic home of the Capitoline Museums. A short detour past the city's edges, to Ostia Antica and along the Appian Way, will bring you even closer to the distant past.

Ancient Rome, Myth & Legend

As much a mythical construct as a historical reality, ancient Rome's image has been carefully nurtured throughout history. Intellectuals, artists and architects have sought inspiration from this skilfully constructed legend, while political and religious rulers have invoked it to legitimise their authority and serve their political ends.

Rome's original myth-makers were the first emperors. Eager to reinforce the city's status as *caput mundi* (capital of the world), they turned to writers such as Virgil, Ovid and Livy to create an official Roman history. These authors, while adept at weaving epic narratives, were less interested in the rigours of historical research and frequently presented myth as reality. In the *Aeneid,* Virgil brazenly draws on Greek legends and stories to tell the tale of Aeneas, a Trojan prince who arrives in Italy and establishes Rome's founding dynasty. Similarly, Livy, a writer celebrated for his monumental history of the Roman Republic, makes liberal use of mythology to fill the gaps in his historical narrative.

Ancient Rome's rulers were sophisticated masters of spin and under their tutelage, art, architecture and elaborate public ceremony were employed to perpetuate the image of Rome as an invincible and divinely sanctioned power. Monuments celebrated imperial glories, while gladiatorial games highlighted the Romans' physical superiority. The Colosseum, the Roman Forum and the Pantheon were not only sophisticated feats of engineering, they were also impregnable symbols of Rome's eternal might.

However cynical and world-weary you may be, it's difficult to deny the thrill of seeing the Colosseum for the first time or of visiting the Palatino, the hill where Romulus is said to have founded the city in 753 BC.

Be a Gladiator for a Day

If you want to ruminate on the ancient wonders of Rome, the Colosseum should be at the top of your list. An awesome, spine-tingling sight, it is the most thrilling of Rome's ancient monuments. It was here that gladiators met in mortal combat, and condemned prisoners fought off wild beasts in front of baying, bloodthirsty crowds.

To any gladiator facing the prospect of meeting the gods via a lively and heated encounter with a bear or lion, the idea that someone more than 2000 years later would pay for a similar experience might seem perverse. Still, for 20 years the Gruppo Storico Romano has been hosting gladiator training classes on the Appian Way: your next stop after visiting the Colosseum.

'Senator Marcus Valerius Messala Barbatus' (real name Pietro Giusto), a gladiator trainer, begins the task of uniting students with their inner Russell Crowe. He teaches students the craft of killing tall Germanic hordes (by sneaking between their legs and slitting their femoral artery) and using a tribulus (spikes hidden in the grass to injure enemies too uncivilised to wear sandals). But before going outside to fight, Marcus schools his students in Roman honour: upholding the ideals of culture and art.

Right **Colosseum**, Rome

Cycle the Appian Way

All roads lead to Rome, but none do so more gracefully than the Appian Way. Built as the king of all Roman highways in 312 BC, it is a road more storied than any other in history. Olympic sprinters have raced down it, armies fought along it in WWII, 6000 followers of Spartacus were crucified by the roadside and St Peter heard Christ's footsteps beside his own on its cobbles. These days, divine apparitions in the lay-bys are uncommon – although this doesn't stop modern Roman cyclists pedalling the nine-mile-long stretch closest to the city.

Bearing south from the gridlocked streets of southern Rome, the blaring of car horns soon recedes to a distant toot. The scent of wild mint hangs in the air as the road passes crumbling Roman villas and medieval towers. Technically the Appian Way is open to all traffic – very occasionally a car passes with the driver jabbing at their satnav in confusion. But much of the time cyclists find themselves alone but for the ghosts of wayfarers past.

Explore Ostia Antica

Near the coast 25km west of central Rome are the remarkably well-preserved ruins of Ostia Antica, ancient Rome's main seaport – one of Italy's most compelling and under-appreciated archaeological sites.

The main thoroughfare, the Decumanus Maximus, leads from the city's entrance to highlights such as the Baths of Neptune, the floor of which features a famous mosaic of Neptune driving his seahorse chariot. Next door is the steeply stacked amphitheatre, built by Agrippa and later enlarged to hold 3000 people.

Above Appian Way, Rome

Ancient Rome on Screen

→ *Spartacus* (1960; Stanley Kubrick)

→ *Quo Vadis* (1951; Mervyn LeRoy)

→ *Gladiator* (2000; Ridley Scott)

→ *I, Claudius* (1976; BBC)

→ *Rome* (2005–07; HBO, BBC)

The original city of Ostia was founded in the 4th century BC at the mouth of the Tiber and developed into a major port, but decline set in after the 5th century when barbarian invasions and outbreaks of malaria led to its abandonment and slow burial in river silt. Thanks to the silt it has survived very well, allowing visitors to walk the ancient town's streets, among shops, and into its impressive amphitheatre – and get about as close to 2000 years of history as they possibly can.

Celebrations

Join Romans to celebrate the city's birthday, the Natale di Roma, on 21 April. The program varies each year but events and historical re-enactments are generally held around Via dei Fori Imperiali, the Campidoglio and the Circo Massimo.

To read about:
Pompeii see page 56
Mosaics see page 108

Left **Mosaic floor detail**, Ostia Antica

The Ruins of Pompeii

Nothing piques human curiosity like a mass catastrophe, and few beat the time-warped ruins of Pompeii, a stark reminder of the malign forces that lie deep inside Mt Vesuvius.

The ghostly ruins of ancient Pompeii (Pompei in Italian) make for one of the world's most engrossing archaeological experiences. Much of the site's value lies in the fact that the town wasn't simply blown away by Vesuvius in AD 79 but buried under a layer of *lapilli* (burning fragments of pumice stone). The result is a well-preserved slice of ancient life, where visitors can walk down chariot-grooved Roman streets and snoop around millennia-old houses, temples, shops, cafes, amphitheatres, and even a brothel.

Pompeii's origins are uncertain, but it seems likely that it was founded in the 7th century BC by the Campanian Oscans. Over the next seven centuries, the city fell to the Greeks and the Samnites before becoming a Roman colony in 80 BC.

In AD 62, a mere 17 years before Vesuvius erupted, the city was struck by a major earthquake. Damage was widespread and much of the 20,000-strong population was evacuated. Fortunately, many had not returned by the time Vesuvius blew, but 2000 men, women and children perished nevertheless.

After its catastrophic demise, Pompeii receded from the public eye until 1594, when the architect Domenico Fontana stumbled across the ruins while digging a canal. Exploration proper didn't begin until 1748. Of Pompeii's original 66 hectares, 44 have now been excavated.

How the Tragedy Unfolded
24 August AD 79

8am Buildings such as the Terme Suburbane and Foro were still under repair after the AD 63 earthquake. Despite earth tremors overnight, residents had little idea of the catastrophe that lay ahead.

Midday Peckish locals poured into the Thermopolium di Vetutius Placidus. The lustful slipped into the Lupanare (brothel), and gladiators practised for the evening's games at the Anfiteatro, which is now the oldest known Roman amphitheatre in existence. A massive boom heralded the eruption. Shocked onlookers witnessed a dark cloud of volcanic matter shooting 14km above the crater.

3pm–5pm *Lapilli* rained down on Pompeii. Terrified locals began to flee; others took shelter. Within two hours, the plume was 25km high and the sky had darkened. Roofs collapsed under the weight of the debris, burying those inside.

25 August AD 79

Midnight Mudflows buried the nearby town of Herculaneum. *Lapilli* and ash continued to rain on Pompeii.

4am–8am Ash and gas avalanches hit Herculaneum. Subsequent surges smothered Pompeii, killing all remaining residents, including those in the Orto dei Fuggiaschi. This volcanic 'blanket' safeguarded frescoed treasures like the asa del Menandro and Villa dei Misteri for almost two millennia.

To read about:
Ancient Sardinia see page 214
Ancient Sicily see page 242

Where the Art Is

Italian art's long history underpins that of all Western art, from the classical, Renaissance and baroque, to Arte Povera in the 20th century. From quiet beginnings in Florence, the Renaissance erupted across Italy and then Europe. Painters such as Giotto, Botticelli, Leonardo da Vinci and Raphael led the way, while all-rounder Michelangelo achieved immortality, producing masterpieces such as David and the Sistine Chapel frescoes.

Before the Renaissance

Italian art as we know it today was born out of the so-called Dark Ages. The merchants, princes, clergy, corporations and guilds who lived in the small independent city-states created a culture of artistic patronage that engendered the great innovations in art and architecture that would define the Renaissance. Clarity of religious message outweighed the notion of faithful representation in the art of the medieval period. To the modern eye, the simplicity and coded allegorical narrative of both the painting and sculpture of this period can look stiff, though a closer look usually reveals a sublimity and grace that speaks across the centuries.

Greek colonists settled many parts of Sicily and southern Italy as early as the 8th century BC, naming it Magna Graecia and building great cities such as Syracuse and Taranto. In art, as in so many other realms, the ancient Romans looked to the Greeks for inspiration. Sculpture flourished in southern Italy into the Hellenistic period and also gained popularity in central Italy, where the art of the Etruscans was greatly refined by the contribution of Greek artisans, who arrived to trade.

The Gothic style was much slower to take off in Italy than in the rest of Europe. When it did, it marked the transition from medieval restraint to the Renaissance, and saw artists once again drawing inspiration from life itself rather than concentrating solely on religious themes. Occurring at the same time as the development of court society and the rise of civic culture in the city-states, its art was both sophisticated and elegant, highlighting attention to detail, a luminous palette and an increasingly refined technique.

The Renaissance

The new Florentine style that started sprouting across the city during the Trecento (14th century) and proliferated in the Quattrocento (15th century) became known as Renaissance or 'rebirth', and it really started to hit its stride after architect Filippo Brunelleschi won a competition to design the dome of Florence's *duomo*. Brunelleschi was heavily influenced by the achievements of the classical masters, but he was able to do something that they hadn't been able to – discover and record the mathematical rules by which objects appear to diminish as they recede from us. In so doing, he gave local artists and architects a whole new visual perspective and a means to glorious artistic ends.

To decorate the new buildings, artists enjoyed a bonanza of commissions to paint heroic battle scenes, fresco private chapels and carve busts of the latest power players – works that sometimes outlived their patrons' clout. The members of the Peruzzi family had risen to prominence in 14th-century Florence as bankers, with interests reaching from London to the Middle East. They set the trend for art patronage by commissioning Giotto to fresco the family's memorial chapel in Santa Croce, completed in 1320, and their legacy set the tone for the artistic flowering of Florence.

But the patrons with the greatest impact on the course of art history were, of course, the Medicis. Patriarch Cosimo the Elder was exiled in 1433 by a consortium

Right **Capella Brancacci**, Florence

of Florentine families who considered him a triple threat: powerful banker, ambassador of the Church, and consummate politician with the savvy to sway emperors and popes. But the flight of capital from Florence after his departure created such a fiscal panic that the banishment was hastily rescinded and within a year the Medicis were well and truly back in town. To announce his return in grand style, Cosimo funded the 1437 rebuilding of the Convento di San Marco (now Museo di San Marco) by Michelozzo, and commissioned Fra' Angelico to fresco the monks' quarters with scenes from the life of Christ.

The High Renaissance

The decades leading up to and beginning the Cinquecento (16th century) are often seen as a kind of university faculty meeting, with genteel, silver-haired sages engaged in a collegial exchange of ideas. A bar brawl might be closer to the metaphorical truth, with artists, scientists, politicians and clergy mixing it up and everyone emerging bruised. The debate was never as simple as Church versus state, science versus art or seeing versus believing; in those days, politicians could be clergy, scientists could be artists, and artists could be clergy.

Inspired by Masaccio, tutored by Fra' Filippo Lippi and backed by Lorenzo de' Medici, Sandro Botticelli was a rising Florentine art star who was sent to Rome to paint a fresco celebrating papal authority in the Sistine Chapel. The golden boy who'd painted the *Birth of Venus* for Lorenzo de' Medici's private villa in 1485 (now in Florence's Galleria degli Uffizi) could do no wrong until he was accused of sodomy in 1501. The charges didn't stick,

Above Botticelli's *Birth of Venus*, Galleria degli Uffizi, Florence

but the rumours did, and Botticelli's work was critiqued as too decadently sensual for religious subjects. When religious reformer Savonarola ousted the Medici and began to purge Florence of decadent excess in the face of a surely imminent Armageddon, Botticelli paintings went up in flames in the massive 'bonfire of the vanities'. Botticelli repudiated mythology and turned his attention to Madonnas, some of whom bear a marked family resemblance to his Venus.

Michelangelo, a Tuscan village lad from Caprese (today Caprese Michelangelo) in the remote Tuscan outback of Casentino in eastern Tuscany, was another of Lorenzo de' Medici's protégés. His classically inspired work was uniformly admired until the Medicis were ousted by Savonarola in 1494. By some accounts, Savonarola tossed rare early paintings by Michelangelo onto his bonfires. Without his Medici protectors, Michelangelo seemed unsure of his next move: he briefly hid in the basement of San Lorenzo and then roamed around Italy. In Rome he carved a *Bacchus* for Cardinal Raffaele Riaro that the patron deemed unsuitable – but this only seemed to spur Michelangelo on to make a bigger and still more sensuous statue of *David* in 1501. It's now exhibited in Florence's Galleria dell'Accademia.

Leonardo, who hailed from Vinci, southwest of Florence, had so many talents that it is hard to isolate only a few for comment. In his painting, he took what some critics have described as the decisive step in the history of Western art – namely, abandoning the balance that had previously been maintained between colour and line and choosing to modulate his contours using shading. This technique is called *sfumato* and it is perfectly displayed in his *Mona Lisa*. Few of his works remain near his birthplace; the exceptions are his *Adoration of the Magi* and *Annunciation*, both in the Uffizi.

In 1542 the Inquisition arrived in Italy, marking a definitive end to the Renaissance exploration of humanity in all its glorious imperfections and Tuscany's leading influence in art and architecture.

Renaissance Frescoes

One of the highlights of a visit to Tuscany is the abundance of churches featuring frescoes, seemingly in every town. They may look like ordinary bible stories now, but in their heyday Renaissance frescoes provided social commentary as well as religious inspiration. In them, human adversity looked divine, and vice versa. Fantastic examples are found throughout Tuscany; here are some of the very best:

Collegiata, San Gimignano There are hardly any undecorated surfaces in this cathedral, with every wall sporting huge, comic-strip-like frescoes by Bartolo di Fredi, Lippo Memmi, Domenico Ghirlandaio and Benozzo Gozzoli. The highlight is Taddeo di Bartolo's gleefully grotesque *Final Judgment* (1396).

Libreria Piccolomini, Duomo, Siena Umbrian artist Bernardino Pinturicchio extols the glory of Siena in 10 vibrant fresco panels (c 1502–07) celebrating Enea Silvio Piccolomini, aka the humanist Pope Pius II. St Catherine of Siena makes a cameo appearance.

Museo di San Marco, Florence Fra' Angelico's frescoes portray religious figures in all-too-human moments of uncertainty, reflecting the humanist spirit of the Renaissance. The highlight is his *Annunciation* (c 1440).

Museo Civico, Siena Magnificent is the only word to use when describing Ambrogio Lorenzetti's *Allegories of Good and Bad Government* (1338–40) and Simone Martini's *Maestà* (Virgin Mary in Majesty; 1315).

Cappella Brancacci, Florence Masaccio's *The Expulsion of Adam and Eve from Paradise* and *The Tribute Money* (c 1427) showcase architectural perspective and sly political satire.

Cappella Bacci, Chiesa di San Francesco, Arezzo Piero della Francesca's *Legend of the True Cross* (c 1452–66) displays a veritable encyclopaedia of Renaissance painting tricks (directional lighting, steep perspective etc).

Chiesa di Sant'Agostino, San Gimignano Benozzo Gozzoli's bizarre fresco of San Sebastian (c 1464) shows the fully clothed saint protecting the citizens of San Gimignano, helped by a bare-breasted Virgin Mary and a semi-robed Jesus. Wins the prize for weirdest religious iconography.

Cappella dei Magi, Palazzo Medici-Riccardi, Florence More Gozzoli, but this time there's nothing strange about his subject matter, which has members of the Medici family making a guest appearance in the *Procession of the Magi to Bethlehem* (c 1459–63).

To read about:
Architecture see page 64
Florence see page 146

Left **Donatello's bronze *David*,** Museo Nazionale del Bargello, Florence

Left **Michelangelo's *La Pieta*,** St Peter's Basilica, Rome

Left **Caravaggio's *Madonna and Child*,** Galleria Borghese, Rome

Left **Raphael's *Transfiguration of Christ*,** Pinacoteca Vaticana, Rome

Right Ghiberti's *Gates of Paradise*, Battistero di San Giovanni, Florence

Right Caravaggio's *St Matthew and the Angel*, Chiesa di San Luigi dei Francesi, Rome

Right Michelangelo's *David*, Galleria dell'Accademia, Florence

Right Michelangelo's *Moses*, Basilica di San Pietro in Vincoli, Rome

Italian Architecture

Italian architecture has an enduring obsession with the 'classical', a formula that pleases the eye and makes the soul soar. The Greeks, who established the style, employed it in the southern cities they colonised; the Romans refined and embellished it; Italian Renaissance architects rediscovered and tweaked it; and the fascist architects of the 1930s returned to it in their powerful modernist buildings.

Classical: 8th Century BC–4th Century AD

Only one word describes the buildings of ancient Italy: monumental. The Romans built an empire the size of which had never been seen and went on to adorn it with buildings cut from the same pattern. From Verona's Roman Arena to Pozzuoli's Anfiteatro Flavio, giant stadiums rose above skylines. Spa centres like Rome's Terme di Caracalla were veritable cities of indulgence, boasting everything from giant marble-clad pools to gymnasiums and libraries. Aqueducts like those below Naples provided fresh water to thousands, while temples such as Pompeii's Tempio di Apollo provided the faithful with awe-inspiring centres of worship.

In pre-Roman times, the Greeks had built theatres and proportionally perfect temples in their southern colonies at Agrigento, Syracuse and Paestum, while the Etruscans concentrated on funerary art, creating elaborate tombs at Tarquinia and Cerveteri. Coming in their wake, the Romans specialised in roads, aqueducts and monumental amphitheatres. Having learned a few valuable lessons from the Greeks (consider Rome's Colosseum, with its ground tier of Doric, middle tier of Ionic and penultimate tier of Corinthian columns), the Romans refined architecture to such a degree that their building techniques, designs and mastery of harmonious proportion underpin much of the world's architecture and urban design to this day. Just witness Rome's exquisitely proportioned Pantheon: the temple's huge but seemingly unsupported dome showcases the Roman invention of concrete, an ingredient as essential to the modern construction industry as Ferrari is to the F1 circuit.

Byzantine: 4th–6th Centuries

After Constantine became Christianity's star convert, the empire's architects and builders turned their talents to the design and construction of churches. His successors in Constantinople went on to build churches in the style that became known as Byzantine. Brick buildings built on the Roman basilican plan but with domes, they had sober exteriors that formed a stark contrast to their magnificent, mosaic-encrusted interiors. Finding its way back to Italy in the mid-6th century, the style expressed itself on a grand scale in Venice's Basilica di San Marco. The true stars of Italy's Byzantine scene, however, are the Basilica di San Vitale in Ravenna and the Basilica di Sant'Apollinare in nearby Classe, both built on a cruciform plan.

Romanesque: 8th–12th Centuries

The Romanesque period saw the construction of fortified monasteries and robust, bulky churches. Pisa's striking *duomo* (cathedral) displays a characteristic Tuscan variation on the style. The next development in ecclesiastical architecture in Italy came from Europe. The European Romanesque style became momentarily popular in four regional forms – the Lombard, Pisan, Florentine and Sicilian Norman. All displayed an emphasis on width and the horizontal lines of a building rather than height, and featured churches where the *campanile* (bell tower) and *battistero* (baptistry) were separate to the church.

Right **Dome of St Peter's Basilica**, Rome

Above Palazzo Ducale, Venice

The use of alternating white and green marble defined the facades of the Florentine and Pisan styles, as seen in iconic buildings like Florence's Basilica di Santa Maria Novella and *duomo* baptistry, as well as in Pisa's cathedral and baptistry. The Lombard style featured elaborately carved facades and exterior decoration featuring bands and arches. Among its finest examples are the Lombard cathedral in Modena, Pavia's Basilica di San Michele and Brescia's unusually shaped Duomo Vecchio. Down south, the Sicilian Norman style blended Norman, Saracen and Byzantine influences, from marble columns to Islamic-inspired pointed arches to glass tesserae detailing. One of the greatest examples of the form is the Cattedrale di Monreale, just outside Palermo.

Gothic: 13th & 14th Centuries

The Italians didn't wholeheartedly embrace the Gothic: its verticality, flying buttresses, grotesque gargoyles and over-the-top decoration were just too far from the classical ideal that seems to be integral to the Italian psyche. The local version was generally much more restrained, a style beautifully exemplified by Naples' simple, elegant Basilica di San Lorenzo Maggiore. There were, of course, exceptions. The Venetians used the style in grand *palazzi* (mansions) such as the Ca' d'Oro and on the facades of high-profile public buildings like the Palazzo Ducale. The Milanese employed it in their flamboyant *duomo,* and the Sienese came up with a distinctive melange in Siena's beautiful cathedral.

Renaissance: 14th–17th Centuries

It's the Renaissance that is the most stunning and most unique period in Italian architecture, from Florence's elegant streetscapes to the otherworldly beauty of Venice's *palazzi*. 'Mess with Florence, and you take on Rome' was the not-so-subtle hint delivered by Florentine architects, who made frequent reference to the glories of the ancient power and its classical architecture when designing their new churches, *palazzi* and public buildings. Architects Brunelleschi and Bramante rewrote the rule books with their beautifully proportioned basilicas, not least of which is Florence's *duomo*. This rebirth of classical culture – harmonious, in mathematical proportion and designed to appeal to both emotion and reason – became more ornamental and decorative as the period advanced.

Baroque: Late 16th– Early 18th Centuries

Dominating the 17th century, the extravagant baroque style found fertile soil in Italy. Noteworthy for its exuberant – some would say decadent – form, the baroque took its name from the Portuguese word *barroco,* used to denote a misshapen pearl. Compared to the classical lines of Renaissance buildings, its output could indeed be described as 'misshapen' – Andrea Palma's facade of Syracuse's cathedral, Guarino Guarini's Palazzo Carignano in Turin, and Gian Lorenzo Bernini's baldachin in St Peter's in Rome are curvaceous and downright sexy structures that bear little similarity to the classical ideal. Lecce's *centro storico* (historic centre) and the baroque towns of southeastern Sicily are other fine examples.

The show-stopping qualities of the baroque were not lost on the Catholic Church. Threatened by the burgeoning Reformation to the north of the Alps, the Church commissioned a battalion of grandiose churches, palaces and art to dazzle the masses and reaffirm its authority. Bernini expressed the popes' claim to power with his sweeping new design of St Peter's Square, its colonnaded arms 'embracing' the faithful with a majesty that still moves visitors today.

Glowing in the wealth of its Spanish rulers, 16th-century Naples drew driven, talented architects and artists in search of commissions and fame. For many of the city's baroque architects, however, the saying 'it's what's inside that counts' had a particularly strong resonance. Due in part to the city's notorious high density and lack of show-off piazzas, investments went to lavish interiors. The exterior of churches like the Chiesa e Chiostro di San Gregorio Armeno gives little indication of the opulence inside, from cheeky cherubs and gilded ceilings to polychromatic marble walls and floors. The undisputed meister of this marble work form was Cosimo Fanzago, whose pièce de résistance is the church inside the Museo Nazionale di San Martino in Naples – a mesmerising kaleidoscope of inlaid colours and patterns.

Considering the Neapolitans' weakness for all things baroque, it's not surprising that the Italian baroque's grand finale would come in the form of the Palazzo Reale in Caserta, a 1200-room royal palace designed by Neapolitan architect Luigi Vanvitelli to upstage France's Versailles.

Siena: An Open-Air Museum Celebrating the Gothic

Siena is a city where the architecture soars, and so too do the souls of many of its visitors: it's a feast for the senses and an essential stop on every Tuscan itinerary. For much of the 13th and 14th centuries, Siena was ruled by the Consiglio dei Nove (Council of Nine), a bourgeois group constantly bickering with the feudal nobles. It enjoyed its greatest prosperity during this time, and the Council commissioned many of the fine buildings in the Sienese-Gothic style that give the city its striking appearance, including lasting monuments the *duomo,* Palazzo Pubblico and Piazza del Campo.

A plague outbreak in 1348 killed two-thirds of Siena's 100,000 inhabitants, leading to a period of decline that culminated in the city being handed over to Florence's Cosimo I de' Medici, who barred inhabitants from operating banks, thus severely curtailing its power. This centuries-long economic downturn was a blessing in disguise, because the lack of funds meant that Siena's city centre was subject to very little redevelopment or new construction. In WWII the French took Siena virtually unopposed, sparing it discernible damage. Hence the historic centre's Unesco World Heritage listing as the living embodiment of a medieval city.

To read about:

Left **Duomo**,
Milan

Left **Duomo**,
Syracuse

Left **Basilica di San Vitale**,
Ravenna

Left **Cattedrale di Monreale**,
Monreale

Right Reggia di Caserta,
Caserta

Right Basilica di San Marco,
Venice

**Right Basilica di Sant'
Apollinaire in Classe,**
Ravenna

Right Duomo,
Pisa

Know Your Grapes: A Short Guide to Italian Wine

A sit-down meal without vino in Italy is as unpalatable as pasta without sauce. Not ordering wine at a restaurant can cause consternation – are you pregnant or a recovering alcoholic? Was it something the waiter said? Italian wines are considered among the most versatile and 'food friendly' in the world, specifically cultivated over the centuries to elevate regional cuisine.

ITALY-WIDE / FOOD & DRINK

Some Italian wines will be as familiar to you as old flames, including pizza-and-a-movie Chianti or reliable, summertime fling pinot grigio. But you'll also find some captivating Italian varietals and blends for which there is no translation, and intriguing Italian wines that have little in common with European and New World cousins of the same name, from merlot and pinot nero (aka pinot noir) to chardonnay.

Many visitors default to carafes of house reds or whites, which in Italy usually means young, fruit-forward reds to complement tomato sauces, and chilled dry whites as seafood palate-cleansers. But with a little daring, you can pursue a wider range of options by the glass or half-bottle.

DOC & Friends

Italy boasts a complex grading system for its wines and wine regions that gives an indication of where the quality is, but it is by no means definitive. A broad understanding of these will stand you in good stead.

DOC *(denominazione di origine controllata)* Wines that meet a set of quality criteria in terms of grape variety, methodology etc. There are 23 DOC areas in Lombardy, 42 in neighbouring Piedmont, 29 in the Veneto and nine in Trentino-Alto Adige.

DOCG *(denominazione di origine controllata e garantita)* Top-notch wines – only wines that have had DOC status for at least five years can be awarded this status. There are 70 such wines or areas in Italy. Additional terms that indicate quality are *riserva, speciale* and *superiore,* which can denote ageing conditions or other factors that make the wine stand out.

IGT *(indicazione geografica tipica)* High-quality wines from specific areas or varieties not covered by the DOC system and for which the rules are more relaxed.

Know Your Regions

Perhaps the most famous wine region in Italy, and something of a viticultural powerhouse, is Tuscany, in Central Italy. Among the myriad full-bodied, highly respected reds from this region that excite wine buffs are Chianti, Brunello and 'Super Tuscans'.

Also from Central Italy is Campanian wine, revered by the ancients, snubbed by modern critics, but once again becoming hot property. Lauded producers are returning to their roots, cultivating ancient grape varieties like the red Aglianico and the whites Falanghina, Fiano and Greco. Campania's three main wine-producing zones are centred on Avellino, Benevento and Caserta. Other wine-producing areas include the Campi Flegrei (home to DOC-labelled Piedirosso and Falanghina vines), Ischia and the Cilento region, home to the DOC Cilento bianco (Cilento white) and the Aglianico Paestum.

In the north, bordering Switzerland, the Valtellina cuts a broad swathe down the Adda valley, where villages and vineyards hang precariously on the slopes of the Orobie Alps. The steep northern flank is carpeted by Nebbiolo grapes, which yield a light-red wine.

Winemaking in the south dates back to the Phoenicians. Yet, despite this ancient viticulture, oenophiles had often dismissed local wines. However, in little more than two decades, Southern Italy has transformed itself into one of the world's in-the-know wine regions, with renewed pride in native varieties and stricter, more modern winemaking practices.

Recommended Drops

Brunello di Montalcino (Tuscany)
Brunello is up there with Italy's most prized wines. The product of Sangiovese grapes, it must spend at least two years ageing in oak. It is intense and complex with an ethereal fragrance, and is best paired with game, wild boar and roasts. Brunello grape rejects go into Rosso

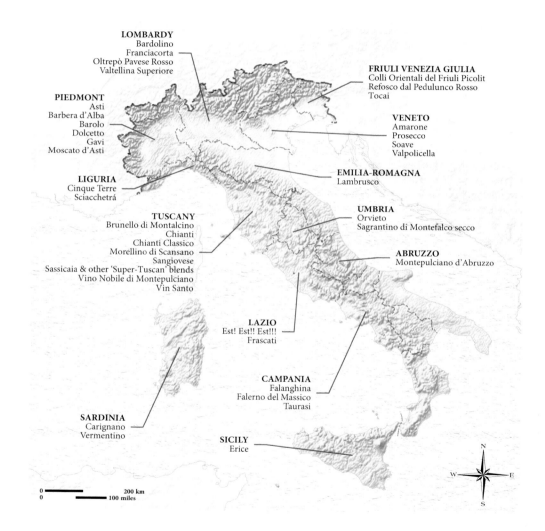

LOMBARDY
Bardolino
Franciacorta
Oltrepò Pavese Rosso
Valtellina Superiore

FRIULI VENEZIA GIULIA
Colli Orientali del Friuli Picolit
Refosco dal Pedulunco Rosso
Tocai

PIEDMONT
Asti
Barbera d'Alba
Barolo
Dolcetto
Gavi
Moscato d'Asti

VENETO
Amarone
Prosecco
Soave
Valpolicella

LIGURIA
Cinque Terre
Sciacchetrá

EMILIA-ROMAGNA
Lambrusco

UMBRIA
Orvieto
Sagrantino di Montefalco secco

TUSCANY
Brunello di Montalcino
Chianti
Chianti Classico
Morellino di Scansano
Sangiovese
Sassicaia & other 'Super-Tuscan' blends
Vino Nobile di Montepulciano
Vin Santo

ABRUZZO
Montepulciano d'Abruzzo

LAZIO
Est! Est!! Est!!!
Frascati

CAMPANIA
Falanghina
Falerno del Massico
Taurasi

SARDINIA
Carignano
Vermentino

SICILY
Erice

0   200 km
0   100 miles

N
W   E
S

di Montalcino, Brunello's substantially cheaper but wholly drinkable kid sister.

Carignano (Sardinia) Once known as a low-quality grape, Carignano is now coming into its own as a rich, spicy, light-tannin red that is affordable and goes well with meaty and spicy dishes.

Chianti (Tuscany) Cheery, full and dry, contemporary Chianti gets the thumbs up from wine critics. Produced in eight subzones from Sangiovese and a mix of other grape varieties, Chianti Classico is the best known, with its Gallo Nero (Black Cockerel) emblem that once symbolised the medieval Chianti League. Young, fun Chianti Colli Senesi from the Siena hills is the largest subzone; Chianti delle Colline Pisane is light and soft in style; and Chianti Rùfina comes from the hills east of Florence.

Erice (Sicily) Representing more than a dozen local wine producers, the Associazione Strada del Vino e dei Sapori Erice DOC celebrates certain wines that are produced in the province of Trapani, western Sicily. The Erice DOC appellation recognises several indigenous grape varieties from the region, including Catarratto, Nero d'Avola, Grillo, Insolia, Frappato, Perricone and Zibibbo. These grapes owe their distinctive flavour to the fact that they're grown in vineyards that lie between an altitude of 250m and 500m but are also located close to the sea.

Falerno del Massico (Campania) The province of Caserta is well known for producing this DOC-designated wine grown in the very same area as Falernum, the most celebrated wine in ancient Roman times.

Super Tuscans (Tuscany) Developed in the 1970s, these are wines that fall outside the traditional classification categories. As a result they are often made with a combination of local and imported grape varieties, such as merlot and cabernet. Sassacaia, Solaia, Bolgheri, Tignanello and Luce are all super-hot Super Tuscans.

Taurasi (Campania) This full-bodied wine is considered one of southern Italy's finest drops. Sometimes called the Barolo of the south, its notes range from dark berries and leather to roasted coffee and Mediterranean herbs. The wine is also one of only four in the region to carry Italy's top quality rating, DOCG.

Valtellina Superiore (Lombardy) This red made from the Nebbiolo grape, with good body and alcohol content, has held the DOC regional quality-standard classification since 1968.

Vermentino (Sardinia) A light-bodied dry white with complex flavour that can be matched with medium-weight dishes, especially richer fish. The northeastern part of Sardinia produces the highest-quality Vermentino di Gallura DOCG.

Vino Nobile di Montepulciano (Tuscany) Prugnolo Gentile grapes (a clone of Sangiovese) form the backbone of the distinguished Vino Nobile di Montepulciano. Its intense but delicate nose and dry, vaguely tannic taste make it the perfect companion to red meat and mature cheese.

To read about:
Friuli Wine Trails see page 74
Aperitivo Time see page 182

Types of Italian Wine

Know what you like but still unsure how to translate that into an order?

Sparkling wines Franciacorta (Lombardy), prosecco (Veneto), Asti (aka Asti Spumante; Piedmont), Lambrusco (Emilia-Romagna)

Light, citrusy whites with grassy or floral notes Vermentino (Sardinia), Orvieto (Umbria), Soave (Veneto), Tocai (Friuli), Frascati (Lazio)

Dry whites with aromatic herbal or mineral aspect Cinque Terre (Liguria), Lugana (southern Lake Garda), Gavi (Piedmont), Falanghina (Campania), Est! Est!! Est!!! (Lazio)

Versatile, food-friendly reds with pleasant acidity Barbera d'Alba (Piedmont), Montepulciano d'Abruzzo (Abruzzo), Valpolicella (Veneto), Chianti Classico (Tuscany), Bardolino (Lombardy), Sangiovese (Tuscany)

Well-rounded reds, balancing fruit with earthy notes Brunello di Montalcino (Tuscany), Refosco dal Pedulunco Rosso (Friuli), Dolcetto (Piedmont), Morellino di Scansano (Tuscany), Oltrepò Pavese Rosso (Lombardy)

Big, structured reds with velvety tannins Amarone (Veneto), Barolo (Piedmont), Sagrantino di Montefalco secco (Umbria), Sassicaia and other 'super-Tuscan' blends (Tuscany)

Fortified and dessert wine Sciacchetrá (Liguria), Colli Orientali del Friuli Picolit (Friuli), Vin Santo (Tuscany), Moscato d'Asti (Piedmont)

Wine Trails: Friuli

FRIULI VENEZIA GIULIA / FOOD & DRINK

In the snowy mountains and fertile plains of northeast Italy, the diverse landscape is reflected in the variety of its wines, from intense reds to fragrantly sweet whites. Explore the region at your own pace on a journey to some of the region's most memorable vineyards.

The rugged Friuli region stretches from the shores of the Adriatic up to the Alps, forming a wedge between Italy's border with Eastern and Central Europe. Vineyards spread along the flat plains of the Piave, Italy's 'sacred river', where rough Raboso wine was a great favourite of Ernest Hemingway, to the Carso, a rocky peninsula running up towards Trieste, where cantinas are often hewn into underground caves.

Inland, the Collio Orientale – the eastern hills around Cividale – are famous for fascinating reds with such intense local grapes as Refosco and Pignolo, but the jewel in Friuli's crown is the Collio, a 50km necklace of hills. The clay and sandstone soil here produce some of the finest white wines in Italy: fruity indigenous grapes like Ribolla Gialla; the unique Picolit, late harvested for a luscious dessert wine rivalling Sauternes; and the local favourite, Friulano, still referred to here as Tocai, even though this name can now only be used by Hungary's famed sweet wine.

Many Collio winegrowers have opened up their estates as B&Bs, often inviting guests to whizz around the vineyards on signature bright-yellow Collio Vespas, and as Friuli is still very much undiscovered, you are sure of a warm welcome. The same is true of eating out; all over the countryside there are rustic *agriturismi* (farm stays) that open at the weekend and offer traditional Friulian fare, which is more influenced by Central European cuisine than Italian.

Plump gnocchi stuffed with susina plums are perfect with a sharp Friulano, and the more characteristic Ribolla Gialla goes well with juicy baby squid sautéed with slightly bitter red radicchio. A

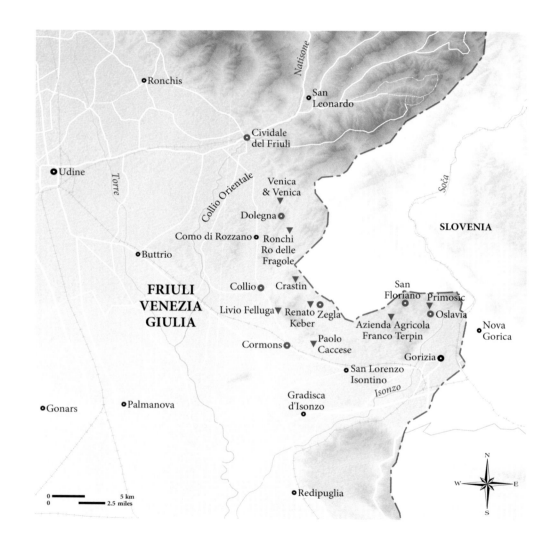

favourite with everyone is Friuli's rich goulash stew; to go with it, it's worth opening a bottle of one of the region's stellar reds, Livio Felluga's Sosso, a potent combination of merlot and Refosco.

Venica & Venica

Just before you drive into the sleepy village of Dolegna, a small sign on the right directs you down a narrow route to one of the Collio's most important wineries. Venica & Venica refers to two brothers, Gianni and Giorgio, who have turned the small vineyard that was founded by their grandfather 80 years ago into a slick, modern estate spanning 37 hectares. They have made a name for their innovative, award-winning wines, but are also pioneers of oenotourism.

They opened a luxurious B&B with a pool and a tennis court way back in 1985, and while the cellar is always open for tastings (apart from Sunday), you can call in advance to reserve a full two-hour tour with a detailed explanation of how the wines are made. The one wine not to miss here is Ronco Bernizza, a surprising, steely chardonnay perfect with *spaghetti alle vongole* (spaghetti with baby clams).

Ronchi Ro delle Fragole

It takes some determination to drive up through the woods that cling to the hillside above Dolegna – don't count on the GPS working – but the reward at Ronchi Ro is to discover a small, new *azienda* (enterprise) where the *vignaiolo*, Romeo Rossi, is brimming with enthusiasm for the wine he is making, while his companion, Carolina, has created an idyllic B&B in their ancient stone farmhouse.

Romeo comes from a winemaking family and worked for many years for leading estates in the Collio. In 2005 he leapt at the chance to buy 3 hectares here, and devote himself to the cultivation of a single grape – sauvignon. Romeo's approach is very technical, and when his wine ages, it is true that he achieves something similar to the mineral 'Fumé' quality that so marks sauvignon from Pouilly and Sancerre in the Loire. But Romeo is also a Friulian traditionalist, and after discovering a parcel of 50-year-old vines of the local Friulano grape, he also set about making a cuvée that, for him, does justice to this iconic wine.

Crastin

Marked by the belltower of a medieval church, Ruttars sits right on the border with Slovenia and is the highest point of the Collio. The road descends into Crastin, a tiny hamlet with just a single ancient farmhouse where Sergio Collarig cultivates a small 7-hectare property.

He is a rough-and-ready *contadino*, what might romantically be termed a peasant farmer, who lives and works in the house he was born in, aided by his sister Vilma. Together they have progressed from producing *vino sfuso* (wine sold in bulk) to creating a small garage cellar producing 30,000 bottles of wine. And it's not just the Friulano and Ribolla Gialla whites that Collio is famous for, but also merlot and cabernet franc aged in oak barrels. Each weekend there are crowds of visitors as the Collarigs open as an *agriturismo,* with Vilma preparing plates of ham, sausages and cheeses while Sergio opens bottles for the tastings.

Livio Felluga

Presided over by the 100-year-old patriarch Livio Felluga, this is the family winery that has set the benchmark for excellence in both the Collio and adjoining Collio Orientale vineyards, where the vast estate stretches over a total of 160 hectares. Felluga recalls that though there were many doubters 60 years ago, when he started planting, he was sure this was the ideal place to grow white grapes like Friulano, sauvignon and pinot grigio, and the indigenous red Refosco.

The cantina is located just outside Cormons, where visitors are welcomed by appointment in a designer tasting room. And just across the road, you can savour Felluga's wines in Terra & Vini, a bustling osteria opened by Livio's daughter, Elda, where *viticoltori* noisily gossip at the long bar and food lovers feast on traditional Friulian *frico* (melted cheese with creamy polenta) accompanied by Felluga's signature Terre Alte, the perfect blend of Friulano, pinot bianco and sauvignon.

Paolo Caccese

The hamlet of Pradis stretches over a series of rolling vine-clad hills overlooking Cormons, the winemaking capital of Collio. The only inhabitants are a dozen *viticoltori,* who all make exceptional wines.

Paolo Caccese's cantina sits atop the highest hill, an ancient stone house alongside three tall cypress trees, surrounded by his 6-hectare vineyard. Caccese is a genuine eccentric, dressed like a country gentleman, and resembling more the lawyer that he trained to be than a producer of a dozen elegant wines. His classic Friulano and Malvasia are delicious, but

ask to also try such oddities as the fruity Müller-Thurgau, aromatic Traminer and a luscious late-harvest Verduzzo. Caccese ignores trends and fashions, still uses old-fashioned cement vats, and explains that he only has to do minimal interfering with the grapes because they are grown in such rich soil in an incredible location.

Renato Keber

The meandering road out of Cormons towards San Floriano is marked on both sides by the Collio's distinctive winemaker signs, and at Zegla, a narrow lane leads you to Renato Keber, a one-of-kind *vignaiolo*. A quiet, unassuming man, Keber has built a swanky tasting room with panoramic views over his vineyards, where he loves surprising visitors with his spectacular wines. He believes that making great wines is all in the ageing, rather than releasing them when they are too young.

The terroir around Zegla is marl and sandstone, and the harvest of these low-yield vines is hand-picked. Keber then waits seven years before bringing out each merlot and cabernet vintage, and he follows the same philosophy with his whites, so it is quite a shock when he opens, say, a comparatively long-in-the-tooth pinot grigio or sauvignon. But, as Keber says, his wines are marathon wines.

Azienda Agricola Franco Terpin

Franco Terpin is an anti-establishment artisan winemaker, the guru of a group of natural, no-sulphite wine producers. Certified organic, and favouring long maceration, natural yeast and no chemicals, Terpin's wine spends a year in the barrel, another in steel vats, then three years ageing in the bottle. He produces 90%

white wines on the estate, which includes vines across the border in Slovenia. They have an incredible orange colour, known here as *vini arancioni*.

Call in advance for a tasting and be prepared for an unforgettable experience. He swears his wines are the only kind he drinks now – that he can no longer stand 'chemically induced' flavours in other non-natural wines.

Primosic

Friuli's Collio region runs out by the border with Slovenia in the village of Oslavia, where at the end of Main St stands the old Frontier Post between two countries divided at the end of World War II.

Back in the 19th century, the Primosic family supplied wine to be sold in Vienna, capital of the Austro-Hungarian Empire, which then included tiny Oslavia, but today Sylvester Primosic and his sons Boris and Marko have created a modern, dynamic winery very much in tune with modern Europe. They are at the forefront of a movement to recognise the potential of the long-neglected indigenous Ribolla Gialla grape, so be sure to try the sparkling Ribollanoir, where 10% of tannic pinot nero is added to the mineral Ribolla.

A few houses down the road is the cantina of one of Collio's most original winemakers, the reclusive Josko Gravener. Although he rarely opens his door to visitors, you can try Gravener's wines in Oslavia's Osteria Korsic. They are something very special, fermented in vast terracotta amphoras buried in his cellar.

To read about:
Harvest Time see page 128
Making Limoncello see page 286

Italian Design

Better living by design: what could be more Italian? From the cup that holds your morning espresso to the bedside light you switch off before you go to sleep, there's a designer responsible, and almost everyone in Italy will know their name. Design here isn't merely functional, it's a way of life.

While the modernist ideal of creating useful objects is at the core of Italian design, it's not so easy to define its style. Design in Italy is suffused with emotion. Whereas mass-produced goods are staid and uncommunicative – specifically designed to work for everyone, everywhere – Italian products are expressive, playful, even outrageous. Not only is the country's rich Renaissance history and cultural bravado evident in its creations, the memory of Latin animism – wherein ancient Roman household objects had a spirit – is present, too. Lounge on Zanuso's Lady chair, tear around on a Piaggio Ciao, toss something into Enzo Mari's *in attesa* wastepaper basket: these objects *breathe*.

Food, fashion, architecture, automobiles, furniture, interiors – Italy is a global trendsetter. Today the country exerts a vast influence on urban, industrial and fashion design worldwide, securing the Made in Italy brand a 30% stake in the €32 billion global design market. Fashion mecca Milan bustles with over 12,000 fashion and design companies, while the annual April Salone del Mobile trade fair is the Super Bowl of the design world, attracting some 270,000 designers, architects and fashionistas in search of inspiration in its city-wide shows.

But how is this possible when Italian production is miniscule compared with that of the USA and other big manufacturing countries? Large-scale industrial production came late to Italy. With the exception of the rich Bourbon Kingdom of the Two Sicilies in the south, the rest of the country was fragmented politically and geographically until Unification in 1861. This meant that the decorative joy inherent in hand-crafted objects persisted longer despite the advancing modernist rigour of the Industrial Revolution.

At the advent of the 20th century, when the era of luxury goods began to emerge, Italian furniture designers such as Vittorio Ducrot and architects such as Ernesto Basile were able to draw on a huge artistic tradition of smithcraft, glass making, carpentry, ceramics, masonry, weaving and textile production. Basile's fusion of Roman classicism and medieval baroque traditions with the modern elements and exquisite craft details of art nouveau led to a revolution in design and architecture that transformed Palermo.

Where ornate 'Stile Liberty' (Italian art nouveau) captured the imagination of a genteel pre–world war Europe, the dynamic style of Italian futurism was a perfect partner for the modernist design movement. Like cogs in a political wheel, fascist propaganda co-opted the radical, neoclassical streamlining that futurism inspired and put it to work in posters, architecture, furniture and design. In 1923, the Novecento Italiano movement was launched at an exhibition in Milan, with Mussolini as a keynote speaker.

The proliferation of factories and the fascist tendency to hierarchical organisation and centralisation boosted Italian manufacturing. Through an inherent eye for purity of line, modern Italian design found beauty in balance and symmetry. This refreshing lack of detail appealed greatly to a fiercely democratising war-torn Europe where minimalism and utility came to represent the very essence of modernity.

Clockwise from top left **Valentine typewriter, Moka coffee pot, Vespa scooter, Chairs at La Triennale di Milano**

After WWII, the military industrial complexes in Turin and Milan became the centrepieces of a new, global consumer-centric economy. Turin's strength was industrial design, from Lavazza espresso machines to the Fiat 500 car; Milan focused on fashion and home decor. Italian films and pioneering magazines such as *Domus* and *Casabella* showcased these newly mass-produced design objects, making them seem both desirable and, more importantly, attainable.

Milan's philosopher-architects and designers – Giò Ponti, Vico Magistretti, Achille Castiglioni, Carlo Scarpa, Gruppo 7, Gae Aulenti, Ettore Sottsass and the Memphis Group, and Piero Fornasetti – were imbued with a modernist sense of optimism. They saw their postwar mission was not only to rebuild the bomb-damaged country but to re-design the whole urban environment.

You can view their ground-breaking work alongside emerging design talent at La Triennale di Milano, which exhibits the very best of Italian design, urban planning, architecture and media arts, emphasising the relationship between art and industry.

Far from being mere intellectual theorists, Italy's architect-designers combine centuries of craft know-how with an ability to innovate – take architect Stefano Boeri's Vertical Forest model for reforesting cities being deployed to create the first 'Forest City', Liuzhou, in southern China by 2020. Their style emerges from traditions that have been handed down through families for generations. It is this attention to our human relationships both with each other and the world around us that ultimately defines 'Italian style'.

Right Alessi bird-whistle kettle

Iconic Italian Designs

Alessi Bird-Whistle Kettle Designed by American Michael Graves, Alessi's bird-whistle kettle was designed not only to boil water, but to bring users joy when it sang its song. Launched in 1985, it has been a bestseller ever since.

Vespa Piaggio Renzo Spolti and Vittorio Casini's 1944 scooter transformed the lives of urbanites with its pressed steel unibody, foot floorboard and hand-mounted controls, which ensured riders could maintain their *bella figura* on the go.

Moka Pot The *macchinetta del caffè* (small coffee machine) is a stove-top coffee maker that produces coffee by passing boiling water, pressurised by steam, through ground coffee. It was patented by inventor Luigi de Ponti for Bialetti in 1933.

Arco Floor Lamp Designed by Achille Castiglioni for FLOS in 1962, this is the rock star of floor lamps, designed to provide lighting without the need for mounted fixtures. Its looks earned it a role in the James Bond movie, *Diamonds Are Forever*.

Valentine Typewriter This sleek, simple typewriter was created by avant-garde designer Ettore Sottsass for Olivetti in 1968.

To read about:
Vespas see page 84
Violins see page 132

Design Icon: The Vespa

In a country of zig-zagging alleyways and where locals embrace a dodgem-car driving style, the Vespa scooter might be your best bet for navigating your way around Italy, not to mention a stylish ride. One of the most enduring symbols of Italian design, the Vespa embodies the Italian obsessions of innovative engineering, elegance and comfort. Its launch by Piaggio in 1946 revolutionised travel.

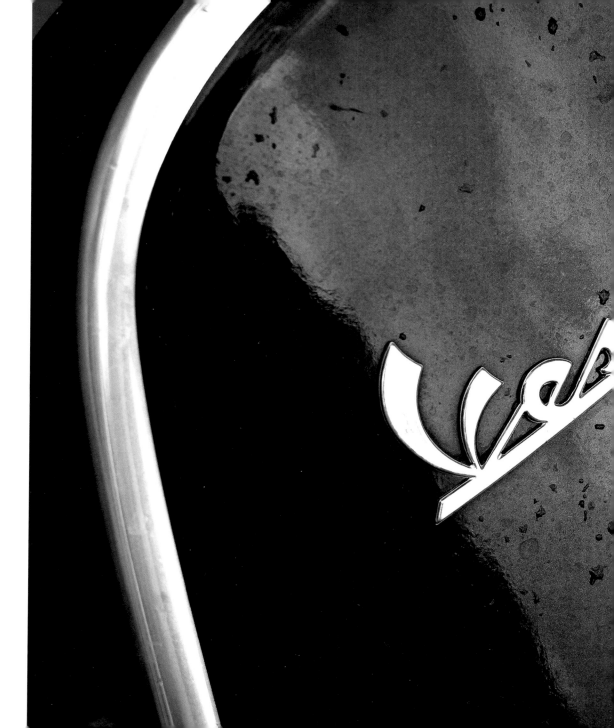

The Vespa prototype was produced by designers Renzo Spolti and Vittorio Casini for Piaggio in 1944 and modified by aeronautical designer Corradino d'Ascanio. It was radically different from any motorcycle design seen before, comprising a pressed steel unibody with a cowling concealing the engine ensuring that clothes remained free from dirt and grease. The step-through seat design and flat floorboard allowed for easy mounting and a comfortable new riding position, while the tall splash guard protected the rider from wind and spray. In addition to the bodywork, the design included handlebar-mounted controls, forced air cooling and wheels of a small diameter that could be easily changed. On seeing it for the first time, Enrico Piaggio exclaimed, *'Sembra una vespa!'* (It's like a wasp!), giving the friendly little *motorino* its name. Since its launch, the 'wasp' has been restyled 120 times, culminating most recently in the vintage-inspired GTV and LXV models, yet the essential design remains timeless.

The complete Vespa story, from the Genovese company's arrival in Tuscany in 1921 to its manufacturing of four-engine aircraft and hydroplanes, to its WWII destruction and rebirth as Europe's exclusive Vespa producer, is grippingly told at Museo Piaggio in a former factory building, 25km southeast of Pisa in Pontedera.

Should Vespa's carefree spirit take hold, hook up with Tuscany by Vespa – operated by Florence Town in Florence – for a Vespa tour.

To read about:
Rome City Life see page 86
Milan Design see page 200

ROME
The Eternal City

A fast-talking, hot-blooded, spaghetti-twirling livewire of a capital city, Rome balances on the ruins of an ancient empire and seven hills. La città eterna (the eternal city) is the ultimate Italian icon, pulsing with urban life, buzzing with Vespas that dart like fireflies past baroque piazzas, bauble-domed basilicas, ancient ruins and jam-packed streetside cafes.

Beyond its traffic jams and tourist traps, Roma is a wholly lovable, livable city that will quite simply floor you with the colossal weight of its past and the full-throttle lifestyle of its present. If you have a peculiar sense of déjà vu when you first set foot here, it's most likely because you *have* been here before – if not in reality, then in a book, a film or a song.

A romp around ancient Rome, once *caput mundi* (capital of the world), opens up a compelling 3000-year history textbook. The Italian capital rose to become Europe's first superpower and the spiritual centre of the Christian world, usurping its would-be rivals in ingenuity and achievement. Naturally, the Romans didn't do things by halves and they built a city to out-pomp them all. Bloodthirsty tales of gladiators battling wild beasts at the 50,000-seat Colosseum, the ruins of the Palatino blushing at sunset, the grandstand views of the Roman Forum and its sprawling ruined temples and basilicas – these are 'wow, I'm in Rome' moments once seen, never forgotten.

The history-loaded Centro Storico is every inch as astonishing, presided over by the 2000-year Pantheon with its echoing dome and marble-clad interior that beggars belief, and spiralling around fountain-splashed Piazza Navona, with its street artists and baroque *palazzi*. Sitting over the river, there's the Vatican, the world's smallest sovereign state, where Michelangelo's marble-wrought *Pietà* moves some to tears among the rich artistry of St Peter's Basilica and his show-stealing frescoes dance across the ceiling of the Sistine Chapel.

To make Rome your own, dive into less explored, thoroughly local neighbourhoods. Alley-woven Trastevere and Gianicolo hide exquisitely mosaic-lined churches, Testaccio heaves with kicking bars, trattorias offering nose-to-tail dining and pizzerias churning out thin, crispy pizzas quicker than you can say *delizioso!* Tridente, Trevi and the Quirinale beckon with the 135 Spanish Steps – the perfect people-watching perch, Renaissance churches brimming with Caravaggio masterpieces, blockbuster art galleries and the Trevi Fountain. Toss in a lucky coin to ensure to you return to Rome – just as countless millions have before you.

Right Trevi Fountain

TEN WAYS TO FALL IN LOVE WITH ROME

ROME / CULTURE

A heady mix of haunting ruins, awe-inspiring art and vibrant street life, Italy's hot-blooded capital is one of the world's most inspiring and romantic cities. While the big-ticket monuments certainly leave their mark, you might just find yourself falling for the city's smaller-scale charms down cobbled lanes and around hidden corners.

Peek Through a Secret Keyhole

Walking around Rome and peering through keyholes will typically result in concerned phone calls to the local *carabinieri*. One exception to this rule is the Villa del Priorato di Malta – a building with a metal gate that contains a tiny keyhole framing one of the finest views in the city. Those who press their eyes to the metal witness a perfectly composed scene: a path shaded by cypress trees and rosebushes, the tower of Santa Maria in Trastevere rising on the far bank of the Tiber and the hulking dome of St Peter's at the centre. It's a composition so perfect, no one can say for sure whether the locksmith (or the gardener) intended it or whether it was a happy accident.

Visit the Pope's Gardens

As holiday homes go, Castel Gandolfo is not the most discreet: a 17th-century pile the size of a football field outside Rome, with a magnificent garden overlooking the shores of the Tyrrhenian Sea. It is precisely this grandeur that meant its lawful resident (the humble Pope Francis) chose not to spend his summer holidays here as his predecessors did – instead opening his gardens to the public for the first time in 2016. Visitor numbers are strictly limited, so entering the grand wrought-iron gates can feel like entering a secret garden.

Drink from a 'Big Nose'

On roasting hot summer days, the saviour of every Roman citizen is the *nasone* or 'big nose'. This is no genetic quirk, but a nickname for the 2500 drinking fountains dotted about the city. So called because of the shape of the spout, the fountains were first installed in the late 19th century,

but are part of a proud Roman tradition dating back to the great aqueducts of ancient Rome. *Nasoni* are used variously by locals, thirsty sparrows, bathing dogs, kids starting water fights and curiously few tourists – and while the iron spout can get very hot, the water is always clean and miraculously cool.

Swim in a Fascist Swimming Pool

Rising mightily over the northwest bank of the Tiber, far from the itineraries of wandering tourists, the Foro Italico sports complex is one of the city's unsung wonders – a monolithic park inspired by the glories of ancient Rome. It underwent some tactful rebranding some 70 years ago: upon construction in the 1930s it was known as the Foro Mussolini after its founder. The fascist leader envisaged it as a factory for a new, all-conquering Italian master race. The ideology went long ago – but Mussolini's impressive if questionable artistic taste remains: nowhere more so than the swimming pool, where visitors can splash about beneath soaring ceilings and marble surfaces.

Find a Vatican Euro Coin

Some come to the Vatican for spiritual enlightenment, others to step into the cool colossus of St Peter's on a hot summer's day. But for a few, crossing into the Holy See is the chance to go in search of a chunk of metal with a maximum face value of €2 (the biggest coin in the set). Among collectors, a Vatican euro coin is a Wonka's golden ticket of currency: a cherished oddity from the smallest nation on Earth. The Vatican minted its first euros a decade ago, but only in recent years have they entered circulation. Admittedly the

odds of finding one in a handful of change from the Vatican Post Office aren't huge. But if you happen upon one, don't spend it – a rarer coin might fetch as much as €65 from a collector.

Eat Grattachecca

Ice cream is everywhere in Rome, flavoured with every possible ingredient and served in Pavarotti-sized portions. But curiously the capital claims a different frozen dessert all of its own – *grattachecca*. Translated as 'shaved ice', the recipe isn't much more complicated than the name would suggest, with chunks of ice coated in syrup and topped with fresh fruit. A dubious legend tells that the Emperor Nero invented *grattachecca,* ordering his grunts to fetch ice from the mountains around Rome and consuming it to cool his angry moods. Though sadly something of an endangered species today, *grattachecca* is a traditional accompaniment to an evening stroll: bought from a stall, and ideally slurped on a bench overlooking the sluggish current of the Tiber as the city stirs with early evening life.

Check Out Pasquino

This unassuming sculpture is Rome's most famous 'talking statue'. During the 16th century, when there were no safe outlets for dissent, a Vatican tailor named Pasquino began sticking notes to the statue with satirical verses lampooning the Church and aristocracy. Soon others joined in and, as the trend spread, talking statues popped up all over town. The sculpture is now off-limits to disgruntled Romans but there's a convenient board next to it where people still leave messages, traditionally known as *pasquinade*.

Spend the Evening in Trastevere

Nowhere is better for a night out than the picture-perfect neighbourhood of Trastevere. Over the river from the historic centre, its medieval lanes, hidden piazzas and pastel-hued *palazzi* harbour hundreds of bars, cafes, trattorias and restaurants catering to a nightly crowd of up-for-it Romans and besotted visitors. Locals meet up at 'the steps', the wide short flight of stairs leading up to the 17th-century fountain on Piazza Trilussa. For a real carnival atmosphere head to the summertime pop-up bars along Trastevere's riverside quays between Ponte Mazzoni and Ponte Cesto and beyond.

Visit Keats and Shelley in the Non-Catholic Cemetery

Dating to the 18th century, Rome's Non-Catholic Cemetery is a leafy plot of land most famous as the resting place of John Keats. He died in Rome aged 25, and lies beside the ashes of his friend Percy Bysshe Shelley. A steady trickle of pilgrims potter around the wisteria-lined pathways to pay their respects to the poets. But they are only part of the story: lying around are a whole cast of characters from across the world who breathed their last in Rome.

Go Rowing at the Villa Borghese Gardens

At clocking-off time, the Villa Borghese Gardens are Rome's rallying point: a hilltop refuge of cypress-lined colonnades, and a serene spot from which to marvel at the mayhem of the city below. Perhaps its quietest corner is the boating lake in the north of the park. Here visitors and locals cast off in rowing boats, navigating the still waters among paddling terrapins, falling leaves and quacking ducks. It pays not to be in a hurry (you could row from one side to the other in a few seconds), so many are content to rest their oars, lie back in the hull and let their boats be carried by the cooling hilltop breeze.

To read about:

The Vatican see page 92
Grand Giardini see page 296

Above 'Big nose' drinking fountain

Left Trastevere

THE VATICAN

ROME / RELIGION, ART

Nestled inside Rome, the Vatican is the world's smallest independent nation. Established under the 1929 Lateran Treaty, it comprises the last vestiges of the Papal States – the papal fiefdom that ruled Rome and much of the Italian peninsula until unification in 1861. Its name comes from the Etruscan settlement, Vatica, meaning 'garden' and the city sits atop a hill amid gardens that were laid out by Agrippina the Elder in the 1st century AD.

The Vatican's association with Christianity dates back nearly two thousand years. In Agrippina's gardens, her son – the Emperor Caligula – built a circus for charioteers, in the centre of which he erected the Egyptian obelisk of Heliopolis, which still stands in front of St Peter's Basilica. It was here, tradition says, that St Peter was martyred, crucified head down by the Emperor Nero between AD 64 and 68. To commemorate this the Constantinian basilica was built in 326 over what was believed to be Peter's tomb. According to Catholic doctrine, the current pope, Francis, is the direct successor to St Peter, whose bones were put on public display for the very first time in 2013.

In this city of outstanding churches, none holds a candle to St Peter's, Italy's largest and richest basilica. Built atop the earlier 4th-century church, it was consecrated in 1626 after 120 years' construction. Its lavish interior contains many spectacular works of art, including three of Italy's most celebrated masterpieces: Michelangelo's *Pietà*, his soaring dome, and Bernini's 29m-high baldachin over the papal altar (the site of St Peter's grave), at which the pope is the only priest permitted to serve. For an extra perspective on the church, you can clamber the 871 steps up to the dome; descend to the grottoes to view the tombs and sarcophagi of previous popes; or, between October and May, go on a seminarian-run tour.

For centuries St Peter's Basilica stood alone at the centre of a densely populated quarter. It wasn't until the 12th century that the Palazzo Apostolico Vaticano – the Pope's official residence – was built. It was revamped to great effect in the 15th and 16th centuries by a series of ambitious Renaissance popes. One of them, Julius II, established the Vatican Museums, which today house one of the world's greatest art collections.

The collections of the museums and the Apostolic Library are deemed of the highest historical, scientific and cultural importance by Unesco, which added the Vatican to its list of Heritage Sites in 1984. It is the only listing to consist of an entire state. Touring the collection is an exhilarating experience. Exhibits are displayed along 7km of hallways, and range from Egyptian mummies and Etruscan bronzes to Roman busts and modern paintings. There's enough art on display to keep you busy for years but highlights include a unique collection of classical statuary in the Museo Pio-Clementino, a suite of rooms frescoed by Raphael, and the Michelangelo-painted Sistine Chapel.

Home to two of the world's most famous works of art – Michelangelo's ceiling frescoes (1508–12) and his *Giudizio Universale* (Last Judgment; 1536–41) – the Sistine Chapel is the one place everyone wants to see, and on a busy day you could find yourself sharing it with up to 2000 people. Michelangelo's ceiling design, which is best viewed from the chapel's main entrance in the far, east wall, covers the entire 800-sq-m surface. With painted architectural features and a cast of biblical characters, it's centred on nine panels depicting stories from the book of Genesis.

The chapel's walls also boast superb frescoes. Painted in 1481–82 by a crack team of Renaissance artists, including Botticelli, Ghirlandaio, Pinturicchio, Perugino and Luca Signorelli, they represent events in the lives of Moses (to the left looking at the *Giudizio Universale*) and

The Pope's Encyclical: On Care of Common Home

The power of celebrity is the power to set the agenda, and few people have the celebrity power of the Pope. He heads the world's largest religion and so has 1.2 billion followers in his flock. From his seat in Rome's Vatican City, he addresses the developed world, much of which descended from Christendom; but thanks to his modest Argentinian roots he also speaks to millions of people in the developing world. On those grounds alone, his encyclical on climate change, *Laudato Sì*, which he gave as a gift to visiting US president Donald Trump, stands as one of the most influential documents of our times. Far from a narrow, Christian-centric contribution to the climate debate, it is a sweeping, radical and highly persuasive critique of how we inhabit this planet. It focuses not just on the ecological challenges we face, but offers a remarkable commentary on morality, society and economics. It is available to download in 12 languages for free at w2.vatican.va.

Christ (to the right). Highlights include Botticelli's *Temptations of Christ* and Perugino's *Handing over of the Keys*.

As well as providing a showcase for priceless art, the Sistine Chapel also serves a function as the place where the conclave meets to elect a new pope. Dating to 1274, give or take a few modifications, the rules of the voting procedure are explicit: between 15 and 20 days after the death of a pope, the entire College of Cardinals (comprising all cardinals under the age of 80) is locked in the chapel to elect a new pontiff. Four secret ballots are held a day until a two-thirds majority has been secured. News of the election is communicated by emitting white smoke through a specially erected chimney.

If the Sistine Chapel is the birthing room of the papacy, St Peter's Square is its public platform. Laid between 1656 and 1667, the scale of the piazza is dazzling: at its largest it measures 320m by 240m; there are 284 columns and, atop the

colonnades, 140 saints. It was designed by Gian Lorenzo Bernini to resemble a giant keyhole with two semicircular colonnades, encircling a giant ellipse that straightens out to funnel believers into the basilica. The effect was deliberate – Bernini described the colonnades as representing 'the motherly arms of the church'.

It is here that Pope Francis holds his weekly Wednesday audiences (you can book free tickets at w2.vatican.va), his Easter and Christmas masses and his noonday Sunday blessings. It was also here that he addressed a crowd of over a hundred thousand pilgrims when he launched the 2016 Jubilee, or Holy Year. Under the year's theme of mercy, the Pope signalled his wish to change the Church's

approach from condemnation of wrong-doing to a Church that is more forgiving and understanding of its flock. It is unconventional and compassionate acts such as this, as well as his care for the homeless and hopeless, that has earned the Pope the love and respect of people – even non-religious people – around the world.

To read about:

Saints & Feasts see page 168
Easter Holy Week see page 174

Left Vatican Museums

Above St Peter's Square

Tradizione

Treasured Heritage, Hill Towns & Harvests

The whole Italy thing? We get it. Italy does that to you: it slips under your skin and tugs at your heartstrings, particularly when you look beyond its blockbuster, crowd-pulling sights. You might tell yourself it's going to be somewhere else next year, but secretly you'll be longing to return. Let yourself be slowly absorbed by its rhythms and seasons, the subtler nuances of its food and wine, and its lovingly honed traditions for deeper insights into its fascinating people and culture.

This is a land of lyrical landscapes, which must be lived not just observed. Walk in the oak and chestnut forests of remotest Tuscany, as the autumn mist creeps in. Tour the backroads of Umbria, where alley-woven medieval towns are pinned to hilltops, detouring to Norcia for prized *salumi* and spiritual enlightenment in St Benedict's birthplace. Pick olives in Puglia on a golden October day, then dig into *cucina povera* (peasant cooking). Or find a very different Italy in Piedmont, discussing the terroir of ruby-red Barolo wines at a family-run cantina, touring Turin's graceful *palazzi*, peering up to the outline of snowcapped Alps, or enlisting a *trifulau* (truffle hunter) in Alba to unearth the highly prized *tartufo bianco* (white truffle). Up and down the country, *agriturismi* immerse you in farming life and let you feast on its bounty.

Of course modernity has its place, but the Italians are fierce about protecting their heritage. And when you read Dante down a back lane in Florence; the city enveloped in the chiaroscuro light of a Caravaggio painting; or marvel at the intricacy of Ravenna's sparkling hand-cut Byzantine mosaics; or watch rough-robed Franciscan monks roam Assisi's shadowy backstreets – you can't help but feel they're right to do so.

The Slow Food Revolution

PIEDMONT / FOOD & DRINK

Italy's Piedmont has an overflowing treasure trove of regional specialities, home-grown delicacies and serious culinary kudos as the birthplace of the Slow Food Movement, which celebrates the pleasure and taste of food over speed and convenience.

The Big Fork Manifesto

The year was 1987. McDonald's had just begun expansion into Italy and lunch beyond the bun seemed to be fading into memory. Enter Carlo Petrini and other journalists from small-town Bra, Piedmont. Determined to buck the trend, these *neoforchettoni* ('big forks', or foodies) created a manifesto. Published in the culinary magazine *Gambero Rosso,* they declared that a meal should be judged not by its speed, but by its pure pleasure.

The organisation they founded would soon become known worldwide as Slow Food, and its mission to reconnect artisanal producers with enthusiastic consumers has taken root with around 100,000 members in over 160 countries – not to mention Slow Food *agriturismi* (farm-stay accommodation), restaurants, wineries, and farmers markets across Italy.

Held on even-numbered years in venues across Turin, Italy's top Slow Food event is the biennial Salone del Gusto & Terre Madre. Slow Food's global symposium, it features Slow Food producers, chefs, activists, restaurateurs, farmers, scholars, environmentalists and epicureans from around the world.

Why Piedmont?

In a country blessed with world-famous produce, Piedmont still stands out as a gastronomic star. This region, with vineyard-filled hills and historical links to its earthy soil, is rich in specialities. While Piedmont is rooted in its culinary traditions, it is also one of Italy's most developed and industrial regions, and it's this progressive attitude that has seen a batch of chefs cooking dishes melding tradition and modernity in exciting ways.

Positano, Slow City

Positano is one of more than 75 towns in Italy to have gained Slow City status (an extension of the Slow Food Movement). In order to be considered, certain criteria must be met: towns need to have fewer than 55,000 inhabitants, no fast-food outlets or neon-lit hoardings, plenty of cycling and walking paths, and neighbourhood restaurants serving traditional cuisine with locally sourced ingredients. For more information, check www.cittaslow.org.

The city of Turin is where most Piedmont journeys begin. Turin introduced the world to its first hard chocolate and to vermouth; fostered Italy's *aperitivo* culture; and is home to Europe's largest open-air food market, Porta Palazzo.

It's often touted as 'Tuscany without tourists', and gourmands in the know head to Piedmont for its regional specialities, including *risotto alla piemontese* (risotto with butter and cheese), *tajarin* (a thin tagliatelle pasta), *vitello tonnato* (veal with tuna sauce), Tomino goats' milk cheese, grissini, rare white truffles, Arborio rice, hazelnuts and gelato. Add to this two of the world's most revered wine regions – Barolo and Barbaresco – and it's easy to see why Piedmont is one of the most exciting culinary scenes in Italy today.

To read about:
Farm Stays see page 106
Zero-Kilometre Cuisine see page 128

Following the Foodie Trail

Stock the larder at a sprawling food emporium, savour rare white truffles and compare the nuances of vintage Barolo and Barbaresco wines on this four-day foodie trail of Piedmont. The trail begins in Turin, a city blessed with a hinterland fabulously rich in produce and with an increasing number of young and innovative restaurateurs and chefs.

Porta Palazzo

Start your day at Porta Palazzo market, a vibrant multicultural place that sees hundreds of stalls spilling out on the Piazza della Repubblica every day except Sunday. Stroll by glistening red tomatoes, fresh figs and piles of olives, while locals fill their carts with fruit and veg, and stall owners spruik their wares to hungry shoppers.

There's also a large indoor fish and meat market but the real reason to come here is for the covered deli and separate local and organic produce section. Wind your way around the deli picking up big bags of grissini and small wheels of soft Tomino di Talucco cheese – mainly made from goats' milk – before heading out the back to see what's in season from the farmers' organic section.

Eataly

When Porta Palazzo starts packing up its stalls come midday on weekdays, make your way to one of the world's most famous 'supermarkets' – the food emporium Eataly, which was set up by one of the founders of the global Slow Food Movement.

In a former vermouth factory, it has shelves stocked with a staggering choice of sustainable produce from the region and the country. Cruise the aisles of bulging bags of porcini mushrooms; jars of traditional *ragù*; every shape, size and colour of pasta imaginable; delicate soft cheeses and decadent dark chocolate incorporating Piedmont hazelnuts. Once you've crammed your shopping bags you can prop yourself at the counter for lunch at one of the specialist eateries – dine on pizza, pasta, seafood and gelato.

La Drogheria

You can't leave Turin without experiencing its famous *apericena* culture – an extension of the classic *aperitivo,* where instead of a small offering of complimentary snacks with your drink, you pay a little extra for a whole lot more, usually in the form of a buffet.

You'll find bars offering *apericena* throughout the city, particularly along Via Po, but one of the most impressive offerings is housed in an old pharmacy. La Drogheria attracts a mixed crowd of locals, tourists and Turin's cool students.

Drop in for a pre-dinner drink, typically a vermouth-based cocktail, such as a potent negroni (Campari, gin, vermouth), and then dig in to the heaped bowls of pasta, risottos, salads, cheeses and bruschetta.

Osteria del Boccondivino

The next day, head to Bra: the town where Slow Food started. Today Bra has become a gastronomic pilgrimage site. Spend the morning checking out the independent family-owned food shops that fill the historic centre, then visit Osteria del Boccondivino for lunch. Set within a courtyard on the first floor of the Slow Food Movement's headquarters, this is the place to really get an idea of how amazing the seasonal produce can be on the daily changing menu. Devour the fresh *tajarin* pasta with butter and sage or indulge in veal braised in a local Barolo red wine.

La Vita Turchese

From Bra it's a half-hour drive to Barolo in the wine region of Langhe, known for producing Italy's 'wine of kings' – bold reds made from the Nebbiolo grape.

This tiny village, home to numerous *enoteche* (wine bars) and cellars, also hosts the Museo del Vino a Barolo. Immerse yourself in viticulture history through its installations before moving on to taste test. There's nowhere more welcoming to do so than La Vita Turchese, where knowledgeable staff will guide you through your tasting and help you make your choice of the local wines before pairing a glass or two with a cheese and prosciutto plate – a lovely way to spend an afternoon and wind into the evening.

Truffle Hunting in Alba

Start day three up early with a trip to Alba where you can walk off the calories in search of Piedmont's prized *tartufo bianco* (white truffle) in this beautiful foodie town.

Thanks to its surrounding 'vegetable garden' hills, Langhe vineyards and hazelnut groves, this town has gastronomic cred in bucketloads – not only for its revered white truffle but also for its excellent wine, dark chocolate and gelato.

The nuggets of deliciousness are buried deep beneath the earth and notoriously difficult to find. It can require hours of searching and excavation but don't dismay if you don't uncover any; many local restaurants incorporate truffles into their dishes. The Alba tourist office organises truffle hunts during the season.

Piazza Duomo

If your truffle hunt isn't successful, you may be lucky enough to find the delicacy on the menu at one of the restaurants in Piazza Duomo, Alba's main square.

This Michelin-starred restaurant has been going strong for over a decade and is headed up by chef Enrico Crippa, whose

Above **White truffle**

impressive resume includes being the star protégé of Gualtiero Marchesi – regarded as the father of modern Italian cuisine.

The menu showcases Piedmont's premium seasonal produce, including vegetables from the restaurant garden. Crippa's dishes carry off new flavours while also respecting the country's traditions. Book your table for lunch and expect such expertly crafted dishes as Piedmont risotto, suckling pig, scallops with black truffle, chocolate bonnet and sorrel sorbet.

Al Nido Della Cinciallegra

To round off your trip don't miss the village of Neive. It is worthy of a stop just to wander through its medieval streets with the sun setting in the afternoon over the rolling vineyards but it's also an excellent place to taste-test the magnificent wines of the region – Dolcetto d'Alba, Barbaresco, moscato and Barbera d'Alba.

The best spot to do this is Al Nido Della Cinciallegra. This unassuming *enoteca* doubles as the *tabacchiera* (convenience store) and the labels on its wooden shelves read like a who's who of the region's best wines, so it's no surprise that it's a favourite of local winemakers. Locals and drop-in tourists come here to sample the wine accompanied by a generous *aperitivo* buffet of cured meats, soft cheeses, mini quiches, salty olives and bruschetta. Taste a few wines, fill up on food, enjoy the relaxed atmosphere into the evening then grab a couple of souvenir bottles on your way out.

To read about:
Emilia-Romagna's Soul Food see page 122
Puglia's Peasant Cuisine see page 134

Left **Neive**

Unearthing Treasures

Black truffles, or tartufi neri, are just one of the ingredients that have made Norcia, a town in southeastern Umbria, famous for producing fine food. In the north of Italy, the town of Alba is practically synonymous with the delicacy, and yields both tartufi neri and the even-more-prized tartufo bianco (white truffle).

Alba

November is prime truffle season and the best time of the year to head into the nearby forested hills alongside your *trifolau* (truffle hunter) guide and highly trained truffle dogs that shuffle through the woods with their noses to the ground.

Pigs originally rootled out truffles from their hiding places in the earth among tree roots, but these underground mushrooms – one of the most expensive cooking ingredients – are now largely tracked down by hounds. White truffles (which fetch some €250 per 20g/0.8oz) are dug up during the frosty, golden months of November and December, and blacks over a longer season that starts earlier in the autumn and runs through to March.

Alba's precious white truffle crop is celebrated, bought and sold – for princely sums, sometimes reaching five figures – at the annual Fiera del Tartufo festival, held every weekend from mid-October to mid-November. They also star on local menus at this time of year.

Norcia

Down in Central Italy, in the hills above Norcia, it's just after dawn as truffle-hunter Nicola Berardi parks in the woods and steps into the misty morning air. He opens the trunk of the car, and his two dogs Nina and Lulu jump out, yapping with excitement. Berardi barks an order, and the dogs sit obediently at his feet, each earning a biscuit as a reward. Then with another command, he sends them bolting down the hillside, their barks cracking like gunshots over the quiet woods. The truffle hunt has begun.

It doesn't take long before they make their first discovery. On the edge of the wood, one dog begins to sniff around the roots of a young oak tree, and frantically starts to dig with her front paws. Berardi pulls her away as he excavates the soil carefully with a small trowel. He scoops his hand into the earth and brings it out clasping a knobbly black mushroom the size of a cricket ball.

Hidden away in the Sibillini hills, this old walled town is renowned across Italy for the quality of its ingredients – from organic honey to ricotta and rare-breed pork. It's a poster town for the Slow Food Movement, championing the use of home-grown products and organic farming.

At lunchtime in Norcia's narrow back-streets, its trattorias are packed. Seated at long wooden tables, under stuffed boars' heads and gnarled roof-beams, diners dip chunks of bread into bean soup and rabbit hotpot, or twirl ribbons of wild hare pasta onto their forks. On the street outside, baskets are stacked with wheels of pecorino cheese, bulbs of garlic, bags of risotto rice and salami the size of saplings. The choice – and the smell – is overpowering.

Up in the hills, Berardi and his dogs have finished their hunt. It's been a good morning – well over a kilo of truffles in just a couple of hours. Now he's heading home for his own favourite lunch – black truffle omelette.

Wine Pairing

Truffles are often paired with red wine but they go just as well with complex, mineral-rich whites, such as those produced from Piedmont's lesser-known Timorasso grape, which yields a golden-yellow wine with a big body that stands proud alongside the powerful truffles.

To read about:
Exploring Umbria see page 119
Italian Fine-Dining see page 294

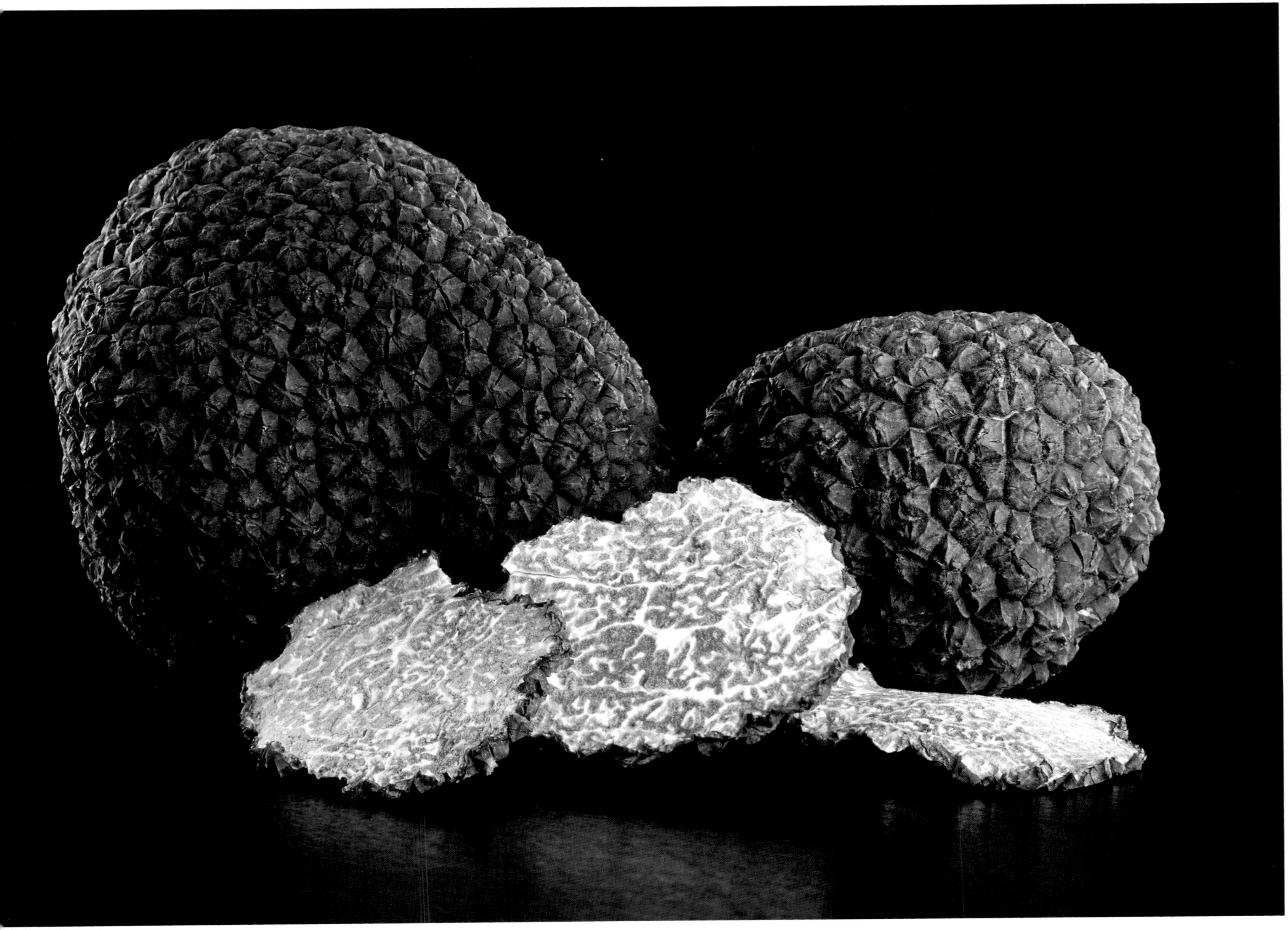

Life on the Farm

ITALY-WIDE / AGRITURISMI

The beauty of Italy extends beyond its world-class cultural riches, glorious cuisine and inimitable fashion and design. The country is also one of Mother Nature's masterpieces, its rural landscapes showcasing extraordinary diversity and soul. And there is no more authentic means of communing with all this sensational natural grandeur than by overnighting at an agriturismo (farm stay).

A traditionally blooming industry in rural regions like Tuscany and Umbria, *agriturismo* accommodation today is gradually becoming as common as muck in the Italian countryside. In keeping with Italy's Slow Food Movement, which reconnects artisanal producers with discerning palates keen to return to a pure grass-roots cuisine, slow travel is increasingly the luxury *de rigueur* for time-smart urbanites wanting to reconnect with nature. At Fattoria Barbialla Novella, a 500-hectare biodynamic farm not far from Florence in northern Tuscany, self-catering guests stay in a handful of exquisitely restored, satisfyingly rustic farmhouses fusing just the right mix of comfort (hip urban-chic decor) and adventure (unpaved roads). Flinging open vintage wooden shutters each morning unveils a glorious green symphony of mist-kissed rolling hills and fields of grazing Chianina cows. The cinematic view never tires. Ditto for breakfasting alfresco on farm eggs and garden-grown cherry-red pomegranates; feeding hay to cream-coloured, long-lashed calves; shopping for velvety olive oil and jars of rich wild-boar stew in the organic farm shop; and tramping through autumn-damp chestnut woods in search of precious white truffles.

Agriturismi (or *masserie* in Southern Italy) are required to grow at least one commercial crop or product. Rural Piedmont, the Dolomites, Abruzzo and Molise, Campania and Puglia in Southern Italy are *agriturismo* hot spots, but with a little pre-trip research (and getting lost down country lanes and unmapped dirt tracks – forget the GPS), life on the farm can be experienced all over the country. Many *agriturismi* on Sardinia (such as Agriturismo

Nuraghe Mannu on the Orosei Coast) and Sicily have spectacular sea, mountain or volcano views.

Addresses range from simple country homes with a handful of olive trees and a donkey to luxury countryside estates with pristine grounds, designer infinity swimming pools, a restaurant and other hotel-like facilities. Some farms produce their own olive oil and wine; others are expansive farming complexes growing wheat, corn and farro or rearing pigs, ducks and livestock.

Simple or sophisticated, all *agriturismi* share a deep-rooted respect for the landscape and a commitment to a rural lifestyle that is slow and venerates local tradition with unfaltering passion. Learning new skills is part of the experience and guests are encouraged to pitch in, be it with the harvest, feeding the animals or foraging for herbs and autumnal mushrooms. Barbialla Nuova offers bread-making and pizza classes. Near Assisi in Umbria, guests at Alla Madonna dei Piatto learn to cook in the farm kitchen using produce from the local market. In Northern Italy, above chic Lake Como, Le Radici ('The Radishes') is all about brushing up on age-old cheese-making techniques and immersing oneself in the bucolic landscape on vigorous hikes. In northeastern Sardinia at Agriturismo Muto Di Gallura, horse riding, donkey trekking and 4WD excursions are big.

Then there is the food – seasonal, zero-kilometre and often organic. Farm accommodation is on a B&B or self-catering basis, meaning breakfast feasts comprising bread and homemade jam, fresh fruit and eggs. Other meals, likewise fuelled by farm products, are served with the

family in the kitchen or in a casual eatery run by the *agriturismo*. At Il Frantoio, an olive farm in Puglia, foodies indulge in lazy eight-course lunches in the whitewashed farmhouse's small cult-status restaurant. In the hills, high above Romeo and Juliet's Verona, Agriturismo San Mattia seduces gourmets with stunning dishes using their own farm-grown fruit, veg, eggs, meat and virgin olive oil. Sparkling white wines and Valpolicella reds from the farm's sun-drenched vineyard are honourable dining companions. For self-caterers, fresh garden herbs add aromatic flavour to evening meals, the scraps of which go straight to the farm pigs – much to the joy of the children for whom an *agriturismo* is, quite frankly, a dream come true.

To read about:
Offbeat Stays see page 208
Palazzi & Villas see page 300

Piecing It Together: Mosaics

ITALY-WIDE / ART

Requiring the patience of a saint and the critical eye of a master jigsaw-puzzle solver, mosaics have been part of Italian interior design for more than two millennia, ever since craftspeople adorned the floors of Roman villas. But, as with other Roman art and architecture, the use of mosaics was derived from Etruscan funerary decoration.

Right **Basilica di San Vitale,** Ravenna

By the 1st century BC, floor mosaics were a popular form of home decor. Typical themes included landscapes, still life, and depictions of gods. Later, as production and artistic techniques improved, mosaics were displayed on walls and in public buildings. At the Museo Nazionale Romano: Palazzo Massimo alle Terme in Rome, you'll find some spectacular wall mosaics from Nero's villa in Anzio.

With the legalisation of Christianity in the 4th century, Christian images began to move into the public arena, appearing in mosaics across the city. Mosaic work was the principal artistic endeavour of early Christian Italy and mosaics adorn many of the churches built in this period.

The Byzantine period was notable for its extraordinary mosaic work. Drawing inspiration from the symbol-drenched decoration of the Roman catacombs and the early Christian churches, the Byzantine de-emphasised the naturalistic aspects of the classical tradition and exalted the spirit over the body, glorifying God rather than humanity or the state.

Byzantine virtuosity with mosaics is showcased in Ravenna, the capital of the Byzantine Empire's western regions for a three-century span beginning in 402. A paradise for mosaic lovers, Ravenna features one of the world's best collections of early Christian mosaic artwork across several churches and baptisteries and enshrined on Unesco's World Heritage List since 1996. Between the fall of the Roman Empire and the advent of the High Middle Ages, Ravenna's citizens enjoyed a prolonged golden age, while the rest of the Italian peninsula flailed in the wake of barbarian invasions. During this time the city became a fertile art studio for skilled craftspeople, who covered the city's terracotta brick churches in beautiful mosaics.

The Basilica di Sant'Apollinare in Classe, the Basilica di San Vitale and Basilica di Sant'Apollinare Nuovo house some of the world's finest Byzantine art, their hand-cut tiles balancing naturalness with a sense of grandeur and mystery.

Those not content to wax lyrical with the aesthetes can pursue a more proactive experience. Ravennate mosaic schools Gruppo Mosaicisti and Mosaic Art School have been teaching students how to mimic, re-create and restore mosaics since the 1940s and '50s.

In Rome, the tilework legacy is upheld by Studio Cassio – a workshop in the yellow streets of the Monti neighbourhood, and a place that offers mosaic-making classes to novices. Home to three generations of mosaic workers, the Cassio family has restored ancient artwork in places like Pompeii, and created new designs, such as the John Lennon memorial mosaic in New York's Central Park.

Surrounded by an assortment of mosaic centaurs, clock faces and saints, students piece together their own creations, while also learning the art of restoring ancient Roman mosaics – handling marble put in place by craftspeople 2000 years ago, and filling in missing chunks.

To read about:
Papier Mâché see page 120
Neapolitan Artisan Traditions see page 260

Above Mosaic, Basilica di Sant'Apollinare Nuovo, Ravenna

Hiking in the Garfagnana

TUSCANY / JOURNEYS

Tucked away in a quiet corner of Tuscany, the Garfagnana is not only a pastoral paradise, preserving a way of life that's hardly changed in centuries – it's also re-nowned for some of Italy's best hiking. So strap on your hiking boots, hit the hills and soak up the culture of this remote mountain valley.

Right **Isola Santa**

As the old proverb goes, 'friends may meet, but mountains never greet,' and this morning the Apuan Alps seem determined to live up to the maxim. For the last two hours, a cloak of cloud has clung to the mountaintops, obscuring both the valley below and the peaks ahead. But the weather hasn't deterred the hikers; they're picking their way along the ridge-lines, kitted out with hats and fleeces, braving the cloud in the hope of better weather down the trail. Their optimism is rewarded; within half an hour, the cloud burns off and they're under a clear canopy of blue, surrounded by summits and lush slopes daubed with wildflowers. It's a reminder of another old mountain adage: if you don't like the weather, sit down and wait.

The weather is the only thing that changes at any discernible pace in the Garfagnana. Hidden away in Tuscany's northwestern corner, 65km north of Pisa, this rural valley preserves a way of life that has hardly changed in centuries. Historically, most families here would have made their living from the land – farming sheep, growing spelt and maize and harvesting chestnuts used to make everything from cakes to bread. Quarrying was the valley's other major industry – seams of white Carrara marble streak the mountainsides, of a purity and clarity valued by Roman architects and Renaissance artists alike.

Today, the Garfagnana is part of a national park, the Parco Nazionale dell'Appennino Tosco-Emiliano, and is renowned for some of Italy's best hiking. Sandwiched between the twin ranges of the Apuan Alps and the Apennines, it's a pocket of unexpected wilderness on Tuscany's northern edge, less well known than the Dolomites, but every bit as beau-tiful. Mouflon and mountain goats roam the high pastures, and old drovers' paths wind through a landscape of lakeside chapels, abandoned quarries and shepherds' bothies. Many of the valley's old farmhouses are now *agriturismi,* and on a clear day, from the top of Monte Prado – the Garfagnana's highest peak at 2054m – the view encompasses three regions of Italy: Liguria to the west, Emilia-Romagna to the north and Tuscany to the south.

The hikers settle down on the grass for lunch: a picnic of salami, fruit, bread and pecorino cheese, all freshly bought from the valley's main town, Castelnuovo di Garfagnana. A troupe of goats trots past along the trail, bells tinkling as they disappear down the near-vertical slope.

Pastoral scenes like these are key to the Garfagnana's appeal. Dotted with tiny villages and sleepy towns – where the streets are lined with old-fashioned cafes and grocers' shops, and family-run trattorias serve up recipes such as wild boar *ragù* – this is a region that celebrates a traditional life. The local calendar is chalked with festivals honouring everything from beer to chestnuts, and one village even holds its own medieval pageant, when jesters and harlequins roam the streets, and locals feast on hog roasts and spelt ale, much as they would have done hundreds of years ago.

To read about:
WWII's Freedom Trail see page 194
Climbing the Dolomites see page 234

A Springtime City Break in Lucca

TUSCANY / LANDSCAPES

Lovely Lucca endears itself to everyone who visits. Hidden behind imposing Renaissance walls, its cobbled streets, handsome piazzas and shady promenades make it a perfect destination to explore by foot – as a day trip from Florence or in its own right. Historic cafes and restaurants tempt visitors to stay a little longer and relax over a glass of Lucchesi wine and rustic dishes.

It's hard to imagine anywhere more romantic than Lucca in the spring. From late March to early June, the surrounding meadows are splashed with colour, as wildflowers run riot, skies are blue and the valleys are lush. The perfect way to enjoy such good weather is to amble through the gardens of Lucca's villas. Villa Reale, 7km north of Lucca in Marlia, was once home to Elisa Bonaparte, Napoleon's sister and short-lived ruler of Tuscany. The house isn't open to the public, but its 17th-century gardens are a theatrical adventure. Neoclassical Villa Grabau, 11km north of Lucca in San Pancrazio, sits among a vast parkland with sweeping traditional English- and Italian-styled gardens, splashing fountains, more than 100 terracotta pots with lemon trees and a postcard-pretty lemon house dating from the 17th century. It even has a clutch of self-catering properties to rent in its grounds should you happen to fall in love with the estate. Also in San Pancrazio, are the gardens of Villa Oliva, surrounding a 15th-century country residence designed by Lucchesi architect Matteo Civitali. Retaining its original design, the fountain-rich park is set across three levels and includes a cypress alley and stables.

Walking Lucca's monumental *mura* (wall) is a great way to see the city. It was built around the old city in the 16th and 17th centuries and remains in almost perfect condition. It superseded two previous walls, the first built from travertine stone blocks as early as the 2nd century BC. Twelve metres high and 4.2km long, today's ramparts are crowned with a tree-lined footpath looking down on the historic centre and the city's vintage botanical gardens with its centurion cedar trees.

Just inside the south end of the *mura* is Cattedrale di San Martino, Lucca's predominantly Romanesque cathedral, which dates to the 11th century. Its stunning facade was constructed in the prevailing Lucca-Pisan style and designed to accommodate the pre-existing *campanile* (bell tower). The reliefs over the left doorway of the portico are believed to be by Nicola Pisano, while inside, treasures include the *Volto Santo* (literally, Holy Countenance) crucifix sculpture and a wonderful 15th-century tomb in the sacristy.

The cathedral's many other works of art include a magnificent *Last Supper* by Tintoretto above the third altar of the south aisle and Domenico Ghirlandaio's 1479 *Madonna Enthroned with Saints*. This impressive work by Michelangelo's master is currently located in the sacristy. Opposite lies the exquisite, gleaming marble tomb of Ilaria del Carretto carved by Jacopo della Quercia in 1407.

During spring, between 22 and 29 April, Lucca pays tribute to its patron saint, Zita, a 13th-century serving maid who gave to the poor. Legend says that when Zita was caught by her master with food hidden in her apron, the offending items turned to flowers, so Lucca honours her memory each year by filling its squares with blooms. In front of the basilica where Zita's body is enshrined, medieval Piazza dell'Anfiteatro is transformed into a garden, blazing with pink, red and orange azaleas and rhododendrons.

To read about:
Florence see page 146
Bologna see page 212

Shakespeare's Italian Plays

ITALY-WIDE / ARTS

William Shakespeare's fascination with Italy is a constant undercurrent of his work, from the lovelorn streets of Romeo and Juliet's Verona and Julius Caesar's murderous machinations in Rome, to the sex, money and intrigue in Othello's Venice. The Italian settings of his plays are so crucial to his plots that they have become characters in their own right.

Right **Juliet's balcony,** Verona

Shakespeare had no idea what he'd start when he set his tale of star-crossed lovers in fair Verona – it's is now regarded as one of the most romantic places in the world, with thousands of lovers visiting each year. And the city has seized the commercial possibilities with both hands – everything from *osterie* (casual taverns) and hotels to embroidered kitchen aprons get the R&J branding. While the play's depiction of feuding families has genuine provenance, the lead characters themselves are fictional.

Undaunted, in the 1930s the authorities settled on a house in Via Cappello (think Capulet) as Juliet's and added a 14th-century-style balcony and a bronze statue of our heroine. Casa di Giulietta is a spectacle – entering the courtyard, you are greeted by a crowd, everyone trying to take selfies with the statue of Juliet. Overhead is the famous balcony with tourists taking their turn to have pics taken.

The decision to set some of his plays outside of England allowed Shakespeare to tackle sensitive political topics without risking the displeasure of England's rulers. Subjects that would have landed him in trouble, such as political assassinations included in Julius Caesar, were not a problem when set in Italy, because at the time Italy was a place where anything could happen with its warring city-states.

It's debatable whether or not Shakespeare ever visited Italy. Some of his Italian plays display a lot of local knowledge, which it would be hard to come by without going there. In *Julius Caesar* he describes an African-style summer thunderstorm in Rome – the type of storm which comes and goes very quickly and is simply not found in England. Some believe that he

Shakespearean Locations

Thirteen of Shakespeare's 36 plays were set or part-set in Italy, where his influence can still be felt.

Two Gentlemen of Verona – Verona, Milan, Mantua

The Taming of the Shrew – Padua

Titus Andronicus – Rome

Romeo and Juliet – Verona, Mantua

The Merchant of Venice – Venice, Belmont

Much Ado About Nothing – Messina

Julius Caesar – Rome

Othello – Venice

All's Well that Ends Well – Florence

Antony and Cleopatra – Rome

Coriolanus – Rome, Antium (present day Anzio)

The Winter's Tale – Sicily

Cymbeline – Rome

could have learned about Italian life from Venetian merchants in London, but it's doubtful as Venice and England had no political relationship at the time. Interestingly, nobody knows where Shakespeare was between 1585 and 1592. Could he have been in Italy?

To read about:
Dante see page 150
Italy on Screen see page 276

Hill Towns of Tuscany, Umbria & Le Marche

CENTRAL ITALY / LANDSCAPES

You're lost on a hairpin-bend-riddled road in the mountains that seemingly leads to nowhere, and no sat nav or map can help you. But then, suddenly, you crest a hill and a tiny village slides into view, surrounded by titanic mountains and sweeping forests. If you're up for an offbeat adventure, get behind the wheel for a head-spinning drive to gloriously remote villages pasted high on a mountain slope.

Right **San Gimignano**, Tuscany

Tuscany

As you crest the nearby hills, the 14 towers of the walled town of San Gimignano rise up like a medieval Manhattan. Once known as San Gimignano delle Belle Torri, or San Gimignano of the Beautiful Towers, there were originally 72 towers, 50 to 60m tall, crammed within the walls of this small, medieval town that crowns a hill in classic Tuscan fashion.

In 1348 plague wiped out much of the population and weakened the economy, leading to the town's submission to Florence in 1353. However, today not even the plague would deter the swarms of summer day trippers, who are lured by a palpable sense of history, medieval streetscapes and an enchanting rural setting.

But you don't have to battle with bands of tourists if you want to get a sense of medieval Tuscany. About halfway between San Gimignano and Siena is Monteriggioni, a small medieval village perfectly preserved within its walls. Two magnificent doorways pierce the walls and there's access to sections that look down on the tiled roofs of houses and their gardens. Monteriggioni has a sense that the men in doublet and hose, ladies in wimples, peasants in jerkins and knights on horseback have just disappeared through the gates – and might return at any minute.

Known globally as the home of one of the world's great wines, Brunello di Montalcino, the attractive hilltop town of Montalcino has a remarkable number of *enoteche* (wine bars) lining its medieval streets, and is surrounded by hugely picturesque vineyards. There's history to explore too: the town's efforts to hold out against Florence even after Siena had fallen earned it the title 'the Republic of

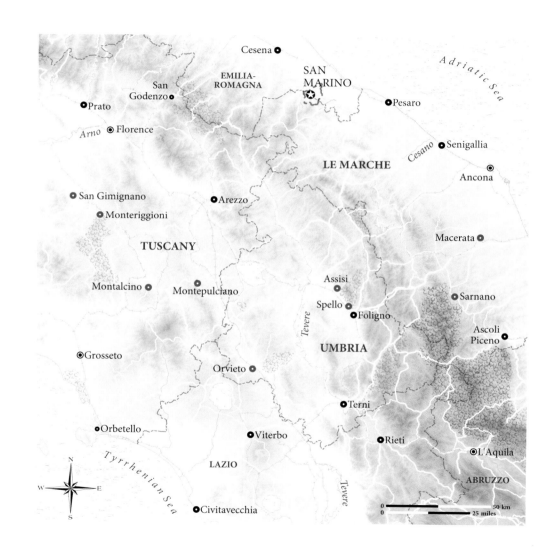

Siena in Montalcino', and there are many well-preserved medieval buildings within the historic city walls.

The serenely beautiful, Romanesque abbey, Abbazia di Sant'Antimo, is just an 11km bus ride, or a two- to three-hour walk, from Montalcino. According to tradition, the original monastery was founded by Charlemagne in 781 and today, the exterior, built in pale travertine stone, is simple except for the stone carvings, which include various fantastical animals.

A late-Etruscan fort was the first in a series of settlements in Montepulciano. During the Middle Ages, the town was a constant bone of contention between Florence and Siena. Florence eventually won the day in 1404 and the Marzocco, or lion of Florence, came to replace the she-wolf of Siena as the city's symbol. The new administration invited architects including Michelozzo and Sangallo il Vecchio to design new buildings and endow this Gothic stronghold with some Renaissance grace and style. That intriguing mix alone makes the steep climbs worthwhile.

Exploring the medieval town, perched on a reclaimed narrow ridge of volcanic rock, will push your quadriceps to failure point. Reward yourself with a generous pour of the highly reputed Vino Nobile while also drinking in the spectacular views over the Val di Chiana and Val d'Orcia.

Umbria

As if cupped in celestial hands, with the plains spreading picturesquely below and Monte Subasio rearing steep and wooded above, the mere sight of Assisi in the rosy glow of dusk is enough to send pilgrims'

souls spiralling to heaven. It is at this hour, when the pitter-patter of day-tripper footsteps have faded and the town is shrouded in saintly silence, that the true spirit of St Francis of Assisi, born here in 1181, can be felt most keenly. Though certainly at its heart a religious destination, Assisi's striking beauty and pristinely preserved medieval *centro storico* and UNESCO-listed Franciscan structures are a fabled haven that will compel and electrify visitors of any motive.

It's a chaotic jumble of styles, built and rebuilt over the course of three millennia. Along one street, columns from a Roman temple prop up the façade of a Renaissance church. On another, a line of Gothic arches is cut off by the addition of a medieval wall. There are dead ends and blind alleys, bricked-up doorways and staircases leading nowhere. Clues lurk in the walls: coats of arms, beastly gargoyles and saintly images loaded with obscure religious significance.

A few miles southeast of Assisi, along a winding road which veers round the wooded flanks of Monte Subasio, Spello demonstrates another feature shared by many of Umbria's hilltop towns: a ring of ramparts, gates and watchtowers, a reminder of the days when a hilltop location was prized not for its prettiness but its protection. As you walk along its battlements, Spello is transformed into an impregnable bastion, bristling with crenels and murder-holes.

Off to the southwest, along quiet lanes that meander through corn fields and cypress trees, lies Orvieto. Perched on a spur of rock high above the plain, this hilltop town had another solution for times

of trouble. Beneath the town's cathedral, a network of tunnels burrows through the limestone, providing escape routes during a siege. Right beneath the townsfolk's feet, centuries of cobwebs drape the walls of this labyrinth of passageways, staircases and galleries. Guides recount tales of people who entered the tunnels, and whose ghosts are still trying to find their way out.

Le Marche

Spilling photogenically down a hillside, its medieval heart a maze of narrow cobbled lanes, Sarnano looks every inch the Italian hill-town prototype, particularly when its red-brick facades glow warmly in the late-afternoon sun. It is a charming, hospitable base for exploring the Monti Sibillini range and home to 11km of ski slopes. In warmer weather, you can navigate over 100km of marked footpaths for walking, cycling and hiking.

To the north lies the ancient hill-top city of Macerata – a less well-known treasure of the Marche region. Its university dates from the 13th century and ensures a lively student population, while the old town, a jumbled maze of cobblestone streets and honey-coloured *palazzi*, springs to life in summer for a month-long opera festival.

To read about:

Lecce: Where the Baroque Meets Papier Mâché

Dubbed the 'Florence of the South' for its operatic architectural ensembles and scholarly bent, the city of Lecce is home to more than 40 churches and at least as many palazzi (mansions) from the 17th and 18th centuries. Many of these churches are ornamented with papier-mâché artworks, while the city's most hallucinatory baroque spectacle has to be the Basilica di Santa Croce, an allegorical feast of sheep, dodos, cherubs and unidentified beasties.

PUGLIA/ ARTS

If Puglia were a movie, Lecce would be cast in the starring role. Bequeathed with a generous stash of baroque buildings by its 17th-century architects, the city has a completeness and homogeneity that other southern Italian metropolises lack. Indeed, so distinctive is Lecce's architecture that it has acquired its own moniker, *barocco leccese* (Lecce baroque), an expressive and hugely decorative incarnation of the genre replete with gargoyles, asparagus columns and cavorting gremlins. Swooning 18th-century traveller Thomas Ashe thought it 'the most beautiful city in Italy', but the less-impressed Marchese Grimaldi said the fantastical facade of Basilica di Santa Croce made him think a lunatic was having a nightmare.

Either way, Lecce is a lively and graceful but relaxed university town, is marvellously illuminated at night, and features some upmarket boutiques and decent Pugliese restaurants. The city also has a strong tradition for painted papier-mâché statues and figurines *(cartapesta),* which are used to adorn churches and other public buildings. Lecce's *cartapesta* culture originated in the 17th century, when glue and paper offered cheap raw materials for religious artists who couldn't afford expensive wood or marble. Legend has it that the first exponents of the art were Leccese barbers who shaped and chiselled their morphing statues in between haircuts.

These days the art is still practised in Lecce and you'll see a number of traditional workshops such as Cartapesta Riso scattered around the old town centre. Also worth perusing is the papier-mâché museum inside the Castello di Carlo V and the decorative papier-mâché ceiling inside the Chiesa di Santa Chiara.

To read about:

Right **Basilica di Santa Croce**

Emilia-Romagna's Soul Food

NORTHERN ITALY / FOOD & DRINK

The rich and wonderful regional cuisine of Emilia-Romagna is the stuff of Italian culinary dreams. Many of Italy's most iconic dishes hail from here: parmigiano reggiano (Parmesan), prosciutto di Parma (dry-cured ham), balsamic vinegar (aceto balsamico) and, of course, ragù play the starring roles in a gourmet pilgrimage to this region.

Cooking in Italy is fiercely regional. This is an exceedingly young country, only unified as a nation in 1861. Before that, it was a collection of city-states. Each has its own traditions, own culture, and even its own language, so it's unsurprising that regional differences remain strong. There's even an Italian word for the fierce local pride: *campanilismo*, which roughly translates as believing your bell tower is the best of the lot. However, even if people from different regions are convinced that theirs is the best cuisine in the country, they will all pay Emilia-Romagna the respect it deserves. If pressed, most Italians will even concur that, after their parents' house, this is the source of Italy's most spectacular gastronomy.

Emilia-Romagna is notable also for the sheer number of premium specialities that it packs into its small area, which is easy to explore by train as well as by car. Take a lazy food-themed journey to try some of these at their source, and you'll soon find yourself delighting in its fiendishly handsome cities and lushly rolling, village-dotted countryside, wondering at how few tourists have discovered this astoundingly well-kept secret.

Spaghetti Bolognese vs *Ragù*

If you came to Emilia-Romagna in search of 'authentic' spaghetti bolognese, you're out of luck. Spaghetti bolognese is about as Bolognese as roast beef and Yorkshire pudding, and Bologna's fiercely traditional trattorias never list it. Instead, the city prides itself on a vastly superior meat-based sauce called *ragù*, consisting of slow-cooked minced beef simmered with pancetta, onions and carrots, and enlivened with liberal dashes of milk and wine. Calling the city's signature meat sauce 'spaghetti bolognese' is like calling Champagne 'fizzy wine'.

So why the misleading moniker? Modern legend suggests that *ragù* may have acted as spaghetti bolognese's original inspiration when British and American servicemen and women passing through Emilia-Romagna in WWII fell in love with the dish. Returning home after the war, they subsequently asked their immigrant Italian chefs to rustle up something similar. Details clearly got lost in translation.

The 'spaghetti bolognese' eaten in contemporary London and New York is fundamentally different to Bologna's centuries-old *ragù*. First there's the sauce. Spaghetti bolognese is heavy on tomatoes while *ragù* is all about the meat. Then there's the pasta. Spaghetti bolognese is served with dry durum-wheat spaghetti from Naples taken straight from a packet. *Ragù* is spread over fresh egg-based *tagliatelle* (ribbon pasta), allowing the rich meat sauce to stick to the thick al dente strands.

Ever keen to safeguard their meat sauce from mediocrity, Bologna's chamber of commerce registered an official *ragù* recipe in 1982, although, ironically, it's still nigh on impossible to find two Bologna *ragù* that taste the same.

La Vecchia Scuola Bolognese

Bologna is not only a place to delight your taste buds, but an autumnal-hued, historic city, with a skyline pierced by medieval towers and kilometres of colonnaded porticos. It's as famous for its leftfield intelligentsia and anarchist bent as it is for its freshly handmade tortellini and tagliatelle.

Start your culinary odyssey by learning a skill that will stay with you forever: how to cook *ragù* just like Nonna (Grandma). At long-established cookery school La Vecchia Scuola Bolognese, you can learn how to make the traditional rich meat sauce and a lasagne to warm the cockles of your heart in a two-hour course (in Italian or English).

Osteria dell'Orsa

All over Italy, unassuming, blink-and-you'd-miss-them trattorias are serving up some of the most spectacularly delicious meals in a simple down-to-earth atmosphere. They're all entirely different and yet resolutely similar, with wood-lined interiors, a few higgledy-piggledy pictures, checked or white tablecloths, a notable dearth of airs and graces, and the family that runs it split between the kitchen and front of house.

Bologna's Osteria dell'Orsa is exactly this kind of stuck-in-time place whose fame has grown through word of mouth. It's a hidden-away trattoria in Bologna's backstreets, where the pasta is freshly handmade by the family in the morning and laid out in trays ready for the day.

In the simple interior, where narrow beams of sunlight sneak in through the windows, you will eat food that will linger in your memory as among the most wonderful meals you've ever had. Not just the light yet substantial punch of *tortellini en brodo*, but the slow-cooked rabbit, which is sprinkled with rosemary and salt and roasted at a low heat for hours to produce a remarkably tender-tasting and aromatic meat.

Finish with a beautifully confected panna cotta, one of the classic Italian trattoria desserts, and accept a *digestivo* of herb-infused liqueur to send you on your way.

Acetaia di Giorgio

Half an hour by train or car from Bologna, the next great foodie stop is the city of Modena, famous for its rich, dark gold that sweetens salads and funks up the world: balsamic vinegar.

The best place to buy it is directly from one of its Modena makers, where the world's best balsamic goes under the official title *aceto balsamico tradizionale di Modena*. When the door opens at the grand, petal-pale villa of Acetaia di Giorgio, you'll be struck by the sweet, acidic scent of fermenting vinegar. This has been a family-run business for generations and if you book a visit, the Barbieri family will talk you through the fermentation process step by careful step.

The vinegar is aged in a series of oak barrels for a minimum of 12 years to more than 25. You'll get to taste a series of sweetly sharp vinegars, a world away from the supermarket version you may have previously drizzled on your lettuce, and then have the chance to buy some to take home with you.

Don Papi

The charming town of Reggio Emilia is a 15-minute train ride from Modena; slightly longer by car. With its pretty piazzas and laid-back traffic, this town is considered the best place to ride a bike in the whole of Italy. The trattoria Don Papi is known for its takes on *gnocco fritto* (fried salted dough), but also serves plenty of other

regional specialities, such as *capeletti zucca* ('little hats' pasta filled with pumpkin).

Gnocco fritto is a light-as-air fried dough parcel that is fast food Emilia-Romagna-style. It varies in shape and size according to the local village or town tradition but, whatever its dimensions, it's an indulgent eat. It's often served as antipasto, with a wafer-thin sliver of *prosciutto crudo* (smoked ham) draped over it, ideally washed down with some local Lambrusco wine.

Salumeria Garibaldi

A half-hour hop from Reggio, notably handsome Parma is particularly pleased with itself, and understandably so. Few provincial towns can say they have contributed quite so much to global gastronomic enjoyment. Shops groan with premium foodstuffs so stock up with goodies to take home.

It's full of stately buildings and kempt piazzas, but the real reason to come here is to try the local Parma ham and taste nuggets from great golden wheels of Parmesan. The town is also responsible for creating the delicious concoction Parmigiana, beloved Italy-wide: layers of fried eggplant and tomato sauce, topped with Parmesan.

Salumeria Garibaldi is one of the town's most venerable delicatessens, whose window display and counter are resplendent with a row of dangling haunches. Sample crumbly morsels of Parmesan before selecting your favourite to be wrapped so you can squirrel it home, and self-caterers can buy luscious portions of Parmigiana.

Antica Corte Pallavicina Relais

In a country where salami is a fine art, the Spigarolis who run Antica Corte occupy a special place in the cured meat canon. On the flat plains around Parma, they produce some of the region's most famous salami in the cellars of a sprawling mansion on the banks of the river Po.

Surrounded by grounds filled with cows, horses and geese, this 1320 homestead is famous for its *culatelli di zibello* (little bums), parcels of cured meat wrapped in a pig's bladder. Aged in the farm's humid cellars, this ham is given the edge by the foggy winters of the region.

The meat is wrapped in twine, which gives the *culatello* its signature pear shape, and the painstaking, elaborate production method includes massaging the parcels and leaving them to rest. The result is a velvety, aromatic meat, one of Italy's most sought after creations.

It has been more than 20 years since Massimo and Luciano Spigaroli took over the farm, which their great-grandfather had worked first as a sharecropper and then as a tenant. They honed the process and now cure meats for clients as diverse as Armani and Prince Charles. They run a superlative restaurant, and you can stay at the farm, or gain an understanding of the *culatello*-making process by arranging a visit to explore the cellars and take part in tastings.

To read about:
Bologna's Food Markets see page 212
Banquets in South Tyrol see page 228

Don't Leave Town Without Trying

Every city in Emilia-Romagna has its gastronomic secrets – weird and wonderful local recipes that you'd be unlikely to find on the menu of your local Italian restaurant back home. Don't leave the following towns without trying these specialities.

Bologna *Tagliatelle al ragù* – thick, meat-heavy sauce served with wide-cut egg-based pasta.

Ferrara *Cappellacci di zucca* – ravioli-like pasta stuffed with pumpkin and nutmeg, and brushed with butter and sage.

Modena *Cotechino di Modena* – pork sausage stuffed with seasoned mince and paired with lentils and mashed potatoes.

Parma *Trippa alla parmigiano* – slow-cooked tripe in a tomato sauce enlivened with Parmesan.

Piacenza *Anolini in brodo* – pasta pockets filled with meat, Parmesan and breadcrumbs swimming in a rich brothlike soup.

Ravenna *Piadina* – thick unleavened bread stuffed with rocket, tomato and local soft squacquerone cheese.

Rimini *Brodetto* – a hearty fish soup served over lightly toasted bread.

Tagliatelle al Ragù

Serves 6–8
Preparation Time 1 hour
Cooking Time 2–3 hours

Art, architecture and food: the three tenets of la bella vita combine with this much loved Bolognese recipe – its ribbons of fine tagliatelle pasta must, according to folklore, be of a measurement that echoes the height of the city's two medieval towers. Chef Mauro Fabbri serves this richly storied dish at Ristorante Diana, at the heart of Bologna's culinary scene since 1909.

First, let's dispel some myths around this, the most classic of Bolognese dishes. Forget spaghetti: flat ribbons of tagliatelle are a better vehicle for this unctuous mince-meat sauce. And come near this recipe with garlic and you risk being strung from Bologna's medieval towers. *Ragù* is only ever flavoured with nutmeg and wine.

According to legend, the width of the tagliatelle should be one 12,270th the height of the Torre degli Asinelli, the taller of the city's two iconic towers that lean away from each other, a precarious question mark over the city's skyline. Said to be modelled after the hair of an Italian noblewoman, pasta with these precise dimensions cast in solid gold can be found at the city's Chamber of Commerce.

Parmesan crowns this dish but Signor Fabbri says its success depends on the choice of meat. A coarse cut, grained with fat and slow cooking will result in a sauce with a full flavour. Made in several stages, this recipe is more time-consuming than the quick 'spag bol' done universally but the results are in the eating. Nutmeg, popular in Bolognese cooking, adds warmth and spice, while an extra egg yolk is added to make the pasta richer.

→ 2 tbsp olive oil
→ soffritto (mixture of onion, carrot and celery – the holy trinity used in Italian sauces): 2 onions, 2 carrots and 3 sticks celery, chopped very finely, so you can taste but not see it
→ 100g (3½oz) fresh, unsmoked pancetta, chopped finely
→ 1kg (2lbs) hanger or skirt steak, coarsely minced by a butcher (important so the meat keeps its shape and doesn't fall to bits during the long cooking time).

Coarsely minced prepacked beef would be a decent alternative but NOT lean.
→ 200ml (7fl oz) red wine
→ salt and pepper
→ half a nutmeg, grated
→ 150g (5½oz) tomato puree
→ 90g (3oz) per head fresh tagliatelle or pappardelle
→ Parmesan, to serve

1. Gently fry the finely chopped onions, carrots and celery in olive oil and add the finely chopped pancetta, until browned.

2. Add the steak. Stir gently and cook until browned, then cover the pan with a lid and braise gently for 40 minutes.

3. Take the lid off and turn up the heat to let any liquid from the meat evaporate.

4. Add the red wine and again let the mixture simmer gently until the liquid has evaporated.

5. Now stir in salt and pepper and freshly grated nutmeg. The chef recommends half a nutmeg but you might want to add slowly to taste.

6. Add the tomato puree and enough water to cover the sauce plus about 2.5cm (1in) extra.

7. Half-cover the pan and simmer sauce very gently (a bare simmer) for two hours, checking and stirring every so often.

8. By the end, the sauce will have absorbed the liquid, leaving a fully flavoured *ragù*. Check and adjust the seasoning.

9. Cook the pasta in boiling salted water for four minutes.

10. Serve the *ragù* over the pasta with freshly grated Parmesan.

Reaping the Harvest

ITALY-WIDE / FOOD & DRINK

In a country where national cuisine translates as an exciting collection of regional cuisines deeply rooted in geography and season, the call of the land is huge. And never more so than at harvest time when Italians celebrate the riches of the earth – and their own hard work in the fields – with exuberance, gusto and inevitable Italian panache.

As the original champions of Slow Food, Italians are natural devotees of zero-kilometre cuisine. Throw a large pinch of fierce loyalty to one's *paese* (home town) into their cooking pot along with an inbred desire to never waste a crumb and the result is sensational: an earthy, wholesome cuisine bursting with rich local flavour and in perfect symbiosis with the land.

Verdant, sun-blessed Italy is so lush in local produce that there is always a harvest happening somewhere, whatever the season. Springtime markets burst with baby violet artichokes, green and pink Mezzago asparagus, fresh garlic, tart radicchio (chicory) and – towards the season's end – plump cherries, figs and zucchini flowers. Early summer sees farm workers head into the fields and fruit orchards to harvest peppers, eggplants, berries and syrup-sweet strawberries. At the Saline di Trapani in western Sicily, salt harvesters rake the first pans for salt in July, watched by a gaggle of fascinated holidaymakers (yes, guided tours can be arranged).

Autumnal joys include foraging for wild fruits of the forests, including a bounty of sweet smoky chestnuts. Piedmont's iconic hazelnut is ripe for picking, while late October opens the sacrosanct season – white and black – in Tuscany, Umbria and Piedmont. Even in winter the harvest continues: in Northern Italy, not far from Lombardy's chic lakeshores, rice and corn crops are brought in among fields polka-dotted with bright orange pumpkins and swathes of green cavolo nero (kale). In the south, fishers hand-harvest Le Marche mussels and *raguse* (sea snails) in the Adriatic Sea and Sardinian sea urchins in the Mediterranean.

Grapes

As the scorching sun mellows and days shorten, September heralds the start of the *vendemmia* (grape harvest) – an utterly glorious moment in the agricultural calendar and a superb time of year to travel in Italy. Summer warmth lingers in much of the country and wine-growing regions burst with celebratory *sagre* (local food festivals) honouring the most revered of autumnal harvests.

Armed with a pair of grape clippers or hooked knife and a wicker basket or red plastic milk crate, pickers head into the vineyards in the early morning to harvest the ripe grapes by hand before the heat of the day blazes down. Great care is taken not to break the skins of the dark purple fruit, swollen with sun-fuelled juice and needing little excuse to start fermenting. Very much a local affair in rural parts of Italy, wine growers rope in their entire family, friends and neighbours to help with the harvest. Amid much banter and gaiety, grape stems are deftly cut, loaded by the crateful into the ubiquitous three-wheeled Ape truck (made by Piaggio and nicknamed 'bee' after its utilitarian, industrious nature), and carted off to the

fattoria (farmhouse) or local cooperative. The sensational pranzone or feast of a lunch that ensues around a shared table is a naturally buoyant, raucous, highly memorable affair.

The further south one travels in Italy, the earlier the harvest. Key wine-growing regions are Tuscany (renowned for its highly prized reds from Brunello di Montalcino and Montepulciano, innovative and complex Super Tuscans, and quaffable Chianti vintages); the Veneto (home of sparkling prosecco and light citrusy Soave whites); and Puglia and Emilia-Romagna. A September visit to the startlingly green, Aeolian island of Salina in Sicily ushers in a fascinating peek at a particularly unusual harvest that sees red Malvasia and now-rare Corinthian grapes picked by hand and laid out to dry on woven cane mats as has been done for centuries. This traditional drying process is a crucial step in the production of local Malvasia wine, a dark-golden or light-amber wine that tastes like honey and is drunk in very small glasses with cheese, sweet biscuits or almond pastries.

Countrywide, overnighting at an *agriturismo* (self-catering farm stay) on a small winery (such as Podere La Casellina Figline in Chianti) ensures a first-hand experience of the grape harvest. While guests cannot always dig in and get their hands dirty, personal guided tours of the vineyards and wine-production areas are common. Or motor romantically along a wine route, visiting vineyards and watching the *vendemmia* (grape harvest) unfold, on well-mapped-out driving itineraries such as the Strada del Vino e dell'Olio Costa degli Etruschi along Tuscany's Etruscan Coast.

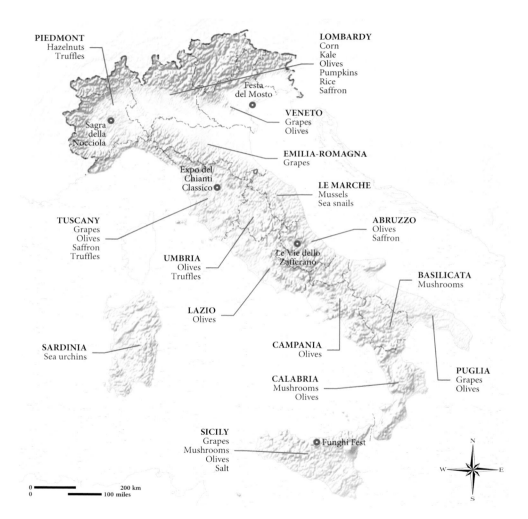

PIEDMONT
Hazelnuts
Truffles

Sagra della Nocciola

LOMBARDY
Corn
Kale
Olives
Pumpkins
Rice
Saffron

Festa del Mosto

VENETO
Grapes
Olives

EMILIA-ROMAGNA
Grapes

Expo del Chianti Classico

LE MARCHE
Mussels
Sea snails

TUSCANY
Grapes
Olives
Saffron
Truffles

ABRUZZO
Olives
Saffron

Le Vie dello Zafferano

UMBRIA
Olives
Truffles

BASILICATA
Mushrooms

LAZIO
Olives

CAMPANIA
Olives

SARDINIA
Sea urchins

CALABRIA
Mushrooms
Olives

PUGLIA
Grapes
Olives

SICILY
Grapes
Mushrooms
Olives
Salt

Funghi Fest

0   200 km
0   100 miles

Mushrooms

While oenophiles are salivating over the season's grape harvest, foodies are deep in chestnut forests, indulging in one of Italy's greatest national pastimes: autumnal mushrooming. *Funghi* (mushrooms) pop up in the lower reaches of the Alps and Apennines, and verdant forests of Calabria and Basilicata in Southern Italy, any time between April and November. But it is September that brings with it an enviable bounty of fresh and sublimely aromatic, brown-capped porcini – the king of Italian mushrooms, whose nutty taste flavours many a gourmet dish, not to mention staple soups, risotto and pasta.

In Sicily, the wild-mushroom season begins in on Mt Etna and in the Madonie and Nebrodi Mountains in October. Tuscan foragers can hook up with Sapori e Saperi and Be Tuscan for a Day, grass-roots organisations that connect visitors with passionate, mushroom-savvy locals.

Saffron

In Abruzzo, a rural and rugged, mountainous region bisected by the spinal Apennines, mid-October opens the month-long saffron harvest. Dubbed 'red gold', *zafferano dell'Aquila* from Abruzzo is among the finest saffron there is and harvesting the purple crocus is back-breaking work – around 200,000 flowers are picked by hand, early in the morning before their six delicate lilac petals unfurl, to produce 1kg of saffron. Their blood-red stigmas are then painstakingly removed, one by one, the same day, after which they are toasted over hot walnut coals to become one of the world's most expensive spices.

Most saffron farmers belong to the local cooperative, Cooperativa Altopiano di Navelli. Its office, inside Agriturismo La Cada Verde in Altopiano di Navelli, is an insider address for buying the local saffron and mucking in with the harvest. Saffron hot spots elsewhere in Italy include San Gimignano in central Tuscany and Lake Como in Lombardy.

Olives

Opportunities to take part in an olive harvest are ripe in Italy, home to 700,000 olive farms and more than 250 million olive trees – silver green and many over 1000 years old. Tuscany, Umbria, Sicily, Campania, Abruzzo, Lazio, Lombardy and Veneto all produce some impressive olive oils but the *olio* (oil) heavyweights are Puglia and Calabria – two regions in the country's blazing hot south where 68% of all Italian olive oil is made.

Olives are harvested between October and December, and in keeping with Italy's reputation for producing fragrant world-class oils, olives are harvested either by hand or by letting the olives fall from the trees into nets. The finest oil comes from olives picked and rushed straight to the mill: olives left for too long after harvesting quickly become acidic. In Puglia there is no finer place to experience the olive harvest than at Masseria Il Frantoio, an organic farm near Ostuni with six hotel rooms and a 1000-year-old olive grove.

In Northern Italy, deep in the Valtenesi hills on Lake Garda's west bank, Comincioli produces some of Italy's finest olive oils – its Numero Uno is legendary. Fourteen generations of the same family have harvested olives here since 1552 and a tutored tasting at the farm-vineyard offers a unique insight into one family's extraordinary love for the land.

To read about:
Farm Stays see page 106
Lake Garda Olive Oil see page 280

Top Five Harvest Festivals

Expo del Chianti Classico, Tuscany (September) Swirl, sniff, sip and spit your way around Chianti's largest wine fair in Greve-in-Chianti.

Festa del Mosto, Venice (October) Garden isle Sant'Erasmo celebrates the grape harvest with parades, farmers markets, food stalls, music and free-flowing *vino*.

Funghi Fest, Sicily (October) Mushroom fans pour into the medieval town of Castelbuono on Sicily's Tyrrhenian Coast for three days of wild mushrooming, mushroom-based recipes from celebrity chefs and music.

Le Vie dello Zafferano, Abruzzo (October) The village of Pio delle Camere celebrates its saffron harvest with a festive street party. La Festa dei Solchi in August celebrates the planting of the crocus bulbs.

Sagra della Nocciola, Piedmont (October) Gourmets go nutty over the Langhe's treasured hazelnut during Castellero's harvest festival.

Viva the Violins!

CREMONA / MUSIC

On a back street in Rome a ceramic-tiled wood stove casts a golden glow on the workshop of an artisan luthier who crafts violins by hand. In portside Genoa, the sound of a solitary violin floats like a will-o-the-wisp through the ancient maze of carruggi (streets). In Cremona music lovers eagerly wait for the concert to begin. Enter the exquisite world of Italian violins…

Violins have a very special place in the Italian heart. The modern-day violin was invented in Italy and the world's finest violins of all time emanate from here – as did the most celebrated of all violin virtuosos.

The story begins in the mid-16th century in Cremona in Lombardy, Northern Italy. It was here that local luthier Andrea Amati (1505–77) discovered that, with a bit of clever adjustment, his old medieval fiddle could be made to sing the sweetest of tunes. All too soon the simple hand-crafted rebecs and viols the master luthier was known for had evolved into the modern-day violin – still in the treble range like the rebec but more elegant in form and minus the nasal sound. In 1555 Amati was commissioned to create an instrument for Lorenzo de' Medici in Florence and a decade on, around 1564, the luthier crafted an entire orchestra of string instruments for the French court of Charles IX. Each piece was crafted from spruce, maple and ebony wood and gilded with the king of France's motto and coat of arms to reflect its royal standing.

Andrea's sons, the Amati brothers (aka Antonio and Girolamo), subsequently took over their father's workshop, but it was Nicolò Amati (1596–1684) – Andrea's grandson and son of Girolamo – who nurtured the pupils who would create the world's best violins. With their family workshops just doors away on the same street in Cremona, master luthiers Antonio Stradivari (1644–1737) and Giuseppe Guarneri (1666–1739) were rivals. The instruments they crafted from spruce, willow and maple wood were masterpieces of classical violin making and to this day a Stradivarius violin is recognised around the globe as the finest violin ever made.

Some 650 Stradivarius string instruments, including 512 violins, are known to exist today – each worth a not-so-small fortune. In 2011 the Lady Blunt Stradivarius (named after Lord Byron's daughter, Lady Anne Blunt, who owned it for three decades) was sold for US$15.9 million. Three years later, armed robbers stole the 'Lipinski Strad' – handmade in Cremona in 1715 and subsequently named after the Polish violinist Karol Lipinski who played it; a reward of US$100,000 was offered for its return and the story (and the violin's later recovery) made headline news.

Most fun of all perhaps, experts remain unable to decide precisely why the sound of a Strad is so utterly unique, superior, sublimely out of this world. Judge for yourself at Cremona's Museo del Violino, a museum showcasing the city's historic collection of violins and exploring its musical heritage. Highlights include a workshop where you can see a luthier at work, a dramatically lit corridor full of gorgeous Cremona-made violins from the 17th century, and a room containing the drawings, moulds and tools Stradivari used in his workshop. Don't miss the enclosed wooden chamber where you can listen to the violin in action as videos of famous performances are projected onto the ceiling – it's as close as you can get to being inside the sound-box of a violin. Come dusk, don a posh frock and revel in a concert at the city's ornate, 19th-century Teatro Amilcare Ponchielli.

The tradition of crafting violins is very much alive and well in Cremona, with some 100 violin-making workshops peppering the medieval streets around central Piazza del Comune. Visits can be arranged (to both admire and buy) through the Consorcio Liutai Antonio Stradivari. Annual events dedicated to violin making include the Concorso Triennale Internazionale degli Strumenti ad Arco that fills Cremona with music by some of the world's finest string musicians every third year – 2018 and 2021 – from mid-September to mid-October. You can catch top violinists and orchestras in action around the same time of year at Cremona's annual Stradivari Festival.

One century after Antonio Stradivari was turning heads in Cremona, Genoa bathed in the musical limelight. Here, in Italy's largest port, violin virtuoso and pioneer of modern violin technique Niccolò Paganini (1782–1849) was born.

The son of a trader and mandolin player, Paganini took up the violin when he was seven. An 11-stop walking tour in his city visits the Genoese churches, theatres and *palazzi* (palaces) where he performed as a young violinist. Inside Palazzo Doria-Tursi, revel in an absorbing collection of Paganini's musical scores, letters, chess set and other personal effects. Pride of place goes to his famous 'Cannone' violin – nicknamed such because of its tremendously rich, canon-sized sound and made by Guarnieri del Gesù in 1743 in Cremona. You can witness world-class violin performances with your own ears in Genoa's biennial homage to Paganini – an international violin festival and competition, Premio Paganini, wherein one lucky musician wins the honour of playing the maestro's violin.

To read about:

Puglia's Peasant Cuisine

SOUTHERN ITALY / FOOD & DRINK

The unsung hero of Italy's food regions, this farm-fringed pocket of fishing villages has its own unique take on Italian cuisine: honest, fresh and hauled from the Med. Cucina povera (literally 'food of the poor') has become increasingly popular, thanks to a recent global obsession with farm-to-table wholesomeness.

Puglia, the foxy heel of the Italian boot, is loved for its rustic cooking as much as for its white-sand beaches and sultry summers. Sleepy for most of the year, in the summer months its seaside towns turn into thronged hubs as holidaymakers descend from Northern Italy and the whole place takes on a carnival feel.

The region is slowly being discovered by international tourists, drawn by the hobbit-friendly conical architecture, rolling hills covered in vineyards and olive groves, silky beaches and translucent water, and white washed and golden-stone coastal towns perched on sea cliffs. They also come for the cuisine. Here, traditional recipes evolved through economic necessity rather than experimental excess. Local people used whatever ingredients were available to them, plucked directly from the surrounding soil and seas, and kneaded and blended using recipes passed down through generations.

Puglia is the source of *burrata*, a cheese even more creamy and delicious than mozzarella; of *orecchiette* ('little ears'), the signature handmade pasta so-called because of its shape; and of *friselli*, dried bread that is soaked in water and served topped with fresh tomatoes and garlic. Meat, though present in *cucina povera*, is used more sparingly than in the north. Lamb and horse meat dominate and are usually heavily seasoned. Unadulterated fish is more common in Puglia, which has a longer coastline than any other mainland Italian region.

A signature Pugliese *primi* (first course) is *orecchiette con cima di rape*, a gloriously simple blend of *rapini* (a bitter green leafy veg with small broccoli-like shoots) mixed with anchovies, olive oil, chilli, garlic and pecorino. Another popular *orecchiette* accompaniment is *ragù di carne di cavallo* (horse meat), sometimes known as *ragù alla barese*. Bari is known for its starch-heavy *riso, patate e cozze*, a surprisingly delicious marriage of rice, potatoes and mussels that is baked in the oven. Another wildly popular vegetable is wild chicory, which, when combined with a fava bean purée, is reborn as *fave e cicorie*.

The region is ideal for a two- to four-day food tour – you won't have to hammer across huge distances in between stops, and yet there's so much to see of great variety. You can go from a pasta-making session in Bari's old town to a rural olive oil press with ease, while stopping to relax on a beach or explore a medieval town in between.

Right **Orecchiette con cima di rape**

Al Trabucco da Mimí

Start your exploration on the Gargano peninsula in northern Puglia. This rocky promontory of land is characterised by wooded hills, sea cliffs, and narrow coastal roads rollercoasting along its edges, and has a very different feel to the rest of Puglia.

Peculiar to the coast are the *trabucchi* – huge wooden contraptions created from a complicated arrangement of wood beams, ropes and wheels to lower a net into the sea and catch the fish as they swim close to the coast.

Some of these you can still see working, and you can even dine on one: Al Trabucco da Mimí is just east of the coastal town of Peschici, the buildings of which seem almost to tumble down the hill to the sea. The restaurant is on an old *trabucco*, jutting over the water, with views across twinkling Prussian-blue sea to locals fishing with rods from the shore. The menu is appropriately fishy, superbly fresh, and tastes all the better for its setting.

Bari Fish Market

Next stop is Bari, the regional capital, about two hours south along the coast. Despite its proud coastal position, 13th-century Frederick II castle and cathedral housing the remains of St Nicholas (yes, that's Santa Claus), Bari is still rather off the tourist trail.

It's a charismatic but not overtly pretty city, with one of the region's liveliest fish markets, which sets up just outside the old city right on the harbour. It's full of fishers, loiterers, fishmongers and hangers-on, big groups playing cards and clusters of people around a lively bar at its centre. Well-weathered men in wellingtons

Above **Handmade pasta,** Bari Vecchia

stomp up and down with buckets of fish, and trays of seafood are laid out for sale, with well-worn scales ready to weigh the catch.

People go crazy for sea urchins along this coast, and the spiky black balls are cut in half to display the creamy orange eggs within, ready to be scooped out and savoured on a piece of bread. In this area people like to eat raw seafood as antipasti, and at the fish market you might be offered raw octopus tentacles as a snack to go with your cold beer – the essential Bari aperitif.

Bari Vecchia

Bari's inner core, the Bari Vecchia (Old Town; Via dell'Arco Basso & Via dell'Arco Alto), is a tangle of narrow lanes that resemble the maze of an Arab medina. Ideally constructed to create shade in the summer heat, a couple of these narrow lanes are famous for their pasta makers, who sit out on the narrow lanes morning and night creating and selling some of Puglia's most quintessential pasta shapes.

The matriarchs make the traditional local pasta, *orecchiette*, by hand pushing the durum flour dough (made only with water, no egg) into an almost shell-like shape, and then laying them on large wood-framed drying racks.

Masseria Brancati

The bucolic area of the Valle d'Itria is less than an hour's drive from Bari. This is one of Puglia's prettiest regions, with gently rolling hills, small vineyards, spring wildflowers, and acre upon acre of twisted, ancient olive trees. Graceful white-stone towns dot the hilltops.

Most gleaming white of all is Ostuni. From the town, olive trees stretch in all directions, their silver and green leaves fluttering, their trunks like strange petrified sculptures. In recent years Italy's olive groves have been ravaged by a bacterium, *Xylella fastidiosa,* which has led to many trees dying, but the endless groves around the Valle d'Itria have survived untainted, thanks to a strict containment policy.

To discover more about the ancient trees and the process of obtaining the oil, you can visit a local olive press. Corrado Rodio of Masseria Brancati has a face burnished by Pugliese sun and a great pride in his ancient olive groves, as he leads visitors around to explain the process and visits some of the most spectacular trees, which date to more than 2000 years ago. You can stay at the *masseria* (farmhouse) or arrange a visit to explore the farm, with its cellar of centuries-old olive-pressing equipment, and taste what is the lifeblood of the region.

Convento San Giovanni Evangelista

Less than an hour's drive away is the beautiful golden-stone university town of Lecce. It's famous for many foodstuffs, such as perfect snack-fodder *rustici* (pastry puffs filled with tomato and béchamel), but perhaps the most enticing culinary adventure is to hunt down the town's *biscotti di pasta di mandorle* – sweets made from almond paste, traditionally eaten during religious festivals.

You can buy these sweets from cloistered local nuns at the 12th-century convent of San Giovanni Evangelista (Via delle Benedettine). The nuns are not permitted to show their faces nor speak to anyone outside, but still manage to keep trade going – ring the bell of the convent and you'll be able to arrange to buy some through the faceless dumb waiter, through which the nuns pass the exquisitely wrapped almond biscuits. The best time to get them is around feast days; you'll be able to spot where to go by the queue.

Stile Mediterraneo Cooking School

Make your last stop this excellent cookery school. The charming chef Cinzia Rascazzo, who's a local but has lived and worked in New York, is a fount of knowledge about Pugliese produce, cooking and food history, such as the time Puglia produced olive oil in underground caverns to supply fuel to light lamps all over Europe.

You'll learn the dazzling yet simple skills of peasant cooking, and work with superlative ingredients to make such dishes as fresh *orecchiette* or *tagliatelle* with tomato sauce, soups with broad beans or eggplant balls and seafood. Stile Mediterraneo is unique in teaching these Puglia classics with a twist, having developed healthier slow-cooking methods in place of frying. You'll learn three recipes, and have a short olive oil tasting session, plus you'll eat the dishes you've prepared; dinner includes wines specially chosen to pair with the food. The school has sites outside Lecce and in town.

To read about:

Sicily's Markets see page 190
Puglia's Coast see page 192

Bread Gnocchi with Black Olive Pesto & Pecorino from the Valle d'Itria

Serves 4
Cooking time 30 minutes

This dish (gnocchi di pane al pesto di olive nere a inchiostro e pecorino della Valle d'Itria) combines some of Puglia's most ubiquitous produce: black olives, pecorino cheese and olive oil. These simple bread gnocchi are on the menu at Trattoria La Tana, in Martina Franca, a hilltop town with VIP views over the Valle d'Itria and its neatly ordered fields dotted with the region's distinctive trulli houses.

It would be easy to think the views from Martina Franca's 14th-century city walls, out over the Itria Valley, were more compelling than the ones within. This sizeable Pugliese town is piled on top of a pointy hill that rises sharply out of the Itrian plains, its shape resembling one of the region's iconic *trulli*. From these heights, panoramic views of Puglia's flat arable lands reveal clusters of these conical-roofed houses – the grace of their dry stone walls, the white symbols painted onto their tapering roofs, of crescent moons, birds and stars.

But step through Martina Franca's Porta di Santo Stefano, the old entrance to town, and you'll find baroque architecture, a basilica and a 16th-century Palazzo Ducale where stables now house one of the town's prettiest restaurants: La Tana. Nicola Colucci, the son of a baker, always wanted to become a chef, studying for the profession as a teenager and starting work when he was 20. He's been running La Tana for 30 years, serving classic Pugliese dishes and creating recipes that showcase its traditional produce. While these gnocchi aren't an 'old' recipe per se, they are very *casalinga* (homely) in spirit – a way to use up hard *casareccio* (home-made) bread, aged cheese and olives so they aren't thrown away.

For the gnocchi
→ 8 tbsp grated hard white bread
→ 4 tbsp semolina
→ 1 clove garlic, chopped
→ 1 tbsp fresh parsley, chopped (put a few whole leaves aside)
→ 1 tbsp pecorino, grated
→ 1 egg
→ water

For the pesto
→ 1 ramekin of black olives
→ 1 clove garlic
→ 1 bunch fresh parsley
→ 200ml (6½fl oz) extra virgin olive oil, from Puglia
→ 1 tbsp pecorino, grated

1. Combine all the ingredients for the gnocchi to make a ball of dough, rolling and kneading gently for a couple of minutes, using flour to stop it sticking.

2. Cut the ball into four or five small pieces then roll out into small sausage shapes about 2.5cm (1in) wide, then chop into little gnocchi – make them a little longer than they are wide.

3. With your thumb, roll each one lengthways along a fork, to get the imprint of the tines. Then leave them to rest for 10 minutes.

4. Put all the ingredients for the pesto in an electric blender until they get to the consistency of pesto or cream.

5. Place the gnocchi in boiling salted water for three or four minutes or until they rise to the surface, then drain, reserving a couple of tablespoons of water.

6. In a separate pan heat the gnocchi water, some olive oil and the few leaves of parsley you've put aside, and salt to taste. Then sauté the drained gnocchi for 30 seconds tossing well to coat in the oil.

7. Serve on a plate that's been glazed with the pesto and coated in a dusting of pecorino. Or simply combine the pesto with the gnocchi in a bowl and grate the cheese on top.

Pinocchio, Pulcinella & Opera dei Pupi

ITALY-WIDE / ARTS

Puppetry is an ancient art that has been entertaining crowds around the world for centuries, with the first written records found in the works of Xenophon in the 5th century BC. From Florence's Pinocchio and Naples' Pulcinella to Palermo's opera dei pupi, Italian puppets have influenced the art form throughout Europe and around the world.

The Real Adventures of Pinocchio

The timeless tale of a wooden puppet that turns into a boy, *Le avventure di Pinocchio* (The Adventures of Pinocchio) is one of the most widely read and internationally popular pieces of literature ever to emerge from Italy.

In the early 1880s, Carlo Collodi (1826–90), a Florentine journalist, wrote a series for *Giornale per i bambini,* the first Italian newspaper for children. Entitled *Storia di un burattino* (Story of a Puppet) and subsequently renamed, the story has been adapted into film a number of times, from Disney's much-loved animated film in 1940 through to Roberto Benigni's 2002 production.

The story, weaving between fantasy and reality, is a mine of references, some more veiled than others, to the society of late-19th-century Italy – a troubled country with enormous socio-economic problems compounded by the general apathy of those in power. Pinocchio waits the length of the story to become a real boy but, while his persona may provoke laughter, his encounters with poverty, petty crime, skewed justice and just plain bad luck constitute a painful education in the machinations of the 'real' world.

A Puppet with Punch

His aliases are many, Punchinello or Mr Punch in Britain and Petruska in Russia. But in his home town of Naples he's simply Pulcinella: the best-known character of the commedia dell'arte and a stock character in Neapolitan puppetry.

In his white costume and black hook-nosed mask, Pulchinella only became a puppet when his character spread to places where the commedia dell'arte was less popular. Upon his adaptation in other regions he took on new names, becoming Kaspar in Germany and Austria, Polichinelle in France, Jan Klaassen in the Netherlands, Mester Jackel in Denmark and, perhaps most famously, as one half of Punch and Judy, where as an anti-authoritarian street philosopher, he is often seen beating the local copper with a stick (hence the term slapstick).

If you'd like to watch Pulcinella puppets being made, Letizia Fiorini's namesake shop in Florence is ideal. Fiorini sits at the counter and makes her distinctive puppets by hand in between assisting customers. Besides Pulcinella, you'll find Arlecchino the clown, beautiful servant girl Colombina, Doctor Peste (complete with plague mask), cheeky Brighella, swashbuckling Il Capitano and many other characters from traditional Italian puppetry.

Opera dei Pupi

Sicily's most popular form of traditional entertainment is the *opera dei pupi* (rod-marionette theatre). Marionettes were first introduced to the island by the Spanish in the 18th century and the art form was swiftly embraced by locals and performances effectively became the soap operas of their day.

Carved from beech, olive or lemon-tree wood, the marionettes stand some 1.5m high, have wire joints and wear richly coloured costumes. The knights are clad in metal suits of armour that make the figures shine and resonate when they engage in swordfights with bloodthirsty Saracen warriors or mythical monsters.

Good puppeteers are judged on the dramatic effect they can create – lots of stamping feet, thundering and a gripping running commentary – and on their speed and skill in directing the battle scenes. You can catch traditional one-hour shows using exquisitely handcrafted *pupi* at the charming Teatro dei Pupi di Mimmo Cuticchio. The Museo Internazionale delle Marionette also stages performances in its beautifully decorated theatre, complete with hand-cranked music machine. The museum also houses more than 3500 marionettes, puppets and shadow figures from Palermo, Catania and Naples, as well as from further-flung places such as Japan, Southeast Asia, Africa, China and India.

To read about:

Opera see page 292
Venice Carnevale see page 306

Over the Horizon: Salina

SICILY / LANDSCAPES

In delightful contrast to the exposed volcanic terrain of the other Aeolian Islands, Salina – the archipelago's second-largest island – boasts a lush, verdant landscape thanks to its natural freshwater springs. Shaped by two extinct volcanoes, the island has inspired poets and filmmakers but still remains relatively unexplored.

Right **Monte dei Porri**

Far left **View to Monte Fossa delle Felci**

Left **Capers for sale**

Right **Salina's whitewashed houses**

Seven Aeolian Islands are scattered in an irregular archipelago across Homer's wine-dark sea between Naples and Sicily. They're not so much a string of pearls as a rope of coral, like that which grows abundantly in the clear, pure waters around them. Their shapes are curious and irregular, blobs of magma from some vast pre-historic eruption, scoured by centuries of wind and sunlight and water. Of them all, Salina is the most beautiful, the greenest and most fertile. Small wonder it has been identified as Homer's Island of the Sirens, and its essence hasn't changed in the centuries since.

Salina's beauty made it the setting for *Il Postino,* the Oscar-winning film about the life of the poet Pablo Neruda. But it isn't the island's legendary status as a setting for Greek epics and contemporary film that makes Salina so seductive. The interior is like a lush hammock strung between two volcanic cones, Monte Fossa delle Felci and the Monte dei Porri, the Mountain of Leeks. From this inland area comes olive oil and Malvasia, a nectar of a wine made from grapes dried on wicker trays in the sun before being pressed.

The area is also famous for its pungent, potent capers – the tiny flavour charge that adds its distinctive character to so many Mediterranean dishes. The caper's importance to the island economy is borne out by a festival celebrating it in June, where locals feast on caper-heavy dishes before partying into the night.

The island's several villages contain characteristic flat-roofed houses that glow brilliant white in the Mediterranean sun but the true beauties of Salina are natural rather than cultural. The interior is filled with wonderful walks, in parts craggy, bare and rocky; in parts covered in abundant chestnut woods, poplars, cypresses, ferns, olives and the distinctive prickly pear cactus. And then there's always the sea: azure, clear, rich in marine life, providing the fish and shellfish that are the mainstay of the island's simple, satisfying dishes, and an endless diversion for anyone drawn to water. If you're looking for high art or ancient monuments, look elsewhere. But if it's tranquillity, peace of mind and the beauty of nature that you're after, then Salina will do very, very nicely.

To read about:

Volcanoes see page 224
Costa Smeralda see page 274

FLORENCE

Cradle of the Renaissance

Stand on the Ponte Vecchio that arcs gracefully across the Arno several times in a day and the nuanced light, mood and view changes every time. From this frame, Florence appears as finely wrought as the frescoes of the Renaissance masters that made the Tuscan capital legendary. This city of water, light and lavishly ornamented buildings conjures giddy romance, with its towers and palazzi, marble basilicas and shadowy back alleys evoking a thousand tales of its medieval past.

Surprisingly small though it is, Florence fires imaginations like few other places on Earth, with a ludicrous stash of world-class art and architecture for a city of its diminutive size.

It was here that those great Renaissance masters really went to town, reaching for the celestial and sublime in works daunting in their scale and splendour. Indeed, you will often be dumbstruck – just as millions have been before you – as you delve into the San Lorenzo and San Marco neighbourhoods, where Brunelleschi's harmonious Basilica di San Lorenzo looms large, Michelangelo's *David* gazes towards Rome in the Galleria dell'Accademia, and Fra' Angelico's spiritually uplifting frescoes adorn the Convent of San Marco.

Central Florence bombards you with artistic brilliance, too – from Brunelleschi's staggering pink, white and green marble Duomo, capped by an octagonal dome, to medieval Piazza della Signoria and the crenellated fortress palace Palazzo Vecchio. The world's greatest collection of Renaissance art hangs out in the Uffizi – Botticelli's *Birth of Venus* and *Primavera*,

Giotto's shimmering altarpieces, Leonardo's *The Baptism of Christ*... Return time and again and you still won't see it all.

Rich in culture and backdropped by history, Florentine lifestyle is anchored by family, faith, food and tradition. Nowhere is this more evident than in Oltrarno on the 'other side of the Arno', Florence's bohemian hood, sprinkled with *botteghe* (artisan workshops). Turn a corner down a narrow passageway and your eyes will alight on jewellers, shoemakers, violin makers, bookbinders, gilders, ironworkers and sculptors – *maestri* (masters) plying their trade just as folk have since Renaissance times.

The city works its magic in little ways, too. Go for an evening *passeggiata* in bar-lined Santa Croce. Linger at a trattoria for a *bistecca fiorentina* (T-bone steak) and a glass of Tuscan red. Watch a fourth-generation goldsmith at work. Florence is one of Italy's capitals of fashion, but its true beauty is timeless.

FLORENCE FROM ABOVE

FLORENCE / LANDSCAPES

Whichever way you look, Florence is a stunner. It's almost impossible not to be seduced by the city's medieval skyline, awash in a rainbow of Tuscan colours. There's the mesmerising sight of the Duomo, the iconic Ponte Vecchio straddling the Arno, and, of course, the terracotta rooftops. You'd be hard-pressed to find a view over this city that doesn't leave you swooning.

One of the finest views is from the top of the *campanile,* or bell tower: a daunting climb up 414 narrow and winding stone steps. Even done slowly, it's a serious test of legs and lungs. The grand roof of the Duomo, which rises up alongside it, looks different after the climb. It becomes harder to separate the soaring beauty of its revolutionary design from the incredible graft it took to build it. The Duomo was 150 years in the making and generations of Florentines climbed and chiselled and carried stones to complete it. From up high, the city, which can be disorientating at ground level, looks strikingly compact. It seems astonishing that so much beauty should have poured out of this place.

Fortunately, there are less arduous ways of appreciating Florence. From the green loveliness of the Giardino Bardini on the south side of the river, you can see the city fall into place around the view of the Duomo. In colder months, the distant peaks of the Apennines will be snow-capped. In summer, the city twinkles with colour: the pink of its terracotta roofs and the yellow of its walls must have been chosen to complement the blue of the sky.

As the sun sets it seems to light up the yellow sweep of the Ponte Vecchio. This medieval bridge is a vivid symbol of the city, functional, beautiful, home to skilled craftspeople – jewellers still occupy some of the shops on the bridge – and also part museum. The astonishing Vasari Corridor runs right across the top of it, identifiable by its regular square windows. The corridor was built in 1564 on the orders of Cosimo I de' Medici so he could walk between his residence in the Palazzo Pitti and the Palazzo Vecchio, from where he ruled the city. A symbol of the Medici family's dominance of the city and an incredible architectural feat, it was completed in a mere five months. The original promenade incorporated tiny windows (facing the river) and circular apertures with iron gratings (facing the street) to protect those who used the corridor from outside attacks. But when Hitler visited Florence in 1941, his chum and fellow dictator Benito Mussolini had big new windows punched into the corridor walls on Ponte Vecchio so that his guest could enjoy an expansive view down the Arno from the famous Florentine bridge.

To read about:

Above Vasari Corridor

DANTE'S FLORENCE

FLORENCE / ARTS

*Prior to the 13th century, Italian liter-
ature was written in Latin. But all that
changed with Florentine-born Dante
Alighieri. The Divine Comedy delivered an allegorical vision of the afterlife
that made an immediate and profound
impression on readers and, through its
wide-reaching popularity, established
the Tuscan dialect as the new standard-
ised form of written Italian.*

When Dante was just 12 he was promised in marriage to Gemma Donati. But it was another Florentine gal, Beatrice Portinari (1266–90), who was his muse, his inspiration and the love of his life (despite him only ever meeting her twice). The *Divine Comedy*, divided into three parts – *Inferno*, *Purgatorio* and *Paradiso*, describes travelling through the circles of hell in search of his beloved Beatrice.

In Dante's *Inferno*, 1300 is an ominous year: our hero Dante escapes from one circle of hell only to tumble into the next – much like life for the writer and his fellow Tuscans, who endured a hellish succession of famine, economic collapse, plague, war and tyranny throughout the 14th century.

Top Dante Sites in Florence

Duomo Down the left aisle, *La Commedia Illumina Firenze* (1465) by Domenico di Michelino depicts Dante Alighieri surrounded by the three afterlife worlds he describes in the *Divine Comedy*: purgatory is behind him, his right-hand points towards hell, and the city of Florence is paradise.

Museo Casa di Dante This house-museum was built in 1910 above the foundations of Dante's dwelling.

Chiesa di Santa Margherita Dubbed Chiesa di Dante, this tiny 11th-century church in an alley near Dante's house is where the poet first spied Beatrice and wed Gemma; both women are buried in the church. Beatrice wed a banker at 22 and died a couple of years later; note the wicker basket in front of her grave filled with scraps of paper on which prayers and dedications evoking unrequited love have been penned. Dimly lit, the church remains much as it was in medieval times.

Basilica di Santa Croce This basilica holds not only Dante's (empty) tomb, but also those of Michelangelo, Galileo and Machiavelli.

Dante Sites Beyond Florence

Tomba di Dante, Ravenna Dante was expelled from Florence in 1302 for political reasons. He finally sought refuge in Ravenna, where he died in 1321. As a perpetual act of penance, Florence still supplies the oil for the lamp that burns continually in this, his real tomb.

Biblioteca Guarneriana, Friuli-Venezia Giulia One of Italy's oldest and most venerated libraries, founded in 1466, it contains 12,000 well-preserved antique books, including a priceless manuscript of Dante's *Inferno*.

Dante Alighieri Statue, Verona The famous, rather pensive statue of Dante looking like a lost tourist, stands on Piazza dei Signori, where he lived from 1312 to 1318. It's the work of Ugo Zannoni and was erected in 1865.

To read about:
Shakespeare's Italy see page 114
Puppet Theatre see page 140

Above Basilica di Santa Croce

FLORENCE DAY-TRIPPER: FIESOLE

FIESOLE / LANDSCAPES

One of the joys of Florence is travelling through the countryside that surrounds it and a trip to Fiesole provides the perfect excuse. Perched in the hills 9km northeast of the city, this bijou hilltop village has seduced for centuries with its cooler air, olive groves, scattering of Renaissance-styled villas and spectacular views of the plain. Boccaccio, Marcel Proust, Gertrude Stein and Frank Lloyd Wright, among others, raved about it.

Founded in the 7th century BC by the Etruscans, Fiesole was the most important city in northern Etruria and its Area Archeologica, off central square Piazza Mino di Fiesole, provides the perfect flashback. Buy a ticket from the tourist office a couple of doors away, then meander around the ruins of an Etruscan temple, some Roman baths and an archaeological museum. Later, pause for thought on the stone steps of the 1st-century-BC Roman amphitheatre.

Afterwards pop into Museo Bandini to view early Tuscan Renaissance art, including fine medallions by Giovanni della Robbia and Taddeo Gaddi's *Annunciation*.

From the museum, a walk along Via Giovanni Dupré brings you to the Museo Primo Conti, where the eponymous artist lived and worked. Inside hang more than 60 of his paintings and the views from the garden are inspiring. Ring to enter.

Meander back to Piazza Mino di Fiesole, host to an antiques market on the first Sunday of each month, where cafe and restaurant terraces tempt. The terrace of Villa Aurora is a classy, classic choice for lazing over an idyllic al fresco lunch. Its panoramic view of Florence has made the four-star hotel and restaurant the place to be in town since 1860.

Alternatively, opt for rustic Tuscan cuisine partaken at a shared table at popular Vinandro, or La Reggia degli Etruschi, an outstanding diner halfway up the steep car-free hill to Chiesa e Convento di San Francesco. La Reggia buzzes on Sunday with knowing Florentines out for the day in Fiesole to feast on first-class Tuscan fare and a mesmerising panorama of their city.

In the afternoon, stagger around Cattedrale di San Romolo, which was begun in the 11th century. A glazed terracotta statue of San Romolo by Giovanni della Robbia guards the entrance inside. Afterwards, make your way up steep walled Via San Francesco and be blown away by the staggeringly beautiful panorama of Florence that unfolds from the terrace adjoining 15th-century Chiesa e Convento di San Francesco. Green afternoon-nap spots abound and the tourist office has brochures about walking trails from here.

Top off your day trip by enjoying an aperitivo with Florentines at local hangout JJ Hill, an atmospheric Irish pub with a tip-top beer list, excellent burgers and other quality pub grub. Or fire up the romantic in you with in a 2½-hour, 21km guided bike ride by sunset back to Florence.

To read about:
Lucca see page 112
Tuscan Hill Towns see page 116

Viva Italia

Modern Life & the Italian Way

Ancient Romans loved to feast, guzzle wine and make merry and some 2000 years down the line, Italians still have plenty in common with their pleasure-seeking, beauty-conscious ancestors. Modern life may sometimes make them hot under the collar – the political scandals, bills to pay and work to do, *che peccato!* (what a shame) – but ultimately Italians are ever the hedonists. They are quick to poke fun and flirt, always up for a party and embrace life to the fullest. Their passionate, tempestuous natures – just watch the gesticulating madness when they are behind the wheel of a car or rooting for their football team when the match is on – adds a pinch of theatre to daily life that transcends the famous north–south divide.

Little encapsulates the Italian psyche like the concept of *la bella figura*, or making a good impression – no matter if you're just doing the supermarket shop, your outfit should match and your hair should be perfectly coiffed. It might seem like vanity, but the national obsession with beauty in all aspects of life gives Italy its undeniable edge in design, cuisine, art and architecture.

Times are changing, but the family still comes first: lunches with *la famiglia* are blow-out affairs from dawn to dusk, weddings are big, showy affairs where every second cousin twice removed is invited. Birth rates are dropping, but the *mammone*, the child who never grows up, is on the rise: as unemployment soars, some two-thirds of young Italians still live with their parents. Many might aspire to luxury – an Armani suit or the latest Ferrari – but even they readily admit that the finer things in Italian life cost little: a friendly chat with neighbours, an *aperitivo* with *amici* (friends), family celebrations and, of course, all the striking beauty right on their doorstep.

All in the Family

Italy's single most successful institution, and the only one in which Italians continually trust, is the family. This devotion is rooted in history. The country's mountainous terrain evolved a mosaic of communities, members of which depended greatly on each other. In these close-knit clans, everyone knows everyone and local matters are more important than world affairs.

Family is the bedrock of Italian society and has been since the Roman era when the institution of the family (*gens* or plural *gentes,* meaning 'people') was highly regulated and structured. At the time, families were much larger and consisted of anyone who shared the same *nomen* (extended family name, rather than just surname) and claimed descent from a common ancestor. Rome's most patrician families, for example, considered themselves related to the first hundred senators chosen by the city's founder, Romulus, to govern the city.

Each Roman family consisted not only of blood relatives, but anyone who was dependent on the *pater familias* (father of the family), including the family's servants, slaves, freed slaves and even other families. The more clients you had the more important and powerful your family. Across the peninsula this web of ties cemented people from different walks of life and ethnic backgrounds – such as the Slovene-Italians in Friuli and the Greek-Italians in the South – into a rich tapestry of dialects and culture.

These distinct regional identities continue to survive in Italy's unique range of customs and festivals, such as Sardinia's Spanish-influenced Cavalcata Sarda and the Nozze Carsiche (*Kraška ohcet*), a Karstic wedding ceremony based on an 18th-century tradition and only held in the fortress town of Monrupino in Friuli-Venezia Giulia. It takes place every two years over a long weekend and is like a mini Carneval with the whole village participating in food stalls, live music and historic *osmizze* (wine tastings).

Family is so significant to Italians that it has shaped not only the cultural and

domestic landscape, but even the physical character of Italian towns. Italian architecture with its numerous piazzas (outdoor living rooms), flower-lined promenades and gardens, encourages people to get outside and socialise. Step out into the *passeggiata* in the early evening in Perugia or Lecce, Verona or Palermo and you'll be swept up in a daily ritual that sees young lovers walking arm in arm, families showing off new babies, children playing and slurping pastel-coloured *gelato* (ice-cream) and old friends nursing a glass of wine on cafe stoops. This is where romances are made, friends catch up, neighbours gossip, and the whole town revels in a warm familial feeling.

But what is it like on the inside of a large, loud and loving Italian family? According to the time-honoured Italian social contract, you'll probably live with your parents until you start a career and a family of your own. Then after a suitable grace period for success and romance – a couple of years should do the trick – your parents might move in with you to look after your kids, and be looked after in turn. As for those who don't live with family members, chances are they're still a quick stroll away, with over 50% living within a 30-minute walk of close relatives. All this considered, it's hardly surprising to hear that famous mobile-phone chorus at evening rush hour: *'Mamma, butta la pasta!'* (Mum, put the pasta in the water!).

While Italy's family-based social fabric provides a protective buffer for many during challenging economic times, inter-generational solidarity has always been the basis of the Italian family. Children are watched over with an eagle eye, embraced frequently and taught to re-spect their elders, giving up their seats for their grandparents and happily fetching and carrying for them.

These cross-generational ties are constantly renewed through various rites of passage, including birthdays, baptisms, confirmations, weddings and funerals. With 80% of Italians identifying as Catholics, Catholicism also plays a significant role in Italian family life. With the country's birth rate one of the lowest in Europe, newlyweds are regularly admonished not only by their *nonni* (grandparents), but by Pope Francis himself.

Stumble across a local wedding on any summer Saturday or Sunday and you'll find the extended Italian family putting on its finest show. A mix of faith and super-stition will also be on display. For example, in some regions the groom still carries a piece of iron in his pocket to ward off the evil eye, while the wedding veil originated in Rome to avoid a couple seeing each other before the ceremony and risking either party calling it off. In the south, the veil should be as long as the couple's love for each other and popular wedding favours include sugared almonds, which symbolise the bitter and the sweet to come. Tradition informs and supports every small detail.

But no tradition is as important to the cohesion of the Italian family as Sunday lunch. Rain, hail or shine, sitting down to Sunday lunch with your family is a non-negotiable part of life. Not a Sunday goes by when family members, friends and neighbours don't crowd around a table to celebrate close bonds and good food. Sunday lunch here isn't just a nice meal, but a way to stay together, to renew close relations through good conversation and to enjoy Nonna's sauce and meatballs.

At Home and at Work

It might score straight As in fashion, food and design, but Italy's performance in the gender-equality stakes leaves much room for improvement. According to a 2009 report by the Uomini Casalinghi (The Italian Association of Househusbands), 95% of Italian men have never turned on a washing machine, and 70% of them have never used a stove. Furthermore, the European Commission's 2017 Report on Equality showed only 52% of Italian women were in the workforce, compared to 80% in Sweden, 75% in Denmark and 66% in France.

Improvements in educational opportunities and changing attitudes mean that the number of women with successful careers is growing – the 2015 Global Gender Gap Index published by the World Economic Forum ranked Italy at number 41 overall in 2015, up a dramatic 28 spots from 2014. That said, the country still sits near the bottom of the list of European nations in regard to political, professional and economic parity between the sexes.

To read about:

Abbey & Monastery Devotions

ITALY-WIDE / RELIGION

Gregorian chant drifts from a high-domed basilica, where Benedictine monks sing in holy worship. A dark-robed Franciscan monk drifts through the pink-stone streets of Assisi like a vision in the fading light of dusk. Pilgrims pray to a bejewelled statue of the Black Madonna in the candlelit twilight of a Renaissance chapel.

Keeping the faith has many different expressions in Italy – from the simplicity of a religious icon on a mantelpiece and clicking rosary beads to the sublimity of the Vatican's St Peter's Basilica, where Michelangelo's *Pietà* is exquisite in its maternal tenderness. But religious belief is not just on the fringes of Italian society; it's entwined in the fabric of daily life. Monks and nuns keep the wheels of faith turning in the country's working monasteries and abbeys – of which there are many.

Take, for instance, the Abbazia di Montecassino in Lazio, lifted to the heavens on a mountaintop. One of the most important Christian centres in the medieval world, it was founded by St Benedict in 529 AD, supposedly after three ravens led him to the spot. Its true wonder is felt as you wander its cloisters in quiet contemplation, glimpse the gold mosaics in its crypt and listen to Gregorian chant echo through its halls during Mass.

The verdant hill country of Tuscany further north is home to some of the country's most magnificent abbeys. Among the most revered is the 14th-century Abbazia di Monte Oliveto Maggiore, concealed amid dense forest in the Chianti region, which is still a retreat for Benedictine monks. Frescoes depicting the life of St Benedict dance across the walls of its cloister, and you can taste Sangiovese red wines at the estate's cellar. A drive south through vineyards, olive groves and farmland brings you to the Romanesque Abbazia di Sant'Antimo, which sits in a remote valley and hides a splendid Carolingian chapel and crypt. Concerts, ranging from classical to sacred, are regularly staged in this lovely setting and if you're looking to polish your monastic skills, the abbey offers lessons in plainchant and manuscript illumination. It also produces its own medieval remedies using the medicinal herbs that grow in the garden, as well as honey, preserves, beer and a bitter digestive liqueur.

The shuffle of centuries of shoes and bare pilgrims' feet has left its mark at Italy's most sacred sites. Pilgrims still seek redemption at the Sacra di San Michele, perched at 962m above the Val di Susa. Devoted to the cult of the Archangel Michael, the Gothic-Romanesque abbey is on the pilgrimage route between Saint-Michel in France and Monte Sant'Angelo in Puglia.

In the mountainous reaches of southern Umbria, Norcia, birthplace of St Benedict in 480 AD, is a fine example of how devotion can be expressed in the modern age. The town was rocked by a huge earthquake in 2016, which left its monastery and basilica in ruins. The enterprising monks – many of whom were brought over from the United States to repopulate the monastery in 2000 – sought salvation in their brewery, Birra Nursia, which had miraculously remained intact. Texas-born Rev Martin Bernhard, the cellarer, is raising funds through selling monastic brews to build a new monastery, where the uplifting sound of Benedictine monks chanting shall soon be heard once again.

To read about:

Right **Abbazia di Montecassino,** Lazio

Viva Italia / **161**

Restoring Italy

While trend spotters in Milan contemplate Gucci's latest logoed T-shirts sporting the provocative question, 'What are we going to do with all this future?' Italians elsewhere are struggling to find a solution to a bigger problem: how can they continue living up to their weighty history? From abandoned villages to disappearing traditions, crafts and recipes, preserving Italy's past is a full-time job.

There's no doubt, Italy is Europe's artistic over-achiever. Italian art, architecture and design underpins much of the cultural history of the Western world. As of 2017, there were 53 Unesco World Heritage Sites in Italy with 40 more on the tentative list. That's more Heritage Sites than any other country in the world, including competitors like China, which comes in second on Unesco's list with 51 sites.

But for all the architecturally important cities and sites that delight travellers, there are scores more where few venture and which now face the prospect of serious decline. According to a 2016 Italian environmental association report, there are nearly 2500 rural Italian villages that are perilously depopulated, some like Civita di Bagnoregio, near Rome, partially abandoned while others such as Craco in Basilicata are already eerie ghost towns.

Protecting Italy's enormous cultural patrimony is an expensive and difficult job, particularly when faced with the challenges of the modern world: rural poverty, rapid urbanisation, mass emigration, financial austerity and natural disasters such as the earthquake that flattened L'Aquila in 2009 and the floods that threatened to sweep away the historic villages of the Cinque Terre in 2011. Even Venice, the jewel in Italy's heritage crown, is increasingly threatened by rising tides.

The financially constrained Italian government can do little to help, so solving the problem falls to locals such as the residents of Prataricca in Tuscany who sold their village for US$3.1 million on eBay, while the mayor of Bormida (population 530) posted an offer on Facebook of US$2100 to anyone who would move there. (He later had to delete the post due to an overwhelming response.) When these towns die, we don't simply lose their architectural and artistic legacies, but a web of unique traditions that are practised by their inhabitants: skills that produce the loom-woven woollen blankets of Santo Stefano di Sessanio; or the *pasta frolla* shortbread biscuits of Molise now made by a single mother and daughter; or the ancient art of the *battiloro* (gold beater) now practiced by a single Venetian using a method that dates to the 18th century.

Recently though, there has been a resurgence of interest both in heritage crafts and the places that sustain them. After all, Alessandro Michele, creative director at Gucci, has made a second home for himself in the fine deserted buildings of Civita di Bagnoregio along with other artists and creatives from Rome and Florence. Young Italians, facing high unemployment, are also turning back to the craft industries that powered the country's post-WWII economy. The masters behind James Bond's sartorial style at august tailor, Brioni, now run a tailoring school in quiet Penne in Abruzzo, while determined entrepreneurs such as Federico Badia and Gabriele Gmeiner spent years working with master cobblers to perfect their trade before opening ateliers in Rome and Venice respectively.

New technology, new finance models and a push by regional governments to assist entrepreneurs are also playing their part. Even the Church is getting in on the act with its crowdfunding 'Adopt a Spire' campaign to help restore Milan's spectacular Duomo. Iconic sites such as the Colosseum in Rome, the Galleria Vittorio Emanuele in Milan and the Rialto Bridge in Venice have secured corporate

Right Craco, Basilicata

sponsorship in the tens of millions; while the new Art Bonus law aims to encourage both individuals and corporate patrons to invest in the restoration of cultural sites by offering a tax bonus equal to a deduction of 65% of their donation. The Italian State Property Agency hopes this will provide the impetus for energetic entrepreneurs to transform more than 100 historic properties which they offered for free in 2017.

Visionaries such as Daniele Kihlgren and Matteo Bisol see the tourism potential in these exquisite places nestled, often, in spectacular landscapes and unique contexts. Both have invested in creating a new style of accommodation knows as an *albergo diffuso*, a 'scattered hotel' of individual houses rented to guests through a centralised hotel-style reception. Bisol has created his in the abandoned fishermen's cottages on the island of Burano in the Venetian lagoon, while Kihlgren has almost single-handedly restored the medieval village of Santo Stefano di Sessanio in Abruzzo.

In the process of his restoration Kihlgren realised that in order to restore Santo Stefano authentically, he needed to use local materials and artisans with traditional skills. The woollen bedspreads for the rooms needed to be woven, the ceramic plates in the restaurant handmade and the food served cooked according to traditional recipes. In the process, Kihlgren has revitalised the village which now hosts thousands of travellers every year. In doing something completely new he discovered a way to hold on to the treasures of the past; a model that gives hope for the future.

To read about:
Subterranean Naples see page 254
Neapolitan Artisan Traditions see page 260

Above **Rialto Bridge,** Venice
Right ***Albergo diffuso,*** Abruzzo

A Snapshot of Cortona

Rooms with a view are the rule rather than the exception in the spectacularly sited hilltop town of Cortona, where large chunks of Under the Tuscan Sun, the soap-in-the-sun film of the book by American author Frances Mayes, were shot.

Beyond olive groves and vineyards, tall pines stretch graciously across the plains. Swallows swirl over red-tiled rooftops, church towers vie with cypresses as focal points, and broad fields, bright with sunflowers, merge into a misty blue horizon of hills. A Grand Tourist would have been enchanted by the sweeping panoramas on offer from almost every corner of Cortona. They might have come here as a relaxing break from the cosmopolitan culture of Florence, if they'd done their homework – in 1502, Leonardo da Vinci sketched this little Tuscan town as a sepia cluster of hilltop houses and towers, combining urban and rural charm in a way that has stood the test of time.

Atop the highest point in town, Fortezza del Girifalco offers stupendous views over the Val di Chiana to Lago Trasimeno in Umbria. The Medici fortress entertains a fabulous season of events that embraces everything from yoga workshops and falconry shows to collective picnics, dinner concerts, DJ sets and dancing after dark.

Pedestrian main street Via Nazionale has plenty of places to linger over coffee, cocktails or a refreshing craft beer. At its west end, cafe terraces spill across pretty Piazza della Repubblica. As the sun warms the flagstones of the piazza, patrons begin to fill the cafe chairs, unfurling their newspapers and ordering espressos. Others merely seek refreshment in preparation for the steep walk up cobbled lanes lined with brick-and-timber houses to the church of San Francesco.

San Francesco's outside staircase is supposed – for obscure reasons – to 'energise' visitors for the testing climb further up to the church of Santa Margherita, where the saint lies mummified, her parched face as brown as the Tuscan soil at the height of summer.

The piazza is busy but the pace is sedate. Cars are diverted from the centre of town and, among the tiny lanes that radiate from it, old women take kitchen chairs outside their houses and knit, keeping a keen ear out for potential gossip.

A latecomer to the town's cathedral opens the door and music floods into the square. Inside, flanked by confession boxes, an organist is thundering out the overture to Mozart's *Don Giovanni:* a libertine with more to confess than most. Later, a busking jazz band will strike up and push on towards midnight. No one seems overly worried about rushing home.

Armchair Experience

Frances Mayes helped put Cortona on the map with her bestselling memoir *Under the Tuscan Sun.* The book – translated into 46 languages and made into a major film in 2003 – describes the restoration of her pink-and-apricot 18th-century villa, called Bramasole ('Yearning for the sun'). At 270 years old, the house is a relative baby in Italian terms, with surrounding houses having notched up as much as 1000 years.

To read about:
Fiesole see page 152
Tuscan Cowboys see page 250

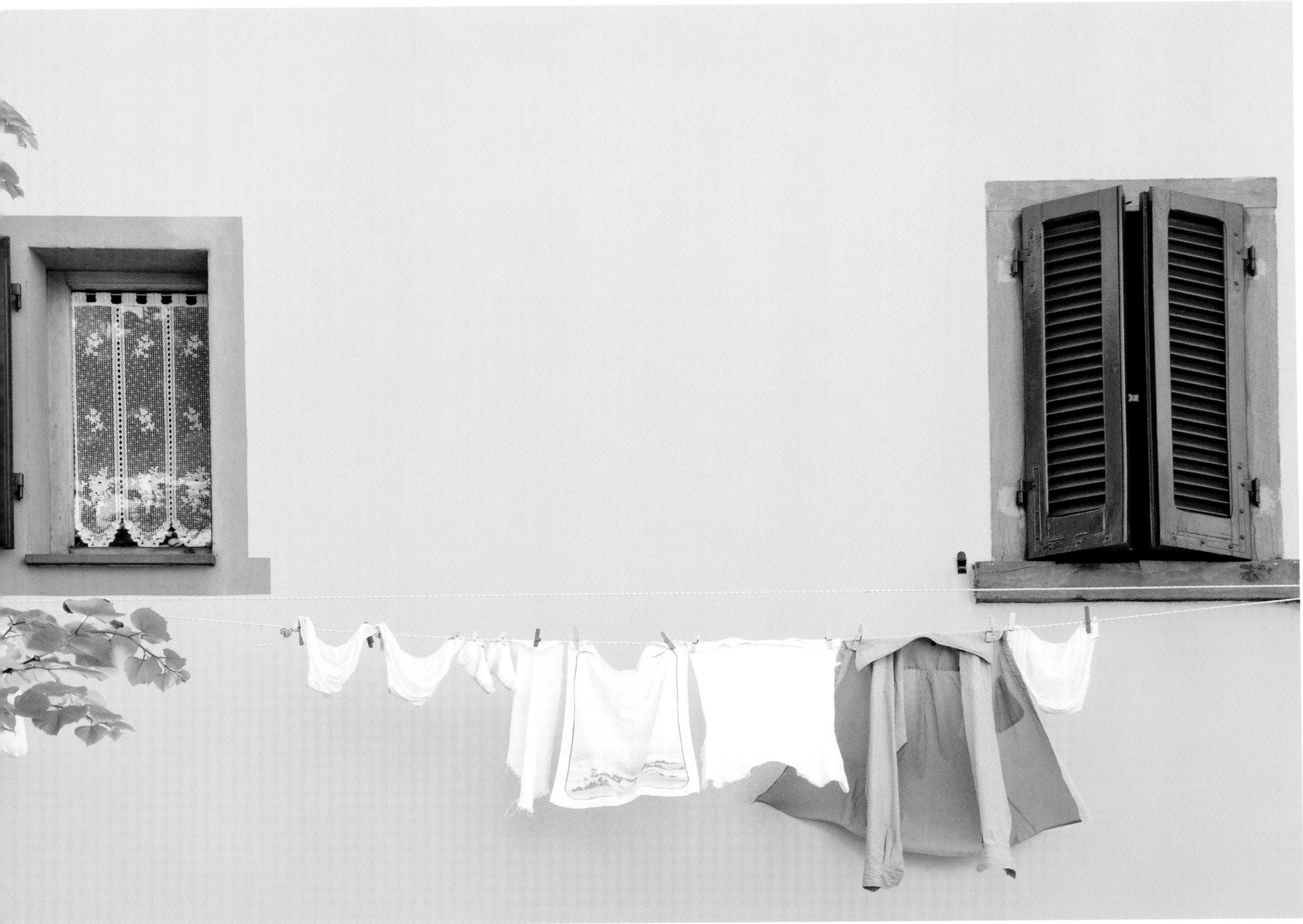

Saints, Feasts & Festivals

ITALY-WIDE / FESTIVALS

To talk of saints in Italy is to enter a complicated religious labyrinth. Every month is filled with a profusion of different saint's days and every settlement from Rome down to the smallest Tuscan hill town honours its own venerated holy deity in an annual festival. Some are solemn, some are exuberant, some attract one million devotees, others are celebrated by a pious trickle, yet all allow a candid, if fleeting, glimpse into Italy's Catholic soul.

Right Il Palio, Sienna

It is not unusual to time a trip to Italy around a religious festival. The busiest celebrations take place in tourist centres like Rome and Venice. Papal Masses are held in the Vatican at Christmas and Easter in St Peter's Basilica, the high church of Catholicism which can accommodate up to 15,000 people. Venice's pre-Lent carnival is famous the world over for its elaborate masks and attracts over three million people in February, although, these days, its religious significance is relatively minor. But, size isn't everything. Hang around the Italian peninsula for long enough, especially in the summer, and you're bound to stumble on some esoteric manifestation of sanctity and folklore, however small.

Befanas & Broomsticks

The feast of the Epiphany, when the Three Wise Men supposedly visited the infant Jesus, is a mainstay of the Catholic calendar worldwide. In Italy, the Epiphany has a bewitching theme. Deviating from standard religious texts, Italian folklore claims that the Wise Men stopped to ask directions at the dwelling of an old woman called *La Befana* (the witch) on their journey to Bethlehem. Consequently, local children are 'visited' over the night of January 5th and 6th by a witch who flies around on a broomstick dispensing sweets and presents to those who've been good, and lumps of coal to those who haven't. The Epiphany has special significance in Venice where the Regata de la Befana climaxes in an aquatic race along the Grand Canal between members of the Bucintoro rowing club theatrically dressed in witch's drag. They are cheered on by supporters who are kept warm with hot chocolate and *mammaluchi* (fritters with

raisins). The most historic Befana festival takes place in the unassuming town of Urbania in Le Marche where a cackling witch zip lines on a broomstick high above the medieval buildings before unlocking the door of her fairy-tale wooden house with a golden key. The festival is anchored by a night-time procession when expectant local children carry an abnormally long stocking through the streets.

Italy's Best-Loved Saint

Assisi in Umbria is synonymous with Italy's joint patron, St Francis, who dwelt in the town in the early 13th century. Francis, who founded the Franciscan monastic order and dedicated himself to a spiritual life, was known for his affiliations with the poor, the natural world and animals. His feast day on 4 October is a fascinating and poignant time to visit Assisi. Don't expect partying and fireworks. St Francis was a humble man and his anniversary is marked by a solemn Mass in the Basilica di San Francesco, followed by a candlelit procession to the Porziuncola chapel inside the Basilica di Santa Maria degli Angeli where Francis took refuge in the early 1200s. The next day, a large market plying local foodstuffs including olives, cheeses and wild-boar sausages is held inside the city walls. Each year a different Italian region is invited to lead the Assisi celebrations and provide the consecrated oil for a holy lamp that guards St Francis' crypt. The same oil is used to light up lamps all over town.

A Tale of Three Cities

If you're confused by the complexity of Italy's religious calendar, you can broaden your options by visiting on 23 and 24 June for the feast of San Giovanni Battista (St John the Baptist), the patron saint of three of Italy's largest cities: Turin, Genoa and Florence.

Turin celebrates the two-day holiday with a giant bonfire crowned by a symbolic bull in stately Piazza Castello on St John's Eve (23 June). Over 50,000 people crowd in to watch the bull motif sizzle and see the ensuing fireworks.

In Genoa, a midsummer party winds its way through the dark alleyways of the old town before ending with another bonfire in Piazza Matteotti. The following morning a more solemn mood prevails when a religious procession from the cathedral shuffles down to the famous port where the Genovese archbishop makes a blessing.

Florence's celebrations are a little less mainstream courtesy of its so-called *calcio storico*, a restaging of an antiquated 16th-century ball game that gets underway in the Piazza Santa Croce on a rough sand-covered pitch. This bullishly combative spectacle, which resembles a cross between rugby, football and all-in wrestling, kicks off with a cannon shot and pitches two teams of 27 players head to head. Graceful it isn't.

Matera's Spectacle of Destruction

If antediluvian football matches strike you as faintly eccentric, the Sagra della Madonna della Bruna, celebrated in the southern 'cave' city of Matera will appear positively bizarre.

The Bruna honours Matera's 'brown virgin'; her image inside the cathedral was given a distinctive brown hue after

Small Town Saints

Large festivals in big cities might lure international tourists, but the celebrations in Italy's smaller towns are often less crowded and more authentic. Here are three worth making a diversion for.

In Camogli in Liguria, the religious feast day of San Fortunato ties in with the Sagra del Pesce, a 60-year-old fish festival held during the second week in May. Events are ignited in a sparkling fireworks display and a bonfire-building competition on the beach between the town's two factions. The next day, locally caught fish sizzle in what is purported to be the world's largest frying pan in the hard-working harbour before being served up in a free feast.

On the idyllic island of Ischia in the Bay of Naples, the feast day of St Anne is celebrated on 26 July with a flotilla of boats decorated in an annual cultural theme. Commemorations culminate with the symbolic 'burning' of Ischia's Aragonese castle in a simulated blaze set off by fireworks, red lights and smoke.

St Ubaldo is hardly a household name, but that doesn't stop fervent celebrations of his 15 May feast day in the Umbrian town of Gubbio. Three colourfully dressed teams race to the Basilica di Sant'Ubaldo atop a steep hill each carrying a 300 to 400kg *cero* (wooden stand topped by a saintly statue) representing San Giorgio, Sant'Antonio and Sant'Ubaldo.

centuries of candle burning (though she's regularly cleaned these days). Festivities start inauspiciously on 2 July when an icon of the Madonna is paraded around the city in a mule-drawn *carro trionfale* (papier-mâché chariot) escorted by an entourage of dandily dressed 'knights'.

Things only start getting weird after the Madonna has been safely delivered to the cathedral whereupon a bevy of boisterous young men scramble out of the crowd and attack the now 'unholy' chariot with their bare hands and tear it to pieces. This seemingly pagan act of destruction is said to signify renewal with the young men representing Matera's shepherds of yore.

Taking home a piece of the chariot is supposed to bring good fortune, although, to unversed outsiders, the sight of it being ripped apart might look more like a minor riot.

The mood remains impassioned in a subsequent fireworks display that lends an unearthly glow to Matera's cavernous *sassi* (cave houses).

Italy's Largest Religious Festival

For sheer size and spectacle, no Italian religious festival can emulate the Festa di Sant'Agata in Catania, Sicily, a fervent parade that envelops the city every February. St Agatha was a rich noblewoman and early Christian devotee who was persecuted and killed by the Romans in AD 251 for practising her faith. It is said that, while she was being tortured, one of her breasts was cut off. Another legend relates how, exactly a year after her demise, Mt Etna portentously erupted in retribution.

St Agatha's legacy is honoured annually for three days beginning on 3 February. Special breast-shaped sponge cakes called *cassatelle di Sant'Agata* filled with sweet ricotta cheese and covered in marzipan are made in her honour. For the festival's grand climax, the volcanic sparks of Etna are replicated in a massive fireworks display that marks the end of a day-long procession in which a statue of the saint is carried in a silver carriage – the *fercolo* – to the cathedral. Over a million people throng the streets of Catania during the procession making it extremely difficult to catch a glimpse of the diminutive *fercolo* as it passes. Shouts of *'Unni ie' a' Santa?'* (Where is the Saint?) have become the festival's rallying cry.

Il Palio

On the surface, Siena's famous Palio is a bareback horse race in which ten of the city's *contrade* (city wards) compete in the tightly packed main square, the Piazza del Campo, in a spectacle of power and pageantry. But, this being Italy, the Palio has strong religious affiliations. The first of the year's two *palios* held on 2 July is officially known as Il Palio di Provenzano after a Sienese manifestation of the Virgin Mary known as the Madonna di Provenzano. The second *palio* takes place on 16 August and ties in with Ferragosto (the Feast of the Assumption), the country's biggest summer holiday. As an annual event, the Palio has run uninterrupted (except during WWI and WWII) since 1633, although its origins can be traced back to medieval times.

To read about:
The Sassi of Matera see page 220
Battle of the Oranges see page 240

Settimana Santa: Easter Holy Week

ITALY-WIDE / RELIGION

The Pope leads a candlelit procession to the Colosseum on Good Friday and blesses from St Peter's Square. In Florence, white oxen pull a wagon laden with fireworks to the cathedral where a dove-shaped rocket sets the thing dramatically ablaze. Hooded penitents walk through the streets of Sorrento and life-size tableaux are carted across the island of Procida. All over Italy, Settimana Santa is marked with well-attended processions and centuries of tradition.

To read about:
The Pope's Gardens see page 89
Carnevale in Venice see page 306

Walk Like an Italian

In Italy, an evening stroll is far more than just a walk in the park, it's an unofficial procession of preening, gossiping, cavorting humanity that snakes at adagio pace through the streets of the nation's historic cities on any given night between 5pm and 8pm. To unversed observers, the spectacle resembles a curious piece of social theatre. To Italians, it's a longstanding evening ritual known as la passeggiata.

The *passeggiata* expropriates streets all over Italy on a daily basis, from Rome's busy Via del Corso to the poetic Piazza Tasso in Sorrento. The spectacle is particularly buoyant in the south where locals congregate in shopping streets or on seaside esplanades to amuse themselves during the lethargic gap between late-afternoon and dinner. Sunday is classic *passeggiata* time, and is most enthusiastically practised in the summer in one of those vaguely grimy Mezzogiorno towns in Calabria or Basilicata where few tourists care to tread.

No time is the tradition more poignant than at sunset in the city of Reggio Calabria on Italy's metaphoric 'toe' where milling throngs crowd the *lungomare*, a 2km-long seaside drive famed for its killer views of Sicily set off by the smoldering cone of Mt Etna across the Strait of Messina.

Of course, rather than just standing there and gawping at it, it's much more fun to join in, whether it be in Florence, Bari or Ventimiglia. The first thing to recognise about the *passeggiata* is that no one is heading anywhere in particular. Instead, strollers are more intent to *fare la bella figura* (create a good impression). Tracksuit bottoms and scruffy running shoes are out. Gucci, Armani and the latest in frizz-reducing hair products are in. The *passeggiata* is a chance to talk, flirt, window-shop, show off your newborn baby and indignantly discuss the latest football scandal as the sun dips below the horizon and the urban birdlife migrates to the trees. Grabbing a pre-dinner gelato or *aperitivo* is perfectly acceptable. Unrestricted people watching as you strike a few attention-seeking poses yourself is practically de rigueur. More than anything, the *passeggiata* is about a sense of culture and belonging; the notion that you are right here, right now, in Italy, engaging, in your own small way, with this all-Italian ritual.

To read about:

Gelato see page 272
Grand Giardini Walks see page 296

The Secret to a Long Life: Acciaroli

CAMPANIA / CULTURE

On the face of it just another sleepy coastal hamlet in Italy's southwest, Acciaroli has recently made headlines because of its disproportionately high number of centenarians – with one in ten living to celebrate their 100th birthday. The secret to their extraordinary longevity? Fresh air, exercise, home-grown food liberally sprinkled with rosemary and an active sex life, apparently.

Wandering around the coastal village of Acciaroli on the Cilento Peninsula, where the light bounces off the sapphire waters of the Tyrrhenian Sea and a broad bay sweeps up to olive groves and rolling hills, you can't help but think that the residents here have got it good. There's that view for one. And the gentle rhythm to life, as though the very sea breezes themselves blow stress away. Down on the beach, there are teenagers flirting and soaking up the rays, families playing in the shallow water and Neapolitan holidaymakers, sharing the sand with an unusually high number of very sprightly eighty- and ninety-year-olds. All seem content with their lot. The general attitude seems to be relax, slow down, chat, laugh, share a glass of wine. *La vita è troppo breve* (life's too short). Except here, of course, it isn't.

It's an attitude that pays off: Acciaroli and the surrounding region have one of the world's highest percentages of centenarians, which make up a staggering tenth of the population of 700. Living to see your 100th birthday in this small fishing village is no great shakes, say locals, with a wry, knowing smile and a shoulder shrug. Many even live to the grand old age of 110.

But scientists seeking the key to longevity want to pin down the reason why, so in 2016 a team of researchers from Rome's Sapienza University and the San Diego School of Medicine spent six months in the region. Their findings were insightful. Firstly, they studied the health of Acciaroli's elderly residents and found they had incredibly good blood circulation for their age due to low adrenomedullin levels – comparable to that of people in their 20s and 30s. They didn't suffer from chronic diseases such as heart disease,

Alzheimer's and obesity, or age-related cataracts. In many ways, despite the odd pot belly, they were as fit as fiddles.

Much of this good health seems to be the direct result of a Mediterranean diet, with a few idiosyncratic twists. Many of Acciaroli's residents rear their own chickens and rabbits and eat fresh anchovies hauled in by local fishermen, rich in omega-3 fatty acids and antioxidants. Olive oil, homegrown vegetables and fruit appear at every meal, as does rosemary. The particularly pungent variety of rosemary that grows in the region, used to flavour oils and season fish or simply as a garnish, is known for its anti-inflammatory, brain- and memory-boosting properties.

While researchers have yet to delve deeper into the genetic pool for answers, their studies revealed several other attributing factors to long-life. Thanks to the glorious weather and way of life, Acciaroli's older residents spend lots of time outdoors, breathing in the clean sea air and socialising with friends on the piazza. Gardening and traipsing up and down the village's steep streets give them plenty of exercise. Then there is the sex, some might tell you with a cheeky wink. Researchers found that many people here remain sexually active way into their 80s and 90s.

So while Italy's birthrate continues to plummet, the average age of the population is increasing. And nowhere more so than in Acciaroli, where the old Italian toast *Cent'anni* (may you live to be a hundred) holds more promise than ever.

To read about:
Mangiare Bene see page 34
Campania's Il Vallone dei Mulini see page 218

Galatina: Home of the Tarantella

SOUTHERN ITALY / CULTURE

With a charming historic centre, Galatina in Puglia is the capital of the Salento peninsula's Greek-inflected culture. It is almost the only place where the ritual of tarantism – a folk cure for the bite of a particular spider – is still remembered. The tarantella folk dance evolved from it, and each year the ritual is performed in June, on the feast day of St Peter and St Paul.

To read about:
Puglia's Peasant Cuisine see page 134
Saints, Feasts & Festivals see page 168

Aperitivo Time

In the culinary heaven that is Italy, few food traditions are as enthusiastically celebrated as the aperitivo, the local take on pre-dinner appetite stimulation. The drill? Saunter into a sociable, urban drinking-establishment (Milan will do just nicely), order a drink, and help yourself from a bountiful spread of complementary 'snacks' laid out on the bar.

Right **Aperol spritz**

The *aperitivo* tradition has been a pillar of Italian culture since Torinese distiller Antonio Carpano invented vermouth in the 1780s. What began as a brief pre-dinner drink supplemented by a handful of nuts and olives, has evolved into something far more sophisticated. These days, magnanimous *aperitivo* spreads have become as quintessentially Italian as the evening *passeggiata*. For the price of a drink (usually between €6 and €12), you can help yourself from a smorgasbord of communal dishes laid out like a Caravaggio canvas in participating bars between around 6.30pm and 8.30pm. What's on offer varies from bar to bar, from small tapa-sized bites, to bowls of piping hot pasta, and regional meats and cheeses. A particularly generous *aperitivo* is called *apericena* and can conceivably replace dinner.

To avoid appearing like a freeloader, it is important to observe a little pre-dinner etiquette. For most Italians, *aperitivos* are an opportunity to whet the appetite, socialise with friends, and show off the latest in Berluti footwear. Savvy drinkers might warm up first with a dry martini, a *spritz* or a negroni (martini, gin, Campari and vermouth) as they mingle and chat. Wine is perfectly acceptable too, and soft drinks are fine if you're teetotal. Next, circumnavigate the food table and fill up your plate. But remember: slowly does it. This isn't an all-you-can-eat buffet at a Caribbean resort.

With a little discretion, there's no reason why cash-strapped travellers can't turn aperitivi into a cheap light supper, while benefiting from a few impromptu Italian lessons and a bit of social anthropology into the bargain.

Above Negroni

Aperol Spritz

Italian summer in a glass. No, make that sunset in a glass. Either way, this glorious cocktail is a rosy *aperitivo* favourite.

Preparation time 5 minutes

→ 90ml prosecco
→ 60ml Aperol
→ 30ml soda water
→ orange slice or wedge
→ ice

1. Drop ice into a large wine glass (approximately 420ml)

2. Pour Aperol, prosecco and soda on top.

3. Garnish with a wedge of orange.

For best results, enjoy alfresco.

First conceived in the cities of Piedmont and Lombardy, the *aperitivo* is a Northern Italian tradition that has gradually spread south and is now trendy in Rome and even Naples. Turin might have invented vermouth, but it was Milan that popularised the *aperitivo* custom in the 1920s and the city remains the best place on the peninsula to sip and graze while showing off your new designer jeans.

To read about:
Coffee Culture see page 186
Limoncello see page 287

Not the Corleone You Know

Having suffered centuries of poverty and a well-documented history as a Mafia stronghold, the town of Corleone, Sicily – best known as one of the settings for Francis Ford Coppola's classic Godfather film trilogy – has been trying to reinvent itself in recent decades, casting off its connections to organised crime.

The concept of the *mafioso* dates back to the late 15th century, when Sicily's rent-collecting *gabellotti* (bailiffs) employed small gangs of armed peasants to help them solve 'problems'. These bandits struck fear and admiration into the peasantry, who were happy to support efforts to destabilise the feudal system. The peasants' loyalty to their own people resulted in the name Cosa Nostra (Our Thing). The early Mafia's way of protecting itself from prosecution was to become the modern Mafia's most important weapon: the code of silence, or *omertà*.

Today, the combined annual revenue of Italy's four main Mafia organisations is equal to around 10% of Italy's entire GDP – a far cry from the days of roguish characters bullying shopkeepers into paying the *pizzo* (protection money). The top money-spinner is narcotics; other sources of revenue include the illegal trading of arms, the disposal of hazardous waste and, now, Italy's ongoing refugee crisis.

Despite the Mafia's global reach, the war against it soldiers on, with frequent police crackdowns and arrests. A worrying trend for the organisations, whose success relies on fear, loyalty and non-interference, is the increase in women within clan families breaking the sacred code of *omertà* and collaborating with police. There is also a growing *anti-pizzo* movement, inspired by the defiance of a Palermitan shopkeeper called Libero Grassi, whose anonymous letter to an extortionist was featured on the front page of a local newspaper in 1991. Grassi was murdered three weeks later.

A further boost in anti-Mafia support came through Sicilian judges Paolo Borsellino and Giovanni Falcone. They contributed greatly to turning the climate of opinion against the Mafia on both sides of the Atlantic, and made it possible for Sicilians to speak about and against the Mafia more freely. Their violent assassinations in 1992 ignited anti-Mafia sentiment across Italy and high-profile arrests in the two decades following the murders included the apprehensions of legendary Mafia kingpins Salvatore 'Totò' Riina in 1993, Leoluca Bagarella in 1995, Bernardo 'the Tractor' Provenzano in 2006, Salvatore Lo Piccolo in 2007 and Domenico 'the Veterinarian' Raccuglia in 2009.

In the 1990s, anti-Mafia activities began to steer towards tourism. Libera Terra (Freed Land), co-founded by Paolo Borsellino's sister Rita, works with member organisations to transform properties seized from the Mafia into agricultural cooperatives, *agriturismi* (farm-stay accommodation) and other legitimate enterprises. Equally encouraging has been the establishment of Addiopizzo, a Sicilian organisation encouraging consumers to support businesses that have said no to Mafia extortion.

The Sicilian town of Corleone is working hard to shake free of the Mafia. It was home to both real-life crime boss Salvatore 'Totò' Riina and the fictional Corleone family of the Mario Puzo novel and the Coppola films. Corleone became infamous as a Mafia stronghold, leading residents to petition for the town to change its name to escape the criminal connotations.

Opponents of the name change suggested that, instead, Corleone should strive to be recognised for fighting the Mafia. The town's anti-Mafia museum, CIDMA (Centro Internazionale di Documentazione sulla Mafia e Movimento Antimafia),

Armchair Mafia

The Godfather Trilogy (Francis Ford Coppola; 1972–90) Marlon Brando and Robert de Niro play an old-school Sicilian-American mobster in this Oscar-winning saga, based on the novel by Mario Puzo.

Gomorra (Matteo Garrone; 2009) An award-winning Camorra exposé based on Roberto Saviano's best-selling book. The film has led to a TV crime series by the same name.

Mi Manda Picone (Picone Sent Me; Nanni Loy; 1983) A cult comedy about a small-time hustler embroiled in Naples' seedy underworld.

In Nome della Legge (In the Name of the Law; Pietro Germi; 1949) A young judge is sent to a Mafia-riddled Sicilian town in this neorealist film, cowritten by Federico Fellini.

recounts the history of Sicily's Cosa Nostra crime, focusing on the efforts of the resistance movement that has sprung up on the island. Photos document the Mafia's historical power over Sicilian society and bilingual tour guides are engaged in the museum's anti-Mafia mission. A huge 'No Mafia' sign greets visitors at the entrance, along with a quote from murdered judge Giovanni Falcone about the unbearable but necessary sacrifice demanded by fighting this just cause.

To read about:
Sicilian Markets see page 190
Ancient Sicily see page 242

Coffee Culture

Italians pretty much invented the way the rest of the world confects, serves and imbibes coffee, from the lingo (cappuccino, latte, macchiato) to the steam-driven espresso machine (first pioneered by Angelo Moriondo in Turin in 1884) and stylish brands (Illy and Lavazza). If coffee has a spiritual home, this is it.

The Flavour

One of the best things about Italian coffee is that, no matter where you are – an obscure mountain village or a cheek-by-jowl Rome piazza – the quality is consistent. As much as Italians like their pasta al dente, they like their coffee to have a heavily roasted, bittersweet flavour with a brown foam or *crema* on top.

The Ordering Drill

Think of your first Italian coffee order as an unofficial initiation ceremony. Rule number one: most Italian coffee orders can be made by uttering a single word. A *caffè* is a strong shot of espresso (the term 'espresso' is rarely used in Italian coffee-bar parlance). A *macchiato* is an espresso with a dash of steamed milk. An *americano* is an espresso with added hot water making for a slightly longer drink.

The king of all white coffees is the revered cappuccino, an espresso topped with frothy milk with an sprinkling of chocolate.

Traditionally, *cappuccini* are taken in the morning. Some cynics suggest that it's a massive faux pas to order a cappuccino after 10am but, while it's unlikely that your Italian *amici* will be sticking milk in their coffee after dinner, late-night cappuccino-drinking is not – as yet – an illegal activity. Just make sure you apologise first.

There are no size differentials in Italy. Requests for a grande or a venti will be met with a confused look. The huge 20oz (590ml) latte – a staple drink in North America – could caffeinate a whole business meeting in Italy. A cappuccino comes in a 180ml porcelain cup and should be warm rather than boiling hot. Take care when ordering lattes. The word *latte* means milk in Italian; order one and that's what you'll get. A *caffè latte* is a glass of warm milk with a drop of coffee in it.

Coffee Variations

Although simple is generally best in the Italian culinary world, coffee culture allows room for a few minor variations, some of them regional. A *caffè corretto* is an espresso 'corrected' with a slug of liquor, usually grappa, and is taken later in the day. A *doppio* is a double espresso, perfectly acceptable if you're hungover or sleep-deprived. A *ristretto* is a short espresso with less water but equal potency. A *cappuccino scuro* is a cappuccino made with less milk. And an ever-growing number of Italian bars in both Northern and Southern Italy now also offer alternatives to cow's milk, making that *cappuccino con latte di soia* (soy-milk cappuccino) or *latte di mandorla* (almond milk) less of an odd request.

The Pausa

Noticeably absent from the Italian coffee scene is the notion of the 'take-away'. Except in train stations, cafes rarely stock disposable take-out cups. Hurry or no hurry, you'll be expected to prop up the bar with the locals, or – for a slight premium – perch at a tiny table. Italians aren't accustomed to hanging around in cafes for hours. A coffee break is known as *'una pausa'* (a pause) and that is quite literally what it is. Take a few bites from a pastry, neck your boiling hot espresso (three gulps maximum) and be on your way. Repeat at intervals throughout the day: seven or eight *pausas* a day isn't unheard of.

A Few Final Tips

→ In bars, coffee is often served with a small glass of water; the water is supposed to be drunk first to cleanse the palate.

→ In some busy bars (especially train stations), you must pay for your coffee upfront at a till and then present your receipt to the barista.

→ Coffee in Italy is refreshingly cheap; if you're paying more than €2 you're paying too much.

→ Italy's best coffee city is a debate that could restart the Risorgimento, but you'd be pushed to find a better stash of historic cafes than those in Turin (home of Lavazza) or Trieste (home of Illy).

To read about:

Gelato see page 272
Chocolate see page 290

Exploring Sicily's Markets

When you're truly ready to experience Italy like a local, head to the market, where fresh produce and bargain wares can draw vibrant crowds on a daily basis. From spices and street food to seafood and designer bags, Sicily is an excellent starting point for exploring the many markets that Italy has to offer.

A feast for the senses, Palermo's Mercato di Ballarò is as much akin to a North African bazaar as to a mainland Italian market: fruit vendors raucously hawking their wares in Sicilian dialect, the irresistible perfume of lemons and oranges, and the crackle of chickpea fritters emerging from the deep-fryer. With its location in one of the street-food capitals of the world, this bazaar might just be ground zero for *buffitieri* – little hot snacks prepared at stalls and designed for eating on the spot.

On the other side of the island, Catania offers an equally evocative street theatre experience. The best show in town is the raucous fish market, La Pescheria. Flanked by some excellent fish restaurants, the market takes over the streets behind Piazza del Duomo every workday morning. Fishmongers gut silvery fish, high-heeled women step daintily over pools of blood-stained water, and tables groan under the weight of decapitated swordfish, ruby-pink prawns and trays full of clams, mussels, sea urchins and all manner of mysterious sea life. Despite its name, the market is not all surf, with meat carcasses, skinned sheep's heads, strings of sausages, huge wheels of cheese and mountains of luscious fruit and veg all rolled together in a few jam-packed alleyways.

Catania's other great market is known locally as La Fiera, a chaotic kasbah peddling everything from curvaceous eggplants and oranges to bootleg CDs and knock-off designer bags.

More of Italy's Best Markets

Rialto Market Shop for lagoon specialities at Venice's centuries-old produce market.

Porta Portese A modern *commedia dell'arte* takes place every Sunday between vendors and bargain hunters at Rome's mile-long flea market.

Mercato di Porta Nolana Elbow your way past bellowing fishing folk, fragrant bakeries and bootleg CD stalls for a slice of Neapolitan street theatre.

Fiera Antiquaria di Arezzo Arezzo's monthly antiques fair is the region's most famous.

Mercato di Luino Lakeside Luino is home to one of Northern Italy's largest flea markets, held weekly on Wednesdays.

Porta Palazzo Turin's outdoor food market is the continent's largest.

To read about:
Slow Food see page 98
Harvest Time see page 128

Right **Mercato di Ballarò**, Palermo

Coastal Life in Polignano & Monopoli

Slow down to appreciate the gentle pace of coastal life on Puglia's Adriatic coast, where the sun and the sea dictate the course of the day. The rhythms of fishing, family meals and time to spend with friends are the pillars of life here.

Tommaso, Giacomo and Agostino sit in the corner of a piazza in Polignano, sharing laughs as they adjust their position according to the movements of the sun. As is the case across much of southern Europe, the square is a men-only club, while women tend to sit outside their houses.

There's a sun-bleached quiet to the town, its pale, narrow streets in shadow, and over it all, the half-hourly tolling of church bells. Mostly wedding-cake white, Polignano seems to have grown out of cavernous limestone sea cliffs. Its top-of-the-world position was once its best means of survival, when Pugliese seaside towns were a favoured pitstop for Turkish pirates and other raiders in the Mediterranean's more lawless days. A few centuries on, life is less fraught, with locals line-fishing from the cliffs, and the town elders keeping an eye on proceedings.

The sparkling appearance of this small town is what draws many of the region's visitors: wandering the streets you'll hear Milanese, French and Spanish accents. In the old town square, a gaggle of elderly women watch from a balcony as some passing Brazilians demonstrate *capoeira*.

Polignano's near neighbour Monopoli lies still closer to the water, defended by an oversized castle. There's something more workaday about this town, and few visitors bother to seek out its picturesque centre and pretty port, cloaked as they are by less appealing outskirts. But it's worth persisting to discover its sheltered harbour of graceful cappuccino-pale buildings fronted by Moorish arches, where bobbing fishing boats provide colour across the water. Just a few decades ago, the sheltered bay would have seethed with boats – Monopoli was once as important a fishing port as Bari and Brindisi, fought over by all from the Byzantines to the Venetians.

Antonello Losito, who grew up here, exudes easy-going Pugliese charm. Like many young locals, he left in search of better opportunities, but later returned to promote the local culture he once took for granted, by operating cycling, boat and cooking tours. He notes the big role that the sea plays in their lives – determining not just the jobs that are available but also the slow pace of life.

The town does indeed appear to be half asleep. The only action in the harbour is a man untangling his fishing net on board his craft. The man explains that he had a problem this morning, because his net got tangled with his friend's. Digging around in a bag on the deck, he takes out a raw crayfish and bites its head off, before eating the rest.

Monopoli's fisherfolk usually head out around 5pm and return at dawn, before going home for lunch. Losito explains why Monopoli becomes a ghost town in the afternoon: people have already worked very long hours and now it's time for family.

To read about:
Yacht Life on the Costa Smeralda see page 274
Driving the Amalfi Coast see page 282

Clockwise from top left **Coastal view**, Polignano; **Mosaic stairs**, Monopoli; **Laneway**, Monopoli; **Wall decorations**, Polignano

Hiking WWII's Freedom Trail

ABRUZZO / HISTORY

Once an escape route used by POWs and Italian freedom fighters escaping Nazi-occupied Sulmona, in the central region of Abruzzo, the Sentiero della Libertà (Freedom Trail) has been turned into a historic long-distance hiking trail that cuts across the peaks and plateaus of the Parco Nazionale della Majella.

Right **Sulmona**

During WWII, with the Allies advancing swiftly through Southern Italy, the inmates at one of the country's most notorious Prisoner of War (POW) camps – Fonte d'Amore (Campo 78), 5km north of Sulmona – began to sniff freedom.

Their excitement wasn't unfounded. When the Italian government surrendered in September 1943, the camp's Italian guards deserted their posts and promptly disappeared. Their boots were quickly filled by German soldiers invading Italy from the north but in the confusion of the changeover, many POWs escaped.

Using the Apennines as a natural refuge, the prisoners fanned out into the surrounding mountains. With the help of local partisans, most fled east across the Majella range from German-occupied Sulmona to Casoli on the Sangro river, which had been held by the Allies since September 1943. The rugged and dangerous escape route – nicknamed the Sentiero della Libertà – was used multiple times by Allied POWs during the exceptionally cold winter of 1943–44, when the Allied advance was temporarily halted by German troops dug in along the Gustav Line (a fortified defensive line built by the Germans across central Italy).

Having to negotiate well-guarded checkpoints and rugged, mountainous terrain, not all the escapees made it. On a windswept mountain pass known as Guado di Coccia, halfway between Campo di Giove and the small mountain village of Palena, a stone monument memorialises Ettore De Conti, an Italian partisan captured and executed by the Germans in September 1943. It's an enduring symbol of the underground resistance.

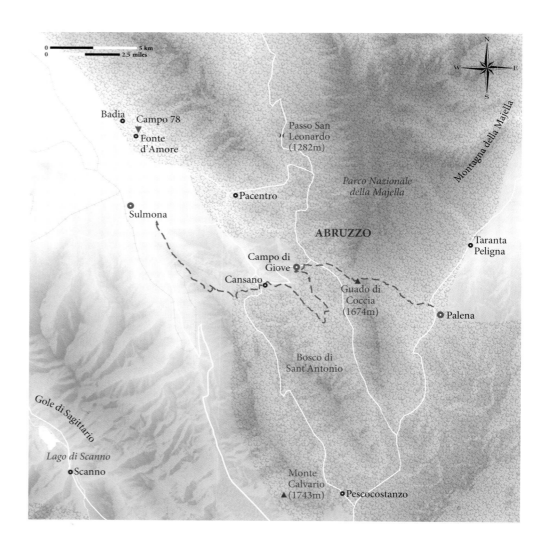

Now well signposted with red and white markers, the path is 60km long. The Sentiero starts in the eastern suburbs of Sulmona and is usually tackled over three to four days. Since 2001, a commemorative communal march along the trail has been held in late April, attracting up to 700 people.

The foreboding fences and watchtowers of the now disused Campo 78 still rise above the village of Fonte d'Amore.

To read about:
WWII in Siena see page 67
Naples' WWII Air-Raid Shelters see page 255

Left **Majella Mountains**

MILAN

Fashion Capital of the World

Italy's second-largest city is the country's self-proclaimed capital of fashion and newfound cool. While much of the country wows you with the weight of its history, Milan makes an entrance with its forward-thinking, artistically progressive ways and looks that are preened to head-turning perfection. Armani, Dolce & Gabbana, Prada, Valentino and Versace: this is where next season's trends are made, born and worn with flair.

Nowhere does the national obsession of *la bella figura* (making a good impression) wield as much clout as here, where everyone gives themselves a once-over in the mirror before heading out. Whether you're doing your weekly shop, sipping a negroni or watching opera in the gilded splendour of La Scala opera house, *per amor di Dio* (for God's sake) do it in style, darlings. Appearances matter, materialism is not frowned upon and luxury is something to aspire to, as reflected in the decadent little details of daily life: from the oysters and gourmet panini at food markets to the turquoise silk lining of a suit and the way boutiques hand-wrap purchases so exquisitely.

Milan works hard for the *bella vita,* but it has substance and soul, too. The beauty of its Duomo, a cathedral that crowns the city like a fairy-tale tiara wrought from pink Candoglia marble, draws the gaze to its forest of pinnacles and fantastical beasts. The Gothic glory is pure Milan: a product of centuries of pillaging, trend spotting, one-upmanship and mercantile ambition. Cross the pale and stately Piazza del Duomo and you're whisked from past to present instantaneously at the Museo del Novecento, a first-class repository of 20th-century art rising up around Umberto Boccioni's futuristic spiral ramp. West of the centre near Corso Magenta, Leonardo da Vinci's Renaissance tour de force, *The Last Supper,* on a wall of the refectory adjoining the Basilica di Santa Maria delle Grazie, attracts a constant train of speechless art pilgrims. While worshippers of fashion gravitate north to the Quadrilatero d'Oro, a quaintly cobbled catwalk of made-in-Milan designer labels presenting high-fashion theatre at its best. Brera is its more alternative, bohemian-flavoured neighbour. But if it's partying in all-night bars you want, you'll have to swagger on south to canal-woven Navigli.

Right Galleria Vittorio Emanuele II

LA BELLA FIGURA: MILANESE STYLE

MILAN / CULTURE

From the choice of clothes on an evening stroll in a perfect Renaissance piazza, to the glint of a well-polished Vespa buzzing past, the ideal of la bella figura – a beautiful appearance – touches every aspect of Italian life, particularly in Milan. Attention to detail can earn you instant admiration – and an admission that, sometimes, non-Italians do have style.

Right **Museo del Novecento**

As a national obsession, *la bella figura* informs every aspect of design, cuisine, art and architecture. Though the country could get by on its striking good looks, Italy is ever mindful of delightful details. They are everywhere you look and many places you don't: the intricately carved cathedral spire only the bell-ringer could fully appreciate, the toy duck hidden inside your chocolate *uova di pasqua* (Easter egg), the absinthe-green silk lining inside a sober grey suit sleeve.

Milan is in many ways the epicentre of the ideal, thanks to the fashion students who flock here, and the city's long record of experimenting in art, architecture and design. The main square is emblematic: to one side of its graceful Gothic Duomo is the Galleria Vittorio Emanuele II – truly a cathedral of shopping, with a soaring glass roof that was revolutionary when it was built in the 1870s. The axis of this space runs between the shopfronts of Prada and its younger rival Versace, to line up with a pair of austere, imposing buildings on the far side of the square. The Palazzo dell'Arengario was built in Fascist times, with balconies from which the crowds could be harangued. The left-hand building has now been put to more enlightening use as the Museo del Novecento, housing a collection of 20th-century Italian art. A mile west is Spazio Rossana Orlandi – a gallery and shop behind a vine-trellised courtyard, which shows a rotating series of works from two-dozen designers each year.

Milanese have strong opinions about aesthetics and aren't afraid to share them. When directed at your garments, the common refrain of *Che brutta!* (How hideous!) may strike visitors as tactless, but consider it from an Italian point of view – everyone is rooting for you to look good, so who are you to disappoint? The shop assistant who tells you with brutal honesty that yellow is not your colour is doing a public service, and will consider it a personal triumph to see you outfitted in orange instead.

While tiny dogs are tugged reluctantly over the thresholds of genteel cafes, newlyweds pose for selfies on the Duomo-facing outside deck of Terrazza Aperol – it takes its name and look from the omni-present Italian pre-dinner drink. The most timeless spot, however, for an Aperol *spritz* – or a ruby-coloured *negroni* – is Bar Basso. In a northeastern district of handsome art nouveau townhouses, this street-corner bar serves its aperitifs in outsize glasses, brought on trays with olives and crostini by waiters in black bow ties and waistcoats. The city's residents are no strangers to this year's trends, but they like the classics too.

To read about:
Italian Architecture see page 64
Italian Design see page 80

BEHIND THE SCENES AT MILAN'S LA SCALA

MILAN / ARTS

Every city has a place that reflects its essence. In Milan, it is the historic opera house Teatro alla Scala that embodies the heart and soul of the city. La Scala isn't simply a place where opera and music are performed; it is the city's cultural compass and beating heart. There is a feeling in Milan that what happens to the theatre is important for the city.

French writer Stendhal described it as the theatre that gives more enjoyment than any other, and he certainly wasn't the last person to find immense delight in the world's most legendary opera house. La Scala is unique thanks to its extraordinary history. Mozart performed early works here, and all the great musicians – Verdi, Rossini, Donizetti, Bellini, Toscanini and Puccini – were at home in La Scala. Performers can't help but rise to the occasion when stepping onto a stage that has seen all the major performers in the history of opera.

The glittering theatre, designed by Giuseppe Piermarini and opened in 1778, has one of the largest stages in Italy and six stories of boxes bedecked in gilt and crimson. When rehearsals are not in session you can stand in boxes 13, 15 and 18 for a glimpse of the jewel-like interior. Similarly dazzling are the audience members, who come to display their finery, particularly on opening night (7 December) when the theatre becomes the centre of the music world.

Beautiful as the theatre is, La Scala is much more than Mario Botta's beautifully revamped auditorium and acoustically perfect stage; it is a world of its own with a world-class ballet company, a symphony orchestra, solo and chamber music recitals, a museum carrying locks of Mozart's hair, the Livia Simone musical library and a range of schools for voice, ballet, orchestral music and theatrical arts.

Step inside the Ansaldo Workshops – a huge hangar-like space of 20,000 sq metres that once served as a steel plant – on a guided tour and you'll find an army of designers, craftspeople and technicians conjuring the theatre's magic. Here in three pavilions devoted to scenography,

costumes and craftsmanship, everything is handmade, from fans and candlestick holders to the 60,000 costumes that are preserved in a vast archive. It is from the calloused hands of these craftsmen and women that the deep rush of excitement emerges as the lights dim and the theatre transports us to a world of thrilling spectacle and tear-inducing emotions.

To read about:
Architecture see page 64
Dante's Florence see page 150

GLAMOROUS ADVENTURES IN MILAN

MILAN / CULTURE

Most Milanese pleasures involve maintaining bella figura, which is hard to do if you're exerting yourself. Activities that keep the effort to a minimum while maintaining maximum bellezza (beauty) include getting steamed, buffed and massaged in Milan's most opulent hammam, having the shave of your life at Puccini's old barbershop, and posing with the locals at the city's biggest water park.

Antica Barbieria Colla Take a pew beside politicians, football stars and businessmen and let jovial Franco Bompieri steam, lather and close-shave you into a state of bliss. Opened in 1904, this is the oldest barbershop in Europe – the brush used on Puccini is proudly displayed – and the shop's range of own-brand shaving creams and colognes is second to none.

Palazzo Parigi Grand Spa This enormous first-floor spa is one of the few in the city that has escaped the basement. As a result, light floods into marble interiors, where a full-length pool, fitness club and hammam await. A hundred euros gets you all-day access to the facilities while the Royal Hammam (€130) includes an aromatic steam bath in your own pink marble pool.

Sauce Milan Tour the best food stalls, high-end delis and wine bars in excellent company. Milan is a serious food town, as professional food writers Sara Porro, Simone Muzza and Jackie DeGiorgio will show you on these convivial half-day tours of the city's finest cafes, markets, bars and street-food stalls.

Ad Artem Explore modern art and medieval architecture on these cultural tours of Milan run by qualified art historians and actors. Highlights include a walk around the battlements of Castello Sforzesco, explorations of the castle's subterranean Ghirlanda passageway, and family-friendly tours of the Museo del Novecento, where kids are invited to build and design their own artwork.

Teatro 7 Rock-star chef Rico Guarnieri is yours, as he blurs boundaries between kitchen and table, cook and diner. Make a meal with the best local produce, using traditional techniques in a dream contemporary kitchen.

Idroscalo Once the liquid landing strip for seaplanes, this artificial lake is now a summer playground. Concerts regularly take place here, including indie-leaning festivals, as well as swimming and water sports.

To read about:
Fine Dining see page 294
Palazzi and Villas see page 300

Che Sorpresa!

Underrated & Unexpected Experiences

Even if you think you know Italy like the back of your hand, this country can throw up surprises when you least expect it. Venture beyond Rome, Venice and Florence and you'll soon find yourself in largely unchartered territory in beautiful, bewilderingly crowd-free places.

If history is your bag, Matera should be on your radar right now as it shapes up to seize the reins as European Capital of Culture 2019. Never heard of it? This gold-stone, 7000-year-old jewel is honeycombed with *sassi* (cave dwellings) that seem to wing you back to the ancient Holy Land. Or take Sardinia, better known for its beaches, whose little-explored hinterland baffles with prehistory at 7000 Bronze Age nuraghic sites. Or Sicily's most enthralling archaeological site in Agrigento, home to some of the best-preserved Greek temples in existence.

There are landscapes that astonish, too – from unsung Monti Sibillini in Umbria during the springtime eruption of wild-flowers, to the smouldering loveliness of Stromboli on the volcanic Aeolian Islands down south. In a remote corner of Tuscany's Maremma region, you can saddle up with *butteri,* Italy's original cowboys, or plunge into the surreal, aqua-blue hot springs of Saturnia. Outdoor action with a twist, you say? Why not white-water raft along the Sesia River in northern Piedmont, tackle a *via ferrata* (iron road) teetering high into the Dolomites or back-country ski over the Slovenian border in Sella Nevea?

Whether you're sipping craft beers in Rome, chowing down on street food like *panelle* (chickpea fritters) in a Palermo market, enjoying a *senza glutine* (gluten-free) lunch in a new-wave vegan cafe in Milan, or exploring an underworld of cisterns, conduits and catacombs in Naples, there's more to Italy than meets the eye. *Aspettare l'inaspettato* (expect the unexpected).

Offbeat Stays

Why overnight in a boring franchise hotel when you can stay in a fortified farm, a conical trullo house, a 14th-century castle, or the highest building in Europe? Travellers looking for accommodation in Italy have plenty of opportunity to embrace the unconventional, eccentric or just plain offbeat.

Monasteries

To get a tangible sense of Italian history you don't need to sell the family jewellery to finance a stay at Rome's Palazzo Manfedi, you just need to book a night in an ancient religious institution. Convents and monasteries have a long tradition as places of refuge in Italy offering food and shelter to travellers. Their hospitality endures. Monastery stays have become increasingly popular in recent years attracting a mix of shoestring travellers, modern-day pilgrims, or just those who want to experience the quiet ebbing and flowing of monastic life. Granted, austere rooms will probably exhibit more crucifixes than pop-art prints, TV and wifi will be non-existent, and breakfast will likely be served at the crack of dawn, but who needs hipster comforts when you've got guaranteed tranquillity, excellent food (what monastery doesn't have a vegetable garden?), and some interesting little extras (Gregorian chanting lessons anyone?). As non-profit enterprises, monasteries rarely charge more than €50 per person per night with some places merely asking for a donation. Hard though it is to believe, you can stay at Venice's magnificent San Giorgio Maggiore monastery with a couple of Tintorettos in its church and spectacular views of Piazza San Marco across the water for a voluntary contribution.

Masserias

The farm-stay movement was born in Italy in the 1970s and '80s and has proved to be hugely popular. Italian farms accepting paying guests are called *agriturismi* and today they attract over one million visitors a year. But not all *agriturismi* are the same. In Southern Italy – most notably Puglia, but also parts of Basilicata and Campania – sprawling country estates are called *masserias*. Modelled on classical Roman villas, *masserias* are fortified farmhouses equipped with oil mills, cellars, chapels, storehouses and accommodation for workers and livestock. The earliest of the estates date from the 16th century when they were built to serve as self-sufficient communities that protected their denizens from Turkish invaders. These days, they still produce the bulk of Italy's olive oil, but many of them have been converted into luxurious hotels, holiday apartments or restaurants. Usually larger and older than their *agriturismi* cousins further north, *masserias* are unique abodes full of salt-of-the-earth southern friendliness and simple *cucina povera* (peasant food) fashioned out of organic home-grown produce. Monasteries they aren't. Expect to pay up to €200 per night although you'll often get access to an array of optional extras, including spas, swimming pools and even golf courses.

Albergo Diffuso

Encouraging historical preservation and cultural immersion in a way not dissimilar to the *agriturismo* movement, *'albergo diffuso'* is an Italian hospitality concept that first emerged over 20 years ago. Intended as a means to revive historic centres in small towns and villages, some of which had become semi-abandoned, the concept allows neighbouring apartments and houses to be rented to guests through a centralised hotel-style reception where you can check-in, pick up information and take breakfast.

Right **Tuscan farmhouse**

Diffuso hotels are usually a feature in more off-the-beaten-track towns where tourism is not yet rampant. Locorotondo in Puglia is a bit of a poster child for the movement. It's a quiet pedestrianised *borgo* where everything is shimmering white aside from the blood-red geraniums that tumble from the window boxes. At Albergo Diffuso Sotto le Cummerse, you'll stay in tastefully furnished apartments scattered throughout the *centro storico* in traditional buildings that have been beautifully restored and furnished.

Another lightly trodden medieval town known for its diffused hotels is Termoli in the Central Italian region of Molise. Termoli is a town of two personalities. Backing its sandy beach is a modern eruption of touristy trattorias and brassy bars built to satisfy the influx of mainly Italian visitors. At the eastern end of the seafront sits the *borgo antico* (old town) jutting out into sea like a massive pier and dividing the sandy beach from Termoli's small harbour. From its seawall you can spy several wave-lashed *trabucchi* (traditional wooden fishing platforms), while in the dense lattice of alleyways surrounding the 13th-century cathedral are two diffused hotels, Residenza Sveva and Locanda Alfieri. With rooms spread all over the town, neither hotel feels generic or utilitarian.

The Trulli of Alberobello

The round dry-stone-wall houses unique to the town of Alberobello in Puglia might have been plucked from a Walt Disney movie, so magical is their appearance. Yet, these so-called *trulli* are a lot older. Historians date the curious structures with their thick limestone walls, tiny windows and conical roofs to the 14th

Above **Locorotondo**

century. While unheard of elsewhere in Italy, there is no shortage of *trulli* in and around Alberobello where over 1500 of the simple abodes crowd the sloping streets of the Zona dei Trulli. Some of the gnome-like houses are available as accommodation – although, since the individual houses are invariably round and small, they are usually clustered together in *diffuso* hotels. If you plan on staying in one, remember that the *trulli* are primitive in design and, due to the lack of windows, bereft of much natural light. However, their diligent owners (who don't wear pointy hats) have done their best to equip them with plenty of modern amenities meaning they offer peace and comfort without sacrificing too much authenticity.

Rifugi

Monasteries aren't Italy's only refuges. Alpine-style *rifugi* pepper Italy's rugged mountain regions and national parks making multi-day hiking sorties through the Alps and Apennines a relative cinch.

Italian *rifugi* are essentially cheap mountain 'refuges' that range in quality from simple sleeping huts to fully staffed high-altitude hostels offering food, dorms, private rooms, and (sometimes) saunas. There are over 600 *rifugi* in Italy, most of them run by the Club Alpino Italiano (CAI) with the best selection nestled among the sawtoothed peaks of the Dolomites. The most famous *rifugio* by a mile is the Capanna Regina Margarita, located a little to west of the Dolomites in the Pennine Alps. Perched at 4554m above sea level, just below the summit of Western Europe's second-highest mountain, Monte Rosa, the Margarita is the highest building in Europe and only reachable by a tricky

two-day hike that includes crossing a glacier. The *rifugio* has been operational since 1893 and offers 70 beds, hot meals, electricity, toilets, a library and – unbelievably – internet. Far best, however, is the extravagant view – an ethereal collection of meat-cleaver mountain summits poking out from beneath a sea of clouds.

To read about:
Restoring Italy see page 162
Italy on Rails see page 266

A Night in a Castle

If you find monasteries too, well, monastic, jump-cut to one of Italy's other historical heirlooms – castles. Sure, you'll pay more money to stay in these kingly domains, but, in the process, you'll feel a lot more like royalty. Italy has countless castles, but for something with four towers, battlements, frescos, heavy drapes and four-poster beds, as well as a gym, spa, fine dining and pleasant gardens, the Castello Bevilacqua 50km southeast of Verona will do just nicely. Dating from the 14th century when the wifi reception probably wasn't quite as good, the Bevilacqua hangs onto its medieval menace with a couple of secret passages and – purportedly – a resident ghost.

Above *Trulli*, Alberobello

La Grassa, La Dotta & La Rossa

Though oft-neglected in favour of other great Italian cites, Bologna deserves your attention. Its medieval core is remarkably free of tourists, and local restaurants serve some of the country's finest food. Most places are within walking distance, so you can saunter between sights and shops, via breaks for historic views and fizzy booze.

Bologna's skyline is pierced by towers – terracotta skyscrapers that are evidence of centuries of noble families trying to outdo one another. They built them to manifest their power in bricks and mortar; to say, architecturally, 'my tower is bigger than your tower'. Significantly, the tallest of all belonged to the city itself: the Torre degli Asinelli. The 498 dark wooden steps that wind up its inside are worn pale in the middle by endless footfalls (though there's a superstition among local university students that if you make the climb before you graduate, you never will). From the top, 97m up, Bologna's buildings stretch out in a restrained rainbow of blush pinks, mustard yellows and burnt umber – anyone wishing to redecorate must pick their colour from a council-approved paint chart.

Bologna is a city with an old soul and a young heart; the latter beating strong in its university culture. The University of Bologna dates back to the 11th century and it's why the city came to be called La Dotta, the learned one.

It was the abundance of terracotta roofs and buildings that earned Bologna the nickname La Rossa: the red one. This rich palette comes alive in the sun, and is best appreciated from the 18th-century hilltop Basilica Santuario della Madonna di San Luca. The walk there from Piazza di Porta Saragozza, under the world's longest portico, is a weekend ritual for locals. Some jog up its 4km length, others stroll with pugs and Pomeranians in tow.

La Grassa, the fat one, is a fine description for the capital of the region that gave the world tortellini, Parmesan, balsamic vinegar and Parma ham. Emilia-Romagna is the larder of Italy – and Bologna's Quadrilatero is its marketplace. This network of narrow streets is lined with the best-looking fruit and veg stalls you'll ever see and delicatessens that smell so invitingly of ham and cheese it's like inhaling a sandwich. Sit at a pavement table at an espresso bar and you'll witness locals in their element: caressing produce to gauge its freshness, discussing what's good that day with vendors, chatting with friends over coffee.

As the day wears on, premises display the best of market produce on platters laid out for *aperitivo*. The sparkling wine of choice for Bolognese locals is not prosecco, but *pignoletto*: light and fruity, with a sweet undercurrent of apple and peach. Shoppers abandon laden bags for a seat, for beers and cured meats stuffed into *tigelle*, little fried-bread parcels. Some have lingered all day, for this is as much a social experience as a retail one.

To read about:
Florence from Above see page 148
Aperitivo Time see page 182

Mysteries of Sardinia's Ancients

Sardinia has been polished like a pebble by waves of history and heritage. The island is scattered with Bronze Age towers, settlements and sacred wells, and Neolithic tombs even more ancient. Stage your own archaeological explorations – down every country lane and in every hamlet, jigsaw-puzzle remnants of prehistory are waiting to be pieced together.

SOUTHERN ITALY / HISTORY

When the first islanders arrived and where they came from are questions that have been puzzling researchers for centuries. The most likely hypothesis is that they landed on Sardinia's northern shores sometime during the lower Palaeolithic period (Old Stone Age).

They were apparently happy with what they found, as by the Neolithic period (8000–3000 BC), Sardinia was home to thriving tribal communities. Excavated ceramics, tools and copper ingots attest to a highly cultured civilisation. The nuraghic people were sophisticated builders, constructing their temples with precisely cut stones and no mortar; they travelled and traded (as revealed by the discovery of seal remains and mussel shells inland); and they had the time, skills and resources to build villages, and to dedicate to arts such as ceramics and jewellery.

Most of the island's *nuraghi* – Bronze Age towers and fortified settlements of the nuraghic people – were built between 1800 and 500 BC and used as watchtowers, sacred areas for religious rites, and meeting places. According to archaeologists the 7000 known examples are just the tip of the iceberg, with at least the same number of *nuraghi* estimated to lie beneath the ground, yet to be discovered.

Nuraghe Su Nuraxi

In the heart of the voluptuous green countryside, Nuraghe Su Nuraxi is the most famous and best-preserved *nuraghe* and Sardinia's sole World Heritage Site. Its focal point is the 1500 BC tower, which originally stood on its own but was later incorporated into a fortified compound. Many of the settlement's buildings were erected in the Iron Age, and it's these that constitute the beehive of circular interlocking buildings that tumble down the hillside.

The site was rediscovered by Giovanni Lilliu (Sardinia's most famous archaeologist) in 1949. Excavations continued for six years and today the site is the only entirely excavated *nuraghe* in Sardinia.

Tiscali

In the twilight of a collapsed limestone cave deep in the Valle Lanaittu, the nuraghic village of Tiscali is another of Sardinia's enigmatic archaeological highlights. Every bit as enchanting as Tiscali itself is the trail through the lush green valley that takes you there – mighty rock faces loom above, birds of prey wheel overhead and only the sound of your footsteps interrupts the overwhelming sense of calm that blankets the valley.

Right **Nuraghe Su Nuraxi**, Barumini

Dating from the 6th century BC and populated until Roman times, the village was rediscovered in the late 19th century. At the time it was relatively intact, but since then grave robbers have done a pretty good job of looting the place, stripping the conical stone-and-mud huts down to skeletal remains.

Despite this, Tiscali is an awe-inspiring sight: jumbled stone foundations amid holm oak and turpentine trees huddled in the eerie twilight of the limestone overhang. The inhabitants of nearby Sa Sedda 'e Sos Carros, a 5-hectare site sprinkled with the remains of some 150 *nuraghe* huts, used it as a hiding place from the Romans, and its inaccessibility ensured that the Sards were able to hold out here until well into the 2nd century BC.

Dorgali

One of Sardinia's most dramatically sited *nuraghi,* the Nuraghe Mannu was first inhabited around 1600 BC. The tower is a modest ruin but that's more than made up for by its spectacular views of the gulf. The site captured ancient Roman imaginations too, and you can see the rectilinear remnants of their constructions alongside the elliptical shapes of earlier buildings.

Santa Cristina

The worship of water was a fundamental part of nuraghic religious practice, and there are reckoned to be 40 sacred wells across Sardinia. This important nuraghic complex has one of the best-preserved Bronze Age well temples on the island.

The first area you come to is a small village centred on an early Christian church dedicated to Santa Cristina. The church and the terraced *muristenes* (pilgrims'

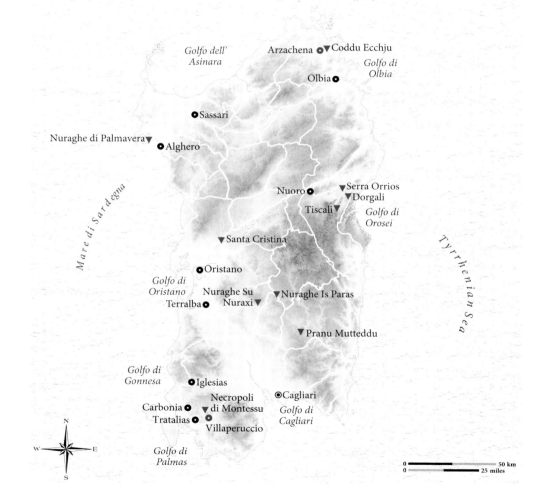

huts) that surround it are opened for only 20 days a year – 10 days preceding each of the twin feast days of Santa Cristina (second Sunday in May) and San Raffaele Arcangelo (fourth Sunday in October).

From the church, a path leads to the well temple. Dating to the late Bronze Age (11th to 9th century BC), the temple is accessible through a keyhole entrance and a flight of 24 superbly preserved steps. When you reach the bottom you can gaze up at the perfectly constructed *tholos* (conical tower), through which light enters the dark well shaft. Every 18 years, one month and two days, the full moon shines directly through the aperture into the well. Every year on the equinoxes (21 March and 23 September) the sun lights up the stairway down to the well.

On the other side of the Christian village is the Nuraghe di Santa Cristina, a single 7m-high tower set in a peaceful olive grove. This once stood at the heart of a nuraghic village, which was inhabited until the early Middle Ages and the remains of which lie littered around the woody glades.

Serra Orrios
Nestled among olive groves, are the remains of Serra Orrios, a ruined nuraghic village that was inhabited between 1500 BC and 250 BC. The remains comprise a cluster of 70 or so horseshoe-shaped huts grouped around two basalt-hewn temples: Tempietto A, thought to be used by visiting pilgrims, and Tempietto B, for the villagers. A third temple has also been discovered, leading experts to surmise that this may have been a significant religious centre.

Nuraghe di Palmavera
This 3500-year-old nuraghic village has at its centre a limestone tower and an elliptical building with a secondary sandstone tower. The ruins of smaller towers and fortified walls surround the central edifice, beyond which are the packed remnants of circular dwellings, of which there may originally have been about 50.

The circular Capanna delle Riunioni (Meeting Hut) is the subject of considerable speculation. Its foundation wall is lined by a low stone bench, perhaps for a council of elders, and encloses a pedestal topped by a model *nuraghe*. One theory suggests a cult to the *nuraghi* themselves.

Necropoli di Montessu
This ancient necropolis occupies a natural rocky amphitheatre in the verdant countryside near Villaperuccio. It dates to the Neolithic Ozieri period (approximately 3000 BC) and is peppered with primitive *domus de janas* (chamber tombs). Many of these appear as little more than a hole in the wall, though some harbour wonderful relief carvings of spirals and symbolic bulls.

Coddu Ecchju
South of Arzachena is a fine example of a *tombe dei gigantic* (giant's tomb), the most visible part of which is the oval-shaped central stele (standing stone) that seals it off. Two slabs of granite, one balanced on top of the other, show an engraved frame that apparently symbolises a door to the hereafter, closed to the living. On either side of the stele stand further tall slabs of granite that form a kind of semicircular guard of honour around the tomb.

Nuraghe Is Paras
This *nuraghe* is notable for its striking *tholos* (beehive-shaped cone) which, at 11.8m, is the highest in Sardinia.

Pranu Mutteddu
Dating to the Ozieri culture (between the 3rd and 4th millennia BC), this funerary site is dominated by a series of *domus de janas* and some 50 menhirs, 20 of them lined up east to west, presumably in symbolic reflection of the sun's trajectory. The scene is reminiscent of similar sites in Corsica and is unique in Sardinia.

To read about:
Ancient Rome see page 52
Ancient Sicily see page 242

Il Vallone dei Mulini

SORRENTO / LANDSCAPES

The beautiful town of Sorrento was once bound by three gorges, but today only one remains. Dating from volcanic eruptions 35,000 years ago, the deep mountain cleft of Il Vallone dei Mulini (Valley of the Mills) is tucked behind Piazza Tasso. The stunning natural phenomenon is named after ancient wheat mills that were once located here, the ruins of which are still clearly visible among lush foliage.

To read about:
Pompeii see page 56
The Sassi of Matera see page 220

The Sassi of Matera

BASILICATA / LANDSCAPES

In the remote southern region of Basilicata, the ancient cave-city of Matera is famous for its stone houses carved out of the caves and cliffs. Haunting and beautiful, the rock-grey facades of the sassi once hid appalling poverty, but in recent years many have been converted into restaurants and swish cave-hotels.

Matera is said to be one of the world's oldest towns, dating back to the Palaeolithic Age and continuously inhabited for around 7000 years. The simple natural grottoes that dotted the gorge were adapted to become homes, and an ingenious system of canals regulated the flow of water and sewage.

The city's history is best immortalised in writer Carlo Levi's book *Christ Stopped at Eboli* – a title suggesting Basilicata was beyond the hand of God, a place where pagan magic still existed and thrived. Inside the cave dwellings, large families lived alongside their livestock and, even as late as the 1950s, without electricity or running water. Despite the clever use of canals these were unhygienic conditions and disease was rife, especially malaria. Reacting to outrage from the general public over the revelations in Levi's book, the government forcibly relocated about 15,000 inhabitants into modern housing in the 'new town' on top of the cliff.

Overlooking the *sassi,* the new town has become a lively place, with its elegant baroque churches, exquisite Romanesque cathedral and elegant *palazzi.*

Ironically, Italy's shame drew curious visitors to the *sassi,* especially after the area was declared a Unesco World Heritage Site in 1993. Matera's fame has since increased, attracting inhabitants back into the caves. Today, many buildings in the *sassi* are crumbling and abandoned but a growing number have been transformed into cosy abodes, restaurants and hotels. The Casa Grotta di Vico Solitario in particular gives an insight into cave furnishings and living conditions of the 1950s.

The best way to experience Matera is to wander through the labyrinthine alleys

Above **Jugs collecting rainwater in a *sassi*,** Matera

The Murgia Plateau

The picturesque landscape of the Murgia plateau surrounding Matera is also pockmarked with abandoned caves, ancient settlements and rock churches. Here, the *Cripta del Peccato Originale* (the Crypt of Original Sin) is known as the Sistine Chapel of the cave churches for its 8th-century frescoes depicting dramatic Old Testament scenes.

and streets of the two *sassi* districts, Sasso Barisano and Sasso Caveoso, where history is etched in the cave dwellings and their traditional house facades, in the stones underfoot and the water cisterns below, and in the rock churches and hermitages cut into the ravine. These *chiese rupestri* (cave churches) were excavated by Basilian monks fleeing persecution during the Byzantine Empire. Inside are faded frescoes painted between the 8th and 13th centuries.

For a stunning view of the *sassi,* head for the Belvedere on the opposite side of the 200m-deep ravine formed by the Gravina river. At dusk, with the cathedral spire rising above the city and evening lights softening the tufa rock, it's not hard to see why Matera has featured in biblical films including Mel Gibson's 2004 *The Passion of the Christ.* Matera's beauty is unique, its *sassi* timeless and enchanting.

To read about:
Subterranean Naples see page 254
Lemon Houses see page 280

A Guide to Explosive Italy

ITALY-WIDE / VOLCANOES

Italy famously teems with World Heritage Sites, but it's less well known that those sites sit in Europe's most volcanically active region. In fact, Italy is home to mainland Europe's only active volcanoes: Vesuvius, Stromboli and Etna.

Vesuvius

Rising formidably beside the Bay of Naples, Mt Vesuvius forms part of the Campanian volcanic arc, a string of active, dormant and extinct volcanoes that include Campi Flegrei's Solfatara and Monte Nuovo, and Ischia's Monte Epomeo.

The Roman town of Pompeii, obliterated by the eruption of Vesuvius in AD 79, continues to draw crowds today, making it Italy's most visited tourist destination. Wandering the deserted streets of this World Heritage Site sends a certain chill up one's spine, especially when viewing the plaster casts of perished Pompeians (created by pouring plaster into voids in the ash made by disintegrated bodies).

As well as being famous for its historic eruptions, Vesuvius is also one of the world's most carefully monitored volcanoes. Another full-scale eruption would be catastrophic. More than half a million people live in the so-called 'red zone', the area most vulnerable to pyroclastic flows and crushing pyroclastic deposits in a major eruption. Yet, despite government incentives to relocate, few residents are willing to leave.

Stromboli

The Campanian arc is part of a large area of intense seismic activity and mountainous terrain that was formed 260,000 years ago as the African continental shelf crashed into Europe. The tips of its peaks now form the eight Aeolian Islands, which stretch southwards to Sicily. They are some of the most beautiful islands in the Mediterranean – Filicudi, Alicudi, Stromboli, Salina, Panarea, Lipari, Vulcano and Ustica.

The island of Stromboli is known as 'the Lighthouse of the Mediterranean', as it constantly throws out incandescent volcanic bombs, which you can see exploding against the velvet night sky.

Stromboli conforms perfectly to one's childhood idea of a volcano, with its symmetrical, smoking silhouette rising dramatically from the sea. It's a hugely popular day-trip destination, but to best appreciate its primordial beauty, languid pace and the romance that lured Roberto Rossellini and Ingrid Bergman here in 1949, you'll need to give it at least a couple of days.

Volcanic activity has scarred and blackened much of the island, but the northeastern corner is inhabited, and it's here that you'll find the island's famous black beaches and the main settlement sprawled attractively along the volcano's lower slopes. Despite the picture-postcard appearance, life here is tough: food and drinking water have to be ferried in, there are no roads across the island, and until relatively recently there was no electricity in Ginostra, the island's second settlement on the west coast.

Etna

Etna is Europe's largest volcano (at 3329m) and one of the world's most active. In ancient times Etna's summit was frequently lit up by spectacular pyrotechnics, and the enormous caldera has spewed ash and lava much more recently (in 1992, 2001, 2002, 2006, 2011, 2015 and 2017). Eruptions make this an ever-changing landscape, where acres of ancient pine forests, such as those at Piano Provenzano, can be swept away, and scarified lava tunnels are created in places like the deep Valle del Bove. It's exciting stuff, as is the ascent to the barren summit to walk the ridge around the caldera.

Looking into the huge, steaming crater, once thought to be home to the giant Tifone (Typhoon), it's easy to see how ancient myths were born.

Despite Etna's ominous power – it makes Vesuvius look like a pimple – there are simple pleasures to be found in its surroundings. You can access the lava fields on foot, take a mineral bath at Terme Stufe di Nerone, drink fine DOC appellation wines and visit the Flavian Amphitheatre, the third largest in Italy after the Colosseum and Capua.

To read about:
Pompeii see page 56
Stromboli see page 226

Left **Volcano crater**, Vulcano

Explosive Stromboli by Night

SOUTHERN ITALY / LANDSCAPES

The hyperactive fire-breathing island of Stromboli has captured human imaginations for eons. To this day, volcano-lovers are drawn to this perfect cone floating in isolation at the Aeolian archipelago's eastern edge.

Stromboli's regular eruptions are legendarily beautiful. The explosions usually occur every 20 minutes or so and are preceded by a loud roar as gases force the magma into the air. After each eruption, you can watch as red-hot rocks tumble down the seemingly endless slope, creating splashes as they plop into the sea.

It's possible to view the fireworks from many different angles – at dusk, hop on a boat to observe the eruptions from the sea. Or hike local areas such as the viewpoint over Sciara del Fuoco, the expanse below Stromboli's craters, where you can watch molten rocks careen down the slopes and crash into the Mediterranean.

Another classic way to experience Stromboli is on a guided night-time hike. Leaving from San Vincenzo church before sunset, a steady climb through yellow broom and wild capers leads above the tree line, revealing bird's-eye views of whitewashed Stromboli village and the sparkling Mediterranean.

A zigzag line of hikers can be seen slogging summit-wards across ashen expanses. Two hours later, the trail emerges into the otherworldly landscape of Stromboli's summit: smoking craters juxtaposed against a twilight sky, with the setting sun and its reflection tracing an upside-down exclamation mark across the sea. Bundle yourself against the cold and enjoy front-row views of the volcano's fireworks. From this exhilarating vantage point above the craters, the steadily hissing steam, punctuated at unpredictable intervals by vertical jets of fire, thunderous explosions and the pitter-patter of sizzling rocks rolling down the craters' flanks is mesmerising. As the skies darken, the eruptions morph from red-freckled billows of grey smoke to vivid fountains of red-orange light – each unique, all beautiful.

What goes up must come down. Eventually you step on to the talus-strewn wasteland of Stromboli's eastern slope and begin the steep descent, with the moonlit sea at your feet, stretching to the twinkling lights of Italy's mainland.

If the mountain gets under your skin, once won't be enough and you'll feel compelled to linger. Exploring the different ways of witnessing this spectacle is well worth it. It's all incredibly exciting. For best viewing, come on a still night, when the livid red Sciara del Fuoco and exploding cone are dramatically visible.

To read about:

Törggelen in South Tyrol

NORTHERN ITALY / FOOD & DRINK

The German-speaking South Tyrol is a region with a dual identity. But there's one thing locals know for sure, and that's how to make the most of autumn. Törggelen is a time of sharing, a tradition of gathering to celebrate the fruits of the harvest.

In his family's farm high in the Dolomites, under white clouds suspended between the mountaintops like spider webs, Stefan Winkler is roasting chestnuts. Wielding a cast-iron pan over a flaming brazier, he flips the nuts to ensure they're cooked evenly, watching their skins blacken and char in the flames, cracking to reveal buttery yellow beneath.

Chestnuts are an essential part of Törggelen and such harvest feasts have been a tradition in the mountains of South Tyrol (Südtirol) since at least the 16th century, when travelling merchants would visit the region's farms and vineyards to taste the year's produce. Keen to show off their goods, farmers would host banquets in their honour – no doubt hoping the merchants might buy a few extra crates of grapes or some barrels of wine in the process.

Visitors to the region are still offered a warm welcome at farms like the Winklers', which offers meals to paying guests during the autumn months. Their simple white farmhouse is festooned with decorations: the doorstep is piled with pumpkins and wicker baskets brimming with apples, and wreaths of corn dangle from the shutters.

Inside, the festivities are well under way. A motley mix of diners – families, tourists, locals, motorbikers, cyclists, hikers – cram around long wooden tables in the pine-clad dining room, warmed by an earthenware stove. At one table, a family dips into bowls of barley soup with chunks of *schüttelbrot:* the flatbread traditionally carried by Tyrolean shepherds. In another corner, a band of bearded Bavarian hikers tucks into roast pork, sausages and thick slices of speck (cured ham), laced with homemade horseradish sauce and sauerkraut. This is a classic Törggelen dish, known as a *schlachtplatte* or slaughter plate. It's an unappetising name, but accurate; half the farmyard seems to be piled on it.

Soon, flagons of beer and jugs of wine arrive, poured by smiling waiters in traditional Germanic peasant costumes. Diners hand around glasses and exchange tales of their day's adventures. One recounts an afternoon picnic beneath the Dolomites' peaks; another recalls the tang of home-brewed apple juice sampled at a local farm. Sipping his beer and wielding a sausage, a man in a leather jacket describes a near-miss on his bike with a dairy cow, joking that it almost ended up on tonight's *schlachtplatte*.

After the main course, bowls of Stefan's freshly roasted chestnuts arrive to

rowdy applause, and the guests peel the hot husks by hand. From somewhere an accordion appears and the room erupts with old folk tunes. Everyone joins in with gusto, although only a few people know the words. More chestnuts arrive, more wine is poured. Outside, dusk melts into darkness, and the party continues into the night.

The word 'Törggelen' is thought to derive from the wooden presses once used to extract wine, known in Latin as *torcolum* and *törggl* in local dialect. Although much has changed in the mountains, the tradition has endured. Südtirolers still attend Törggelen two or three times a season – once with friends, once with family, once with colleagues – and many inns, farmhouses and hostelries across South Tyrol still host these harvest banquets in the old-fashioned way.

At Agriturismo Lafoglerhof, about 20 miles outside Bolzano (Bozen), every table is full, and the waiters are working overtime, topping up jugs of wine, pulling pints of pilsner, preparing platters laden with meat, cheese and sauerkraut. Children chase each other around the farmyard, dodging old barrels and strutting chickens, and their parents chink glasses with a gutsy 'Grüß Gott', the customary greeting of South Tyrol.

The magnificent backdrop to the celebrations, the Dolomites slice through South Tyrol like a dragon's jawbone. The best way to combine this scenery with South Tyrol's harvest-time hospitality is to hike the Keschtnweg, or 'Chestnut Way', a 60km trail that winds along the Isarco Valley (Eisacktal) between the towns of Bressanone (Brixen) and Bolzano. It's named after the old chestnut groves that

carpet the hillsides, planted by Roman settlers 2000 years ago, and has been tramped by shepherds, pedlars and pilgrims for centuries. Once the quickest path across the Alps, it takes around five days to complete – although during Törggelen season, the temptation of stopping for another mountain feast means it often takes considerably longer.

What soon becomes apparent to Keschtnweg hikers is South Tyrol's split personality. One minute the views appear Alpine: green fields, grazing cows, geranium-covered houses. The next, they turn Italian: saintly icons, tumbledown churches, hilltop monasteries. In one hamlet, the church might be dedicated to St Jakobus or St Georg; in the next, it might be Santa Maddalena or Sant'Angelo. Stop in at one bar and you'll be served a shot of grappa; at the next it's as likely to be a glass of schnapps.

Though it's been a province of Italy since 1919, for much of its history the region was part of the Austrian empire. Two-thirds of people identify German as their mother tongue; another quarter speaks Italian, while a further 5% speak Ladin, an old Romance language believed to have its roots in the patois of Roman legionaries. Road signs are always in two languages, sometimes three, every village has both a German and an Italian name, and this is surely the only corner of Italy where locals are equally happy to sit down for a bowl of dumplings as they are to a bowl of ravioli.

At Radoar-Hof, one of the area's renowned organic apple farms, owner Norbert Blasbichler is pouring out glasses of juice and grappa for his guests at a wooden table in the garden. It's surrounded by terraces of fruit trees, stretching away in orderly lines and laden with apples, pears, quince and berries, ripe and ready for harvest, which Norbert reckons is just a week away. He pours an early taste of this year's juice: it's sweet, floral and fruity, with a rich perfume and a twist of acidity that comes from a blend of apple varieties. He urges guests to drink and eat as he lays down a platter of bread and cheese, which is eaten to the bassy drone of the orchard's honeybees and the sputter of a tractor in a nearby field.

Food is a cornerstone of life in South Tyrol, and hiking the Keschtnweg reveals a landscape shaped by agriculture: vines climb the slopes; barns stand in fields of barley; plump cows graze. The region owes its productivity to the climate. The Isarco Valley occupies a buffer zone between the mountains and the sea, benefiting from warm, moist air from the Mediterranean to the south, and cool, dry air from the Alps to the north.

Every inch of land is used for something – all but the mountains themselves that is. The Dolomites are an inescapable presence along the Isarco Valley. Known as the Monti Pallidi, the Pale Mountains, a reference to their milky-white colour, they're a reminder of the wild world that lies beyond the neatly tended fields. Towering above a pastoral patchwork of villages, meadows and farms, the summits spike the skyline like wolves' teeth. As the sun sinks low over the valley, the rocks shift colour, from diamond white to coral pink and copper gold.

At the southern end of the valley, as the Keschtnweg nears its end just outside Bolzano, the region's Italian side comes ever more into focus. Italianate villas appear. Barley fields become vineyards.

Temperatures warm and accents soften. There's also a crispness in the air that hints at autumn's end – for winemakers like Florian Gojer, that means the harvest is drawing to a close.

In his late twenties, with fair skin and a swash of auburn hair, Florian is the latest in a dynasty of Tyrolean winemakers. He looks after the 5000-hectare family vineyards close to Bolzano and believes this is the perfect place to be a winemaker.

He sets up a table high in the vineyard, overlooking Bolzano's terracotta rooftops. From a satchel, he produces two bottles of wine: a white Kerner and a Lagrein red, both signature grapes of South Tyrol. The white is crisp and mineral-rich, the red perfumed and fruity.

Beyond the vineyard's terraces, bare trees stretch along the back roads, and clouds of fallen leaves rattle and swirl in the breeze. Above, the sun is sinking behind the Dolomites, and the summits sparkle with the first dusting of snow. Winter is coming to the mountains but for now, at least, there are a few more days of autumn to enjoy.

To read about:
The Garfagnana see page 110
The Dolomites see page 234

Eating Gluten-Free in the Land of Pasta

ITALY-WIDE / FOOD & DRINK

In a country where pizza and pasta are a staple practically from birth, the idea of passing on a steaming plate of Nonna's homemade spaghetti or the world's original wood-fired pizza margherita with perfect crust in Naples feels tragic. Fortunately for gluten-free diners, life in Italy revolves around food – and no one misses out.

Given their cuisine is one of the world's most revered, it comes as no surprise to learn that Italians live, think and dream food with unfaltering passion, exuberance and – fortunately for coeliacs and the gluten-intolerant – unlimited generosity. Sharing a meal around the kitchen table with family and friends is the essence of social life in Italy, and preparing gluten-free dishes for those unable to eat wheat, barley and rye is rarely too much trouble.

Carefully prepared, gluten-free dishes aside, Italian cuisine is not hard to swallow for diners with coeliac disease. Italy's culinary soul is earthy and rustic, with most regional cuisines growing up over an open wood fire in *la cucina contadina* (farmer's kitchen). Ingredients are simple, seasonal fruits-of-the-land and Italian cooks make use of every scrap: alternative flours milled from chickpeas and chestnuts have been Italian staples for centuries. *Farinata* (flatbread made with chickpea flour) – peppered with olive oil and fresh rosemary or a sprinkling of rock salt – became the ubiquitous street food in the port city of Genoa in the 13th century. Legend says it was cooked up at sea in 1284 during the Battle of Meloria between Pisa and Genoa. A storm hit the victorious Genoese fleet and barrels of chickpea flour spilled across the deck and mixed with sea water – to become a batter which, when dried and baked afterwards in the hot Ligurian sun, tasted quite delicious. Further south, in the Tuscan port of Livorno, *torta di ceci* is the traditional go-to snack, and in Sardinia the same deliciously gluten-free, chickpea pancake is called *fainé*.

The Italian kitchen embraces ample dishes that are traditionally gluten-free such as risotto, osso buco and springtime artichokes, commonly served in restaurants all over Italy. In addition, plenty of restaurants list specific gluten-free dishes on their menu. In Rome, Aroma – one of the capital's top fine-dining restaurants – serves a four-course, gluten-free menu (€115); and Pandalì is a gluten-free bakery selling pizza slices, sandwiches, salads and cakes. In the fashionable Roman neighbourhood of Monti, knowing gourmets lunch on exquisite miniature *panini* with catchy names like Amber Queen, Strawberry Hill and Lady Godiva at glamorous, gluten-free Zia Rosetta on Via Urbana and later gravitate to uber-chic *pasticceria* (pastry shop) Grezzo to hob-nob over exquisite tiramisu miniatures, chocolate tarts, cheesecakes, Sicilian almond and pistachio gelato (made with fresh almond milk) and one-bite pralines – all raw, organic and gloriously gluten-free. (Should you be hankering for a gluten-free dessert in a traditional restaurant, consider creamy panna cotta or *torta Caprese,* a chocolate and almond (or walnut) cake originating on the island of Capri and said to be born in the 1920s when an absent-minded baker reportedly forgot to add flour to the cake mix.)

An ever-increasing awareness in Italy of dietary requirements for coeliacs has seen a whole new breed of eateries mushroom in recent years. And unlike in many other European countries, decent gluten-free dining is not restricted to the capital. The Associazione Italiana Celiachia (Italian Coeliac Society; www.celiachia.it) has more than 4000 registered gluten-free entries in its little black book of go-to addresses in Italy – accessible online or via its smartphone app – embracing every genre of dining, shopping and accommodation countrywide. Pastry chef Luca Montersino's Golosi di Salute brand, known throughout Northern Italy for its biscuits, cakes, tarts and spreads that variously avoid gluten, dairy or sugar, deserves a special shout-out. A native of Alba, his produce (including a killer gluten-free *torta di nocciole* – hazelnut cake made from local ingredients) is available as far afield as New York.

But what about those iconic, utterly irresistible Italian classics – pizza, pasta and gelato? Feast on gluten-free pasta and pizza with sea-view at Le Arcate in Amalfi or with Sardinians at Man.Gia in Caligari. Agonise over the torturous choice of citrus and ricotta, pineapple and ginger, peanut or traditional chocolate at one of several branches of artisanal gluten-free gelateria Fatamorgana in Rome. Join the mob queueing for creamy gelato as rich as a Venetian doge at Suso or Gelateria Il Doge in Venice. And know that foodie Italy has all coeliac-bases covered.

To read about:

Mangiare Bene see page 34
Chocolate see page 290

Left **Farinata**

Iron Roads of the Dolomites

Thrilling vie ferrate (iron roads) speckle northeastern Italy's rocky Dolomites like ant trails. These networks date from WWI, when the mountains were the setting for furious battles between the Italian and Austro-Hungarian armies. Today the cables and stairways provide exhilarating protected climbing.

The Dolomites are not surrounded by gentle foothills. These limestone stacks appear to thrust directly out of the ground. It's savage terrain: great toothy crags rear into the sky, their exposed cliffs, jagged gullies and tiny ledges teetering above yawning chasms of ragged rock. Just imagine trying to cross these mountains amid the combat of WWI, when a network of tunnels and trenches was dug to try to surprise and overtake the enemy; you can still see these at Lagazuoi and Castelletto della Tofana. Natural dangers were even more fearsome than snipers – thousands died from hypothermia or exposure, and around 50,000 from avalanches.

Soldiers on both sides built the tiny spidery supports of the *vie ferrate* into the rock face. Consisting of ladders, cables and bridges, they formed a fine web of iron. Some of the original paths still exist today, monuments to the hardship suffered here, with memorial plaques punctuating the way. Others have been renewed, extended and given an entirely new life as an incredible way to climb across otherwise unthinkable routes.

Crossing this out-of-this-world landscape is an incredible experience, with pinnacles and sheer walls alternating with lush green valleys of forests, meadows, canyons and thundering waterfalls.

Although a good level of fitness is required, there is a great variety of difficulty on these routes. There are easier sections to suit less-experienced climbers, and some which only the extremely proficient should attempt. Other than on broader, unprotected sections along the routes, the basic safety rule is that you use the belaying technique, climbing with two lines. This means that when you move onto a new section, you unclip one line at a time and are never completely unsecured.

Via Bocchette (the Way of the Passes) is the most famous iron road of the Dolomites. One of the first trails to be developed, it offers an experience closer to real mountaineering, with several sections that are completely exposed. You'll need a head for heights because at times you'll inch along narrow ledges with seemingly nothing but cloud swirling beneath you.

To read about:
Hiking the WWII Freedom Trail see page 194
Tuscan Cowboys see page 250

The Wilds of Abruzzo

CENTRAL ITALY / LANDSCAPES

With its thrilling mountain scenery, rural back country charm and snaking roads, the little-known Italian region of Abruzzo makes for exhilarating driving and wild encounters. With its brooding mountains and ancient forests, wide vistas and remote hill towns, age-old traditions still hold sway and little appears to have changed in centuries.

Right **Santa Maria della Pietà**, Rocca Calascio

As the crow flies, Abruzzo is only about 110km from Rome but feels a world away from the bright lights of the Italian capital. Bisected by the spinal Apennine mountains, Abruzzo and the adjacent region of Molise make up Italy's forgotten quarter, blessed more with natural attractions than cultural colossi. A major national-park-building effort in the 1990s created an almost unbroken swathe of protected land that stretches from the harsh, isolated Monti della Laga in the north to the round-topped Majella mountains further south. Dotted in their midst are some of Italy's most unspoilt, picturesque mountain villages. Sometimes, a visit here feels like a trip back to the 1950s – a world of wheezing trains, ruined farmhouses and poppy-filled pastures. All this is good news for prospective walkers, who share the region's ample paths with sheep dogs, mountain goats, abundant bird life and the odd, rarely sighted, human being.

It's also epic driving country, following a route to take you deep into the Parco Nazionale d'Abruzzo, Lazio e Molise and up to the mighty Gran Sasso massif. Start at Sulmona, a handsome provincial town famous for its *confetti* (a sugar-coated almond sweet), where you can get your first taste of local hospitality. At the family-run Hostaria dell'Arco, the owner insists on lighting the charcoal grill just for you. The lamb chops, he insists, just wouldn't taste the same otherwise.

You leave Sulmona's cobbled lanes the next morning and head into the big country of the Parco Nazionale della Majella. Climbing steadily, you weave smoothly through wooded hills while foreboding peaks loom on the blue horizon. A few kilometres beyond the Bosco di Sant'

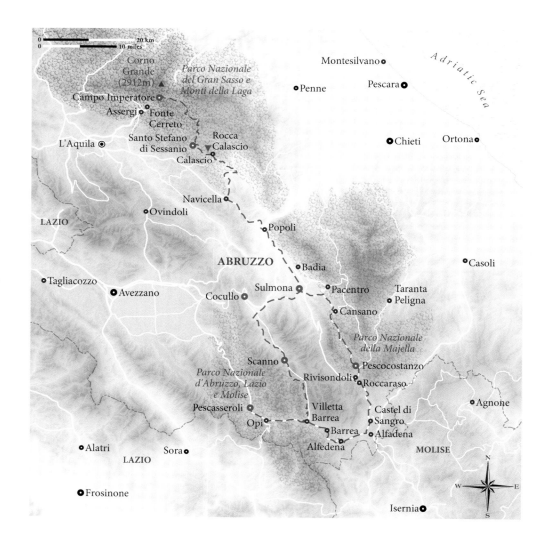

Antonio beech forest lies Pescocostanzo. Set among lush, almost alpine, plains, this surprisingly grand hilltop town harbours a pristine historic core that dates back to its time as one of the most important staging posts on the Via degli Abruzzi, the traditional trans-Apennine route that linked Florence to Naples.

You push on towards Pescasseroli, the primary centre in the Parco Nazionale d'Abruzzo, Lazio e Molise. The going becomes fairly easy by now and it is wonderfully relaxing to meander past the Lago di Barrea on the SS83, enjoying the unspoiled verdant scenery. Pescasseroli is reasonably quiet even at the busiest of times, and it is positively sleepy when you arrive. But you're keen to stretch your legs so you decide to stop over for the night.

The plan for day two is to double back to Sulmona via Scanno, a route that will take you through a gorgeous rocky gorge known as the Gole di Sagittario, and then head further up to the Gran Sasso. This promises some tough climbing, and so it proves as you motor up to the Passo Godi mountain pass at 1630m. From there you can inch your way down a slow, tortuous descent to Scanno: a decidedly picturesque town with steep alleyways and a cluster of slate-grey stone houses grafted on to the mountainside. You pause for a quick look around before heading down to the lake, a couple of clicks beyond the main centre. There isn't a lot going on there but while he watches his grandson play, a local cheerfully regales you with tales of bears and hungry wolves.

The next leg takes you into virgin territory, and on to one of the highlight stretches. The road up to Santo Stefano di Sessanio is a true white-knuckle drive with a series of sharp second-gear switchbacks and sweeping views at every turn. You'll be concentrating too hard to take in the scenery, including the remote Rocca Calascio castle when it comes into view, but there is no denying the drama of the landscape. The fortress was a location for *The Name of the Rose* (1986) but its lonely profile would be ideal for a horror film.

Six kilometres further on, Santo Stefano di Sessanio is similarly haunting. Formerly a 16th-century Medici stronghold, it suffered damage in a 2009 earthquake and many of its stone buildings are still under scaffolding. Popping into a cheese shop, you pick up a hefty wedge of fresh pecorino that makes for a tasty addition to your picnic lunch.

Now you're at an altitude of about 1200m and the rest of the world feels a very long way away. The sense of isolation grows as you push on to Campo Imperatore, a rolling highland plateau known as Italy's 'Little Tibet'. Mussolini was briefly imprisoned here in 1943, and it's a stark and majestic place. Overlooking everything is the great grey fin of Corno Grande, the summit of the Gran Sasso massif and, at 2912m, the highest point in the Apennines. You've long wanted to climb it – it's a tough but doable summer hike – but it will have to wait for another day.

To read about:
Farm Stays see page 106
Hiking in Abruzzo see page 194

Snakes Alive

Some 20km west of Sulmona, Cocullo is home to one of Italy's weirdest festivals. The Festa dei Serpari (Festival of the Snake Catchers) is the highlight of celebrations to honour St Dominic, the village's patron saint, held on the first Thursday of May.

The main focus of attention is a statue of the saint that's festooned with writhing serpents – all caught for the event in the surrounding hills – and paraded through the village.

The Battle of the Oranges

PIEDMONT / FESTIVALS

In the Piedmont region of northwest Italy, the town of Ivrea holds an annual carnival that dates back to 1808 and is one of the oldest festivals in all of Italy. Its highpoint? A fierce and spectacular re-enactment that carpets the streets in smashed fruit.

To read about:
Venice's Carnevale see page 306
Lemons see page 280

Wonders of Ancient Sicily

SOUTHERN ITALY / HISTORY

Seductively beautiful and perfectly placed in the heart of the Mediterranean, Sicily has been luring passers-by since the time of legends. The land of the Cyclops has been prized by many ancient cultures – Phoenicians, Carthaginians, Elymians, Romans and Greeks – whose bones lie buried here. Whether in the perfection of Agrigento's Concordia temple, the monumental rubble of Selinunte's columns or Taormina's spectacularly located Teatro Greco, reminders of bygone civilisations are everywhere.

Right **Tempio dei Dioscuri**, Valley of the Temples

Contradictory Palermo

For millennia at the crossroads of civilisations, Palermo delivers a heady, heavily spiced mix of Byzantine mosaics, Arabesque domes and frescoed cupolas. This is a city at the edge of Europe and at the centre of the ancient world, a place where souk-like markets rub against baroque churches, where date palms frame Gothic palaces and where crumbling staircases lead to gilded ballrooms. The evocative history of the city infuses its daily life, and many of the city's treasures are hidden rather than scrubbed up for endless streams of tourists.

A trading port since Phoenician times, Palermo first came to prominence as the capital of Arab Sicily in the 9th century AD. When the Normans rode into town in the 11th century, they used Arab know-how to turn Palermo into Christendom's richest and most sophisticated city. The incredible Cappella Palatina is the perfect expression of the marriage, with its gold-inflected Byzantine mosaics crowned by a honeycomb *muqarnas* ceiling – a masterpiece of Arab craftsmanship.

Windswept Segesta

Set on the edge of a deep canyon in the midst of desolate mountains, the 5th-century BC ruins of Segesta are one of the world's most magical ancient sites. On windy days its 36 giant columns are said to act like an organ, producing mysterious notes. The city, founded by the ancient Elymians, was in constant conflict with Selinunte, whose destruction it sought with dogged determination and singular success.

Little remains of ancient Segesta today, save its hilltop theatre and Doric temple.

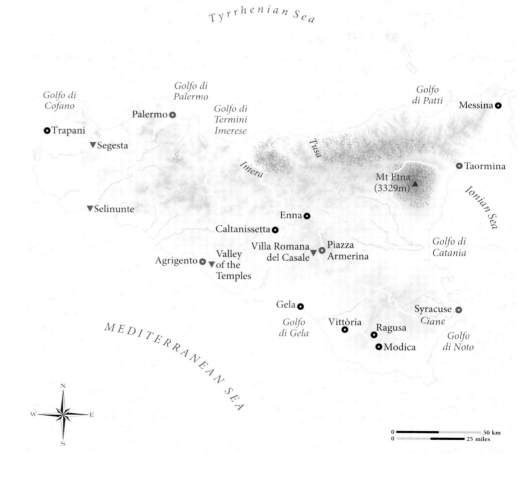

Right Cappella Palatina, Palermo

Villa Romana del Casale

Near the town of Piazza Armerina in central Sicily, the stunning 3rd-century Roman Villa Romana del Casale was once a sumptuous hunting lodge, possibly belonging to Diocletian's co-emperor Marcus Aurelius Maximianus. Buried under mud in a 12th-century flood, it remained hidden for 700 years before its magnificent floor mosaics – considered unique for their narrative style – were discovered in the 1950s. Visit from November to March or early in the day to avoid the hordes of motor-coach tourists.

The temple, which stands in splendid isolation, has retained all of its columns and is topped by a perfectly intact entablature and pediment – though the missing roof and lack of fluting on the columns indicate that it was never completed. The ruins' remarkable state of preservation and the majesty of their rural setting combine to make this one of Sicily's enduring highlights.

Walking Among Wildflowers in Selinunte

Built on a promontory overlooking the sea, the Greek ruins of Selinunte are among the most impressive in Sicily, dating to around the 7th century BC. Selinos (as it was known to the Greeks) was established by a group of settlers from nearby Megara Hyblaea in 628 BC; the plains surrounding the site were overgrown with celery (*selinon* in Greek), which served as inspiration for the new colony's name. Destroyed by the Carthaginians in 409 BC, it finally fell to the Romans around 250 BC, after which it rapidly declined. Today this vast complex of fields and ruined temples beside the Mediterranean is a delightful place to wander, especially in springtime, when the wildflowers are in full bloom.

The most stunning ruin, Temple E, has been partially rebuilt, its columns pieced together from their fragments, while the Acropolis, the heart of Selinunte's political and social life, occupies a slanted plateau overlooking the now-silted-up Gorgo di Cottone. Many of the carvings, the quality of which is on par with the Parthenon marbles, particularly from Temple C, are now in Palermo's archaeological museum.

The Mystical Valley of the Temples
Agrigento's Unesco-listed Valley of the Temples is one of the most mesmerising sites in the Mediterranean. Strung out along the rocky promontory where the ancient Greeks erected them 2500 years ago, the temples' magical aura is enhanced at night, when they are brilliantly floodlit.

The ruins are divided into two main sections, known as the eastern and western zones: the western zone is dominated by the massive ruin of the Tempio di Giove and the hauntingly beautiful, fragmentary remains of the Tempio dei Dioscuri. In the eastern zone, the magnificent Tempio della Concordia (Temple of Concord) is one of the best-preserved ancient Greek temples in existence and has survived almost

entirely intact since it was constructed in 430 BC. On summer evenings, don't miss the chance to walk the eastern zone after dark, an experience unparalleled at any other Sicilian ancient site. A short way up the hill, Agrigento's Museo Archeologico is one of the island's finest museums, with a huge collection of clearly labelled artefacts from the excavated site.

Archaeological Syracuse
Encapsulating Sicily's timeless beauty, Syracuse is a dense tapestry of overlapping cultures and civilisations. Ancient Greek ruins rise out of lush citrus orchards, cafe tables spill out onto baroque piazzas, and medieval lanes meander to the sea. Your visit, like the city itself, can be split into two easy parts: one dedicated to the archaeological site, the other to the island of Ortygia, which is just offshore.

It's difficult to imagine now but in its heyday Syracuse was the largest city in the ancient world, bigger even than Athens and Corinth. The Parco Archeologico della Neapolis is home to a staggering number of well-preserved Greek (and Roman) remains, with the huge 5th-century-BC Greek theatre as the main attraction. In the grounds of Villa Landolina, situated about 500m east of the archaeological park, is the Museo Archeologico Paolo Orsi.

Despite the labyrinthine streets, it is hard to get lost on the island of Ortygia, since it measures less than 1 sq km, and

yet it also manages to encompass 25 centuries of history. Architectural styles vary widely, including ancient ruins and medieval Norman buildings as well as Piazza del Duomo – a masterpiece in baroque town planning.

Ancient Theatre in Taormina
Over the centuries, Taormina has seduced an exhaustive line of writers and artists, from Goethe to DH Lawrence. The main reason for their swooning? The perfect horseshoe-shaped Teatro Greco, suspended between sea and sky, with glorious views to brooding Mt Etna through the broken columns. Built in the 3rd century BC, the theatre is the most dramatically situated Greek theatre in the world and the second largest in Sicily (after Syracuse). From June to August a lively schedule of events is held at the Teatro Greco, where you can watch everything from international film premieres to famous rockers, dancers and divas performing under the balmy night air, all with Mt Etna as the scenic backdrop.

To read about:
Ancient Rome see page 52
Pompeii see page 56

In Hot Pursuit of Targa Florio

SICILY / SPORT

Motor racing started on public roads before it moved to specialised racing tracks, and none of those early road circuits conjures up the magic of the sport better than this ultimate test: the Targa Florio, the world's oldest sports-car race, which was held in Sicily between 1906 and 1977.

The coastal town of Campofelice di Roccella is an easy drive east of Palermo, on the north coast of Sicily. It has a long beach, a church, a 14th-century castle, and nearby there are the Greek ruins of Himera, but it's what happened in the street one Sunday in May 1970 that entranced a large contingent of the local population. Under the building balconies, the citizens of Campofelice were lining the pavements, leaning out into the street, waving ecstatically and cheering loudly for a local Palermo schoolteacher.

The schoolteacher was Nino Vacca-rella and he was hurtling towards them, obviously travelling at something approaching warp speed, in a bright-red, 600-horsepower Ferrari 512S – and he was in the lead of the Targa Florio. He didn't go on to win that year, but he did the following year and again in 1975, when he clinched his third Targa victory. A 1970 photograph summed up what made the race so utterly irresistible: the setting, the enthusiasm and the sheer absurdity of it. You simply do not let people stand in the street, totally unprotected, when racing cars are hurtling past.

From 1906 to 1977, however, the world's oldest sports-car race did exactly that. At first the race was a complete circuit of Sicily, and over the years assorted other routes were tried, but from 1951 the race used the Circuito Piccolo delle Madonie. The Madonie is one of Sicily's principal mountain ranges, and since *piccolo* is Italian for 'little' this was the small racing track in the mountains. The short one, the little track with more than 700 corners.

You went around it 11 times if you were going to win the Targa Florio. And although the long straight that stretches along the coast towards Palermo might have given Signor Vaccarella the opportunity to push his Ferrari to its maximum speed, all those twisting corners as the circuit climbed up into the hills meant that the fastest anyone ever got around the circuit was at an average of just under 129km/h.

Although Nino Vaccarella did drive in a handful of Formula 1 Grand Prix races, sports cars were his speciality, when he could get away from his day job: teaching accounting. He won all sorts of races, including the Le Mans 24-Hour-Race, but it was the Targa Florio where he was always the popular favourite. When he crashed his Ferrari into a wall and out of the race in 1966, the words 'Viva Nino' were soon graffitied on the wall he hit.

From Campofelice, it's about 10km along the coast to where the track turns sharp left and starts to climb – and twist and turn – from sea level towards the town of Cerda, the start and finish point of the Targa Florio. On such a narrow winding track it was impossible to start the cars together so the cars started one by one, 15 seconds apart. The pit counter still stands beside the old starting line, and manufacturers still like to bring their latest creations down to the track to try them out. The impossibly beautiful countryside with its photogenically perfect roads certainly helps.

From Cerda the road really begins to corkscrew as it hairpins its way up to Caltavuturo, the 'Fortress of Vultures', at 635m altitude. From the coast the track has been running south, but now the route turns north and starts the descent back towards the coast, dropping down through Scillato and Collesano before the final breakneck plunge down towards the sea. Collesano has Greek and Arab historic connections, the remains of a Norman castle and an assortment of interesting churches. It also boasts the official Targa Florio Museum, which features a model of every race winner.

Targa simply means 'plate' and the plate in question was presented as a prize by Vincenzo Florio, a wealthy Sicilian businessman, wine merchant and fast-car enthusiast. The name lives on in the Targa Tasmania, an annual race around the Australian island state, and in every Porsche 911 Targa to cruise Rodeo Drive in Los Angeles or the King's Rd in London's Chelsea. Porsche was a Targa Florio specialist; it won the race 11 times, edging out Alfa Romeo by one.

In the Targa Florio's racing days, drivers would often practise when the road was open to everyday traffic, and dodging wayward donkeys was part of the fun. The Circuito Piccolo delle Madonie is still a wonderful road to drive, although you're obviously not going to do it in anything like the sub-34-minute lap record. Two hours and seven minutes is the suggestion from Google Maps, at an average speed of just over 35km/h. Given the 700 corners, the twists, the turns, the climbs, the descents...that's probably quite fast enough.

To read about:
Italian Cars see page 42
Ancient Sicily see page 242

Left Ferrari Dino 206S racing in 1971's Targa Florio

Travel Back in Time with the Cowboys of Tuscany

CENTRAL ITALY / CULTURE

Riding serenely on horseback through pine and beech woods to explore the wild beaches and empty hills of the Maremma is hypnotically calming. This rural slice of southern coastal Tuscany is home to the famous butteri: the Maremmese cowboys.

It's afternoon in the Uccellina hills as guide Daniele Contarino and his riders seek shelter from the fierce heat of the sun under a grove of umbrella pines. Shadows lace the ground like spider webs, and through the canopy there's the cobalt flash of sky and ocean.

After half an hour the trees thin out and the riders emerge near the beach at Collelungo, marooned in swathes of marram grass. Along the coast an old watchtower stands guard, its battlements burning red in the sun. Apart from a couple of walkers and some bleached driftwood, the beach is deserted.

The *butteri* work in the Parco Regionale della Maremma, a strip of hills, beaches and salt-marsh whose unique wildlife and rare ecosystems have been protected since 1975. Parts of the park are farmed to graze the Maremma's long-horned cattle.

Because of the risk of forest fire, much of the park remains off limits in summer without the company of an official guide.

The only way to reach Collelungo (and much of the Maremma's coastline) in the hot months is on foot, by sea or, as in Contarino's case, in the saddle. As a result, its coves stay quiet, even when the bigger beaches beyond the park's borders are heaving.

A little way south lies Cala di Forno, another secluded beach where Contarino often leads his horse treks. Cradled between two rocky headlands and hemmed in by maquis shrubland, it's half an hour from the nearest road, accessed via a dusty forest track or by piloting a kayak along the rocky coastline. It's worth the effort: with its white sand and crystal water, it's a patch of paradise in the middle of Tuscany's busiest stretch of coast.

But there's more to the Maremma than beaches. A century ago, this sunbaked strip of land was Tuscany's answer to the Wild West: a centre for cattle production, with its own breed, the long-horned Maremmana. Traditionally, the cattle

were left semi-wild, roaming freely over the hills until it was time to round up the herd. That's where the *butteri* came in. The profession required steely nerves and superb horse skills – something that still remains the case generations later, even though the days of wild cattle herding are mostly gone. Though the herds these days are smaller, the work of the *butteri* stands as a throwback to another time.

A 400-hectare organic farm on the edge of the park called Terre Regionali Toscani offers visitors a superb insight into the work of the *butteri*. It even allows experienced riders to sign up for a day herding cows with them, and offers shorter guided horseback tours for all experience levels.

To read about:
Hiking in the Garfagnana see page 110
Hill Towns of Tuscany see page 116

Right Two *butteri* in 1959

NAPLES

Italy's Most Intriguing Metropolis

Cities around the world love to wax lyrical about their 'hidden secrets': quirky museums, evocative backstreets, cognoscenti drinking holes. Yet few cities harbour secrets as breathtaking and downright extraordinary as Naples. Here, secrets come in the form of subterranean Roman streets and market stalls, esoteric baroque chapels, and haunting frescoes lurking in dark, silent catacombs.

Naples is ancient. According to legend, Greek traders established the place in around 680 BC, naming it Parthenope in honour of a suicidal siren. Unable to lure the cunning Ulysses with her songs, she drowned herself, washing up on shore. Bittersweetness has defined the city ever since. Loved passionately and exploited ruthlessly by a string of foreign suitors, Naples today is both rich and ravaged. Here, potholed streets lead to citrus-scented cloisters such as those adjacent to the Basilica di Santa Chiara and the Chiesa di San Gregorio Armeno, jewel-like sacristies like the one inside the Basilica di San Paolo Maggiore, or art-graced palaces such as hilltop Palazzo di Capodimonte. One minute you're weaving through a torrent of screaming scooters, the next you're lost in a Caravaggio masterpiece. Nowhere are these contrasts as palpable as they are in Naples' dark, dense centro storico (historic centre), a decadent mess of tag-strewn baroque porticoes, soul-stirring frescoes, jacketed academics and gruff, chain-smoking matriarchs spying on the world from their humble bassi (ground-floor apartments). Spritz-sipping artists share the piazzas with illegal-parking attendants and the odd

cross-dressing cigarette seller. Few raise an eyebrow. This Mediterranean port has seen it all, with a freestyle approach to rules, regulations and life that fills the air with delicious unpredictability and lust. Naples is an intense, fatalistic creature, a city that lives for the moment and a place where human interaction still takes precedence over the tick-tock of a clock.

Espresso machines hiss, hung laundry flaps and Neapolitans banter, love and loathe their way through the highs and lows of another day. Snippets of these daily dramas unfurl on the city's balconies, squares and streets, transforming the metropolis into a stage. Even the city's setting – on the Bay of Naples – recalls a giant amphitheatre. After all, the Neapolitans are Italy's most consummate performers and some of the country's most iconic performers hail from here. Among them is Sophia Loren, whose onscreen personas have often encapsulated the complexity of the screen siren's hometown: elegant yet earthy, proud yet vulnerable, compassionate but cunning. In many ways, Napoli is a synthesis of Italy at its most noble and most depraved. The end result is one of the world's most enigmatic, intriguing urban centres.

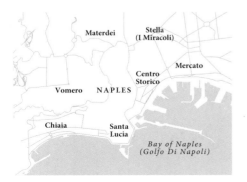

Materdei

Stella (I Miracoli)

Centro Storico

Mercato

Vomero   NAPLES

Chiaia   Santa Lucia

Bay of Naples (Golfo Di Napoli)

Right Basilica di San Paolo Maggiore

NAPLES, THE CITY BELOW

NAPLES / HISTORY

Sacred shrines, secret passageways, forgotten burial crypts: it might sound like the set of an Indiana Jones film, but we're actually talking about what lurks beneath Naples' loud and greasy streets. Subterranean Naples is one of the world's most thrilling urban other-worlds: a silent, mostly undiscovered sprawl of cathedral-like cisterns, pin-width conduits, catacombs and ancient ruins.

Since the end of WWII, some 700 cavities have been discovered in Naples, from original Greek-era grottoes to Palaeo-Christian burial chambers and royal Bourbon escape routes. According to the experts, this is simply a prelude, with another 2 million sq metres of troglodytic treats still to unfurl.

Naples' caving geeks are quick to tell you that their underworld is one of the largest and oldest on earth. Sure, Paris might claim a catacomb or two, but its subterranean offerings don't come close to this giant's 2500-year history. And what a history it is: from buried martyrs and foreign invaders to wife-snatching spirits and drug-making mobsters. The city's inhabitants have been tunnelling into the easily quarriable yellow tuff rock beneath their feet for millennia, leaving a honeycomb of crypts, catacombs and air-raid shelters for visitors to explore.

Hidden down a secret stairway in San Lorenzo Maggiore's main cloister, the often overlooked Greco-Roman city of Neapolis is still on display. Descending just one flight down will land you smack in the middle of the ancient city's marketplace, where you can still stroll among dimly lit shopfronts of diamond-patterned bricks: once premises for the butcher, the baker, even the banker. Passing through an arched cryptoporticus (a covered passageway that was perhaps the city's fish market) and beyond, you'll find precious fragments of frescoes and mosaic floors.

Naples' most famous saint, San Gennaro, was interred in the Catacomba di San Gennaro in the 5th century BC. A millennium later, in AD 536, Belisario and his troops caught Naples by surprise by storming the city through its ancient tunnels. According to legend, Alfonso of Aragon used the same trick in 1442, undermining the city walls by using an underground passageway leading into a tailor's shop and straight into town.

Inversely, the 18th-century Bourbons had an escape route built beneath the Palazzo Reale di Capodimonte. A century later they commissioned a tunnel to connect their central Palazzo Reale (Royal Palace) to their barracks in Chiaia: a perfect crowd-free route for troops or a fleeing royal family.

And while strategic tunnels and sacred catacombs are important features of Naples' light-deprived other-world, the city's subterranean backbone is its ancient aqueduct system. Naples' first plumbing masterpiece was built by Greek settlers, who channelled water from the slopes of Mt Vesuvius into the city's cisterns. The cisterns themselves were created as builders dug out the pliable *tufo* sandstone on which the city stands. At street level, well shafts allowed citizens to lower their buckets and quench their thirst.

Not to be outdone, the Romans built their new 70km aqueduct, transporting water from the river Serino near Avellino to Naples, Pozzuoli and Baia, where it filled the enormous Piscina Mirabilis.

The next update came in 1629 with the opening of the Spanish-commissioned 'Carmignano' aqueduct. Expanded in 1770, it finally met its end in the 1880s, when cholera outbreaks heralded the building of a more modern version.

Dried up and defunct, the ancient cisterns went from glorious feats of ancient engineering to handy in-house rubbish tips. As refuse clogged the well shafts, access to the *sottosuolo* (underground) became ever more difficult and, within a few generations, the subterranean system that had nourished the city was left bloated and forgotten.

But there was a kind of new life to be found in the underground – the Bourbon Tunnel enables visitors to traverse many centuries. Conceived by Ferdinand II in 1853, the never-completed escape route is part of the 17th-century Carmignano system, itself incorporating the 16th-century cisterns. The sheer size and scale of this cavernous cistern-turned-would-be-royal-escape-route are humbling enough, but the cruel reminders of its use as a WWII air-raid shelter will chill you to the bone: low-voltage electricity supplies, toilets, showers, cots, toys and heart-breaking graffiti – messages of hope and fear etched into the walls for posterity.

All across the city it took the wail of air-raid sirens to reunite the city's sunlit and subterranean sides once more. With Allied air attacks looming, many cisterns and former quarries were turned into civilian shelters. Lakes of rubbish were compacted and covered, old passageways were enlarged, toilets were built and new staircases were erected. As bombs showered the city above, tens of thousands took refuge in the dark, damp spaces below.

The fear, frustration and anger of those days lives on in the historic graffiti that covers some of the old shelters, from hand-drawn caricatures of Hitler and 'Il Duce' to poignant messages like '*Mamma, non piangere*' (Mum, don't cry). Many families spent weeks living underground, often emerging to find their homes and neighbourhoods nothing more than rubble. For the many whose homes were

destroyed, these subterranean hideouts became semi-permanent dwellings. Entire families cohabited in cisterns, partitioning their makeshift abodes with bedsheets and furnishing them with the odd ramshackle bed. Traces of this rudimentary domestication survive to this day, from tiled 'kitchen' walls and showers, to evidence of DC battery power.

Alas, once rebuilding began, the aqueducts once again became subterranean dumpsters, with everything from wartime rubble to scooters and Fiats thrown down the shafts. And in a case of history repeating itself, the historic labyrinth and its millennia-old secrets faded from the city's collective memory.

Thankfully, all is not lost, as a passionate league of professional and volunteer speleologists continues to rediscover and render accessible long-lost sites and secrets – a fact not overlooked by the likes of National Geographic and the BBC, both of which have documented the work of these subterranean experts. The city's most prolific speleological association today is La Macchina del Tempo (The Time Machine), which manages the fascinating Museo del Sottosuolo, a DIY ode to speleologists and the treasures they uncover. Hidden away on Piazza Cavour, between the centro storico (historic centre) and the Sanità district, the museum was founded by veteran cave crusader Clemente Esposito, lovingly nicknamed il Papa del sottosuolo (the Pope of the Underground) in local speleological circles.

La Macchina del Tempo runs thrilling speleological tours that take in unexplored nooks few locals will ever see. On these journeys, surprise discoveries are far from rare, whether it's a secret wartime

hideout, an early-Christian engraving or an even older Greek urn.

And yet, not even the infectious enthusiasm of Naples' speleologists is enough to secure the protection and preservation of the city's sottosuolo. The golden era of the 1990s, which saw the city council provide generous funding to speleological research, has since been supplanted by standard Italian bureaucracy and political bickering. As a result, many precious sites uncovered by the city's speleologists remain indefinitely abandoned, with little money to salvage and restore them.

A more positive outcome involved NUg (Napoli Underground group), who discovered a long corridor beneath the Quartieri Spagnoli, part of the ancient Largo Baracche district. The unearthing team called for its transformation into a much-needed community centre – a wish that fell on deaf ears at city hall. Destined to become a squat, its saving grace was a gung-ho group of young community activists called SABU. Giving the space a mighty scrub, the group opened it as a nonprofit art lab and gallery in 2005. The space is also well known for its permanent mural, created by Naples' best-known street artists, cyop&kaf. To see it, you'll need to ask them to turn off the lights – it's the only way you'll catch the glow-in-the-dark creation.

'Underground art' has taken over elsewhere too, with many of the city's metro stations designed or decorated by top-tier artists, both homegrown and foreign. You'll find Mario Merz' blue neon digits at Vanvitelli, a witty Fiat installation by Perino & Vele at Salvator Rosa and Technicolor wall drawings by Sol LeWitt at Materdei. And then there are the snap-

Myth of the Little Monk

It's only natural that a world as old, dark and mysterious as Naples' sottosuolo should breed a few fantastical urban myths. The best known and most loved is that of the municello (little monk), a Neapolitan leprechaun of sorts known for being both naughty and nice. Said to live in a wine cellar, the hooded sprite was reputedly a regular sight in the 18th and 19th centuries. Some spoke of him as a kindred soul, a bearer of gifts and good fortune. To others, the municello spelt trouble, sneaking into homes to misplace objects, steal precious jewels and seduce the odd lonely housewife.

While a handful of Neapolitans still curse the imp whenever the car keys go missing, most now believe that the cheeky municello was actually the city's long-gone pozzari (aqueduct cleaners). Descending daily down the wells, the small-statured pozzari fought off the damp, cool conditions with a heavy, hooded mantle. Naturally, most would pop back up for a breath of fresh air, sometimes finding themselves in people's very homes.

shots by heavyweight Italian photographers at Museo or Jannis Kounellis' eerie shoe installation at Dante.

Most of the city's 'Art Stations' are on the extended Line 1. Among the most striking is Università – brainchild of Egyptian-born industrial-designer Karim Rashid. True to Rashid's style, the station is a playful, candy-coloured ode to the

Above **Toledo station**, Naples

digital age. White tiles clad the station entrance, each one printed with a word originating in the last century. In the station itself you'll find lenticular icons that change perspective and colour, a sculpture reflecting the nodes and synapses of the brain, platform steps decorated with abstracted portraits of Dante and Beatrice, even platform walls adorned with glowing, 'animated' artwork.

Perhaps even more breathtaking is Toledo station. Topping a CNN list of Europe's most impressive metro stations in 2014, its lobby features ruins from an Aragonese fortress and a spectacular wall mosaic by conceptual artist William Kentridge. Depicted in the latter is a medley of Neapolitan icons, from San Gennaro and a *pizzaiolo* (pizza maker) to the Museo Archeologico Nazionale's famous *Farnese Atlante* sculpture. Another Kentridge mural hovers above the escalators (it's said that the cat represents the artist himself). Toledo station reaches a depth of 50m below sea level, a fact not lost on the station's colour scheme, which goes from ochre (representing Naples' iconic tuff stone) to a dazzling blue as you descend the escalators. It's here, 'below the sea', that you'll find a spectacular mosaic porthole, streaming down light from the sky above. The porthole's light installation is by artist Robert Wilson, whose concourse 'Light Panels' ripple as you hurry past them.

Designed by architects Alvaro Siza and Eduardo Souto De Mura, Municipio station (opened in 2015) comes with its own museum space, home to some of the 3000 artefacts unearthed during the station's construction. Among the astounding finds are remnants of the city's ancient Greek

and Roman ports, as well as Roman vessels. The base of a 14th-century Angevin tower – the Torre dell'Incoronata – is showcased in the station's concourse, beside a specially commissioned installation by Israeli artist Michal Rovner. The ancient and the cutting-edge also collide at Duomo station, where a street-level glass-and-steel bubble designed by Italian starchitect Massimiliano Fuksas sheds light on a Roman temple used for the Isolympic Augustan Roman Italic Games, a local version of Greece's ancient Olympics.

For further information on the Naples metro works of art or official guided tours, visit www.anm.it. Grab a metro ticket, head underground and get inspired. And take your time exploring the WWII relics and ancient history down there too – the sunlight up above can wait a bit when there's this much going on beneath your feet!

To read about:
Italian Architecture see page 64
Preserving Cultural Sites see page 162

NEAPOLITAN ARTISAN TRADITIONS

NAPLES / ARTS

Down dark streets, behind unmarked doors and in unsuspecting courtyards, artisan studios litter Naples' World Heritage-listed centro storico. In these secret bolt holes, some of Naples' most intriguing artists celebrate, reinterpret and sometimes subvert Neapolitan traditions. After all, this is a city where the past is always present and where nothing is quite what it seems.

One of the most famous of Naples' many traditions is the *presepe napoletano* (Neapolitan nativity crib). While nativity cribs aren't exclusive to the city, the local version stands out for its meticulous attention to detail, from the life-like miniature *prosciutti* (hams) in the tavern to the lavishly costumed *pastori* (crib figurines or sculptures) adorning the newborn Christ. It's a craft that traces its roots to 1535, when local priest Gaetano da Thiene ditched tradition and dressed his crib characters in Neapolitan garb instead of traditional biblical robes. Da Thiene's crib makeover ignited a passion that would reach its zenith with the 18th-century *presepe del Settecento* (crib of the 1700s), a baroque spin-off set in bucolic, sunlit European landscapes and reflecting the palettes of the era's great artists.

For the nobility and the bourgeoisie of 18th-century Naples, the *presepe* allowed a convenient marriage of faith and ego, the crib becoming as much a symbol of wealth and good taste as a meditation on the Christmas miracle. The finest sculptors were commissioned and the finest fabrics used. Even the royals got involved: Charles III of Bourbon consulted the esteemed *presepe* expert, Dominican monk Padre Rocco, on the creation of his 5000-*pastore* spectacular, still on show at the Palazzo Reale. Yet even this pales in comparison to the epic crib showcased at the Certosa e Museo di San Martino, considered the world's greatest.

Centuries on, the legacy continues, with *presepe* and *pastore* pedlars lining Naples' famous Via San Gregorio Armeno. Sadly, many of these now sell mass-produced reproductions. Only a few workshops or studios in the city completely handcraft their *pastori* the old-fashioned way. Among them are Ars Neapolitana and La Scarabattola, both of which flank Via dei Tribunali, the main east-west *decumanus* (street) of ancient Neapolis. These artisan studios remain true to the *presepe's* golden age, moulding each bust by hand using fine-grain clay and dressing each *pastore* in intricate costumes. Despite their modest appearance, both studios have A-list fans, from European royalty to Italian fashion designers Domenico Dolce and Stefano Gabbana.

A few blocks south Neapolitan traditions get a thoroughly contemporary makeover at the 16th-century Palazzo di Sangro. Hidden away in its basement is the atelier of gregarious Neapolitan artist Lello Esposito, a man intrigued by Neapolitan identity, ambiguity and metamorphosis. It's a fascination that feeds large-scale sculptures and installations that might see an esoteric *corno* (horn-shaped amulet) fused with the head of patron saint San Gennaro, or the classical character of Pulcinella bound like a prisoner; a comment on the city's constant struggle between tradition and progress. According to Esposito, modern Naples is no less baroque than its 18th-century self, a belief evident in the artist's thick, luscious, colour-saturated paintings.

To read about:
Papier-Mâché Sculptures see page 120
Handmade Puppets see page 140

Dolce Vita

Indulging in Italy's Sweet Life

Italians don't aspire to the *dolce vita* (sweet life), they consider it their birthright. This becomes blatantly obvious in any Italian town or city, where the day begins with an expertly brewed espresso and a chat with the barista. Midday on the piazza and restaurant terraces are crowded with people tucking into handmade pasta, fresh fish sprinkled with herbs and homemade *dolci* (desserts). Ask what they're eating and they'll reply, with a shrug: 'just a simple lunch'. The conversation and the wine flows. How good it must feel to be Italian, you think. They would most likely agree.

From Federico Fellini's classic film, where Anita Ekberg famously got drenched in her ballgown in the Trevi Fountain, to *Cinema Paradiso* zooming in on life in small town Sicily and the *Italian Job* showcasing the cinematic beauty of the Alps – *la dolce vita* has been played out on the silver screen time and again.

While you don't have to be rich to enjoy Italy's sweet life, luxury abounds for those who can afford it. This is epicure heaven, whether you're dining by Lake Como's villa-lined waterside, sipping *limoncello* in the twilight romance of Positano and Sorrento, sailing the sapphire waters of Capri, being serenaded by a gondolier in canal-woven Venice, or piazza-side posing on Sardinia's swanky Costa Smeralda. Catch an opera in the gilded splendour of La Scala, roam sky-high Ravello's ravishing gardens at sunset and marvel at how this country moves to its own deliciously relaxed beat. The Grand Tour is still alive in Italy and it's fine to indulge in a little pleasure because *così va la vita* (that's what life is all about).

The Grand Tour: An 18th-Century Gap Year

ITALY-WIDE / JOURNEYS

While Italy has no shortage of pilgrimage sites, its history as a modern tourist destination can be traced back to the late 1700s and the fashion for the Grand Tour. The 18th-century version of a gap year, the Tour was considered an educational rite of passage for wealthy young men from northern Europe, and Britain in particular.

Some saw it as an educational pilgrimage. Others as a trans-continental finishing school, inculcating knowledge and good taste. The Grand Tour, which reached its peak in the late 18th and early 19th centuries, was the prerogative of rich aristocracy and landed gentry. As the Grand Tourists – many of them English, most of them young – moved steadily from Paris through Switzerland to Italy (and sometimes back through Austria, Germany and Holland), they noted the great glories of European culture and, it was hoped, found their minds enhanced, their spirits lifted and their manners polished.

The overland journey through France and into Italy followed the medieval pilgrim route, entering Italy via the St Bernard Pass and descending the west coast before cutting in to Florence and then down to Rome. After a sojourn in the capital, tourists would venture down to Naples, where the newly discovered ruins of Pompeii and Herculaneum were causing much excitement, before heading up to Venice.

Often they travelled by private coach, possibly with a personal tutor or their own cook. Some even took along professional artists to record the 18th-century equivalents of holiday snaps. Not everyone did it in such style – in 1814, the English Romantic authors Mary Shelley and Percy Bysshe Shelley travelled from Paris across the Alps on foot and by donkey. In any case, tours were sometimes gruelling. The Channel crossing could be bilious; the Alps uncomfortable; the food, though invariably interesting, challenging.

Rome, enjoying a rare period of peace, was perfectly set up for this English invasion. The city was basking in the after-math of the 17th-century baroque building boom, and a craze for all things classical was sweeping Europe. Here more than anywhere the Grand Tourist was awakened to an interest in art and architecture. Rome's papal authorities were also crying out for money after their excesses had left the city coffers bare, reducing much of the population to abject poverty.

Thousands came, including Johann Wolfgang von Goethe, who stopped off to write his travelogue *Italian Journey* (1817), as well as John Keats, Lord Byron and the Shelleys, who all fuelled their romantic sensibilities in Rome's vibrant streets. So many English people stayed around Piazza di Spagna that locals christened the area *er ghetto de l'inglesi* (the English ghetto).

Parents back home footed the bill while tourers would spend months, even years, on the road, ticking off cathedrals and colosseums and being suitably awed by sublime views.

Eventually, the tour was democratised for the middle classes by the coming of the railways and, so, while parents may no longer foot the bill, the tradition of the Grand Tour lives on.

To read about:

Italy on Rails see page 266
Italy's Grandi Giardini see page 296

Left Valle d'Aosta

Italy on Rails

ITALY-WIDE / JOURNEYS

With some of Europe's fastest trains and most scenic routes, Italy is a great place to travel by train. The country might be more famous for its deluxe sports cars and challenging driving conditions, but Italian trains are economical, comfortable and direct, offering an insight into local life, and endless views of villas, villages and dilapidated ancient towers.

Travel in Style on Italy's Fastest Trains

If you thought Ferraris were fast, you've clearly never travelled on a Frecciarossa 1000, Italy's high-velocity train that reaches a top cruising speed of 300km/h. The fastest Frecciarossas connect Turin, Milan and Venice in the north before heading further south via Bologna and Florence to Rome, Naples and Salerno.

These rockets-on-wheels are not only faster than Ferraris, they're also invitingly comfortable with leather seats, a complimentary welcome drink (in business class) and a luxurious dining car where the view changes every five seconds.

As a rule, the fastest Rome–Naples trip clocks in at a smidgen over an hour, Rome–Florence zips by in roughly 90 minutes, while Rome–Venice takes three hours 40 minutes, which is still very respectable considering the same journey takes over five hours by car.

Italy's Most Scenic Train Journeys

The speed of Freccia trains means that the scenery is often rendered a blur. For Italy's most spectacular rail journeys, you'll have to abandon any stringent time constraints and seek out small private lines, which crawl from one *campanile* (belltower) to the next.

The epic Centovalli, '100 valleys', line that starts in Domodossola in Piedmont travels across 83 bridges in two hours of condensed alpine splendour to terminate in Locarno in Switzerland.

Another beauty is Sardinia's intentionally slow Trenino Verde, renovated in the 1990s, which runs four summer trains along narrow-gauge track through some of the island's most remote enclaves.

Equally seductive is the Ferrovia Circumetnea which runs out of Catania in Sicily circumnavigating Mt Etna on a diminutive locomotive that looks more like a trolley bus than a train. En route it crosses lemon groves and lava flows, stopping at an endless string of tiny and remote stations.

Rail is also the best way to travel in some of Italy's most scenic destinations, including Cinque Terre, where cheap trains connect the five picturesque cliff-top villages, passing through numerous tunnels in the steep cliffs and giving views of the ocean. The bargainous Circumvesuviana connects Naples with Sorrento via the archaeological sites of Herculaneum and Pompeii, providing views of Mt Vesuvius and the Bay of Naples along the way.

Arriving in Italy by Train

Some of Italy's finest train journeys cross its international borders with its neighbours to the north. The Brenner Pass route that links Munich with Venice over the Alps is sometimes touted as the finest train ride in Europe, while the EuroNight overnight train between Rome and Vienna with two-bed sleepers is a fun option if you've never bedded down on a train.

If you want to imagine you're living in a Graham Greene novel or an Agatha Christie whodunit, take the Venice Simplon Orient Express from London (or Paris) to La Serenissima. This art deco hotel on wheels runs once a week from March to November and was seemingly invented with romance in mind.

Turin's recently refurbished Porta Susa station is a terminus for French TGV trains which provide rapid service to Lyon and Paris. Milan offers Thello overnight trains to Paris or daytime coastal trains to Nice

Tickets & Passes

Rail passes such as Eurail and Inter-Rail won't usually save you money in Italy, because you still have to pay a reservation fee of around €10 for high-speed trains, and tickets for regular trains aren't expensive. It's cheaper to purchase separate tickets for each journey. Although trains rarely sell out, pre-booking can save you a lot of money. You can normally book tickets up to four months in advance.

High-speed train tickets come with a specific seat reservation and must be purchased before you get on the train. Tickets for high-speed trains don't require validation, as they can only be used on the specific service they are valid for.

Regionale trains, which stop at nearly every station, don't require reservations. Just pay for your ticket before departure, jump on the train and grab a seat wherever you like. Regional train tickets aren't dated, you must 'time-stamp' them in a *convalida* machine on the platform before boarding the train.

and Marseilles. By using a mixture of Eurostar and TGVs, it's possible to travel between Milan and London in one day for a cost of around €65 (or Paris for as little as €25) and you get to see awe-inspiring alpine scenery in the bargain.

To read about:

The Dolomites see page 234
Driving the Amlfi Coast Road see page 282

The Sweet Stuff: Tiramisu

The iconic dessert that packs a punch with generous measures of coffee, sugar and, in select versions, liquor, has become a favourite worldwide. Its name comes from the words tira (pull/lift) mi (me) su (up), making it the ultimate pick-me-up pudding. Although some attribute its origins to the Medici courts, there's no sign of it in recipe books before the 1960s.

Most accounts of the origins of this creamy cake place its creation firmly in Treviso, at Le Beccherie restaurant, at the hands of the pregnant owner who needed a lift. Now in her late 80s, Alba Campeol came up with the recipe after being inspired by her mother-in-law's recommendation to eat Savoiardi biscuits dipped in coffee to give her a much-needed boost. Her nascent son, Carlo, went on to make this dessert the star of Le Beccherie's menu, and it's now served in restaurants worldwide as a generic Italian export.

The governor of Veneto, Luca Zaia, has long been campaigning for Treviso to be recognised by the European Union as the official home of tiramisu. His mission received a setback in 2017, when neighbouring region Friuli Venezia Giulia had tiramisu officially added to its set of *prodotti agroalimentari tradizionali,* a list of traditional regional foods published by the Italian Ministry of Agricultural, Food and Forestry Policies. The move came after food writers Clara and Gigi Padovani reportedly found recipes for tiramisu in the Friuli Venezia Giulia region that dated from the 1950s, predating Campeol's claim. Zaia has expressed his horror at the decision, controversially claiming that the ministry may have been misled by Friuli Venezia Giulia.

Though Campeol and her husband still live above Le Beccherie, in 2014 they handed the reins of the restaurant over to new owner Paolo Lai and chef Federico Moro. All three of the tiramisu recipes Moro makes, including Campeol's original and his own version, tiramisu *scomposto* (deconstructed), call for an Italian Savoiardi-style biscuit. Drier and crumblier than the French 'boudoir' variant or ladyfingers, Savoiardi soak up more liquid but remain light and fluffy.

To read about:
Coffee see page 186
Making Tiramisu see page 271

Tiramisu

Serves 6–8
Cooking time 3½ hours, including refrigeration time

→ 5 egg yolks
→ 5 tbsp sugar
→ 500g (17½oz) mascarpone
→ 1 standard packet (around 200g/7oz) Savoiardi biscuits
→ 400ml (13 fl oz) strong coffee/espresso
→ cocoa powder to sprinkle

1. Beat the egg yolks with the sugar.

2. Add the mascarpone and gently fold everything together.

3. In a serving dish, alternate a layer of biscuits quickly soaked in the coffee, with a layer of the mascarpone mixture. Continue, adding two layers of each.

4. Let it stand for at least three hours in the refrigerator.

5. Take the tiramisu from the refrigerator, sprinkle with cocoa powder and serve.

The Scoop on Gelati

Gelato is one of Italy's great social unifiers, and as much a part of Italian life as morning coffee – try it and you'll understand why. Everyone, from elegant matrons to politicians and toddlers, adores the stuff and the country's gelaterie cater to locals as much as tourists.

The Romans treasured the snow, using it to chill their wine, but it was the Arabs who first started the mania for all things icy – including gelato (ice cream). The origins of ice cream lie in the Arab *sarbat* (sherbet), a concoction of sweet fruit syrups chilled with iced water, which was then developed into *granita* (where crushed ice was mixed with fruit juice, coffee or almond milk) and *cremolata* (fruit syrups chilled with iced milk), the forerunner to gelato.

Gelato flavours have come a long way since Nero snacked on snow mixed with fruit pulp and honey. Rome has some of the world's finest ice-cream shops, where they use only the finest seasonal ingredients, sourced from the finest locations. In these artisan gelaterie you won't find a strawberry flavour in winter, for example, and pistachios are from Bronte, almonds from Avola, and so on. A rule of thumb is to check the colour of the pistachio flavour: ochre-green equals good, bright-green equals bad.

There are some excellent places where you can learn how to make your own gelato but Gelateria David in Sorrento is cream-of-the-crop, run by the third generation in the ice-cream business. Its specialities include the deliciously one-off 'Sorrento moon', with almond and lemons, and *veneziana,* a lemon, orange and mandarin sorbet. And if you'd like to become a true *gelataio,* you can enrol at Bologna's Gelato University for its 19-day professional gelato-making program.

The University's adjacent museum is run by Carpigiani, Italy's most famous gelato-machine manufacturer and traces the history of frozen desserts from ancient times to the present, replete with 19th-century ice-cream carts, vintage gelato-making equipment and a Taste Gelato History tour that includes a sample or two.

Finally, test your skills, or get your fill at the nation's annual gelato festival, which sees Europe's finest gelato makers compete for the title of 'best gelato' during days of tastings, demonstrations, classes and foodie goodness. Be aware that suspense runs high; the festival begins in April and doesn't culminate until September, when the finals are held in Florence.

To read about:
Limoncello see page 287
Chocolate see page 290

Yacht Life on the Costa Smeralda

Sardinia's Costa Smeralda is the place to day-dream about a billionaire's lifestyle as you float in an emerald sea past palatial villas and super-yachts. It's one of the world's glitziest beach destinations.

SARDINIA / JOURNEYS

Back in 1962, flamboyant millionaire Karim Aga Khan established a consortium to buy a strip of unspoiled coastline in northeastern Sardinia. Each investor paid roughly US$25,000 for a little piece of paradise, and the coast was christened Costa Smeralda (Emerald Coast) for its brilliant green-blue waters.

These days billionaire jet-setters cruise into Costa Smeralda's marinas in mega-yachts that are like floating mansions, and models, royals, Russian oligarchs and media moguls come to frolic in its waters.

Believe the hype: the Costa Smeralda is stunning. The Gallura's wind-whipped granite mountains tumble down to fjord-like inlets, and an emerald sea fringes a coast that is necklaced with bays like the Aga Khan's favourite, Spiaggia del Princi-pe – a perfect crescent of frost-white sand smoothed by gin-clear water.

Play paparazzo, eyeing up the mega-yachts in millionaires' playground re-sorts, or eschew the high life to seek out secluded coves, embedded in fragrant *macchia* (Mediterranean scrubland), where the views are simply priceless.

Starting at the Golfo di Cugnana, 17km north of Olbia, the Costa stretches 55km northwards to the Golfo di Arzachena. The 'capital' is the yachtie haven of Porto Cervo, although Porto Rotondo, a second marina developed in 1963, is also celebrity-spotting central, attracting pa-parazzi with its Silvio Berlusconi connec-tions and its seafront promenade.

Just over the water, the pink-granite island of La Maddalena offers startlingly lovely seascapes. Divers sing the praises of the sapphire waters here, which are among the cleanest in the Mediterranean and teem with marine life. Over a cause-way from Isola della Maddalena, Isola Caprera was once Giuseppe Garibaldi's 'Eden' – a wild, wonderfully serene island, covered in green pines which look stun-ning against the ever-present seascape and ragged granite cliffs. The green, shady Caprera is ideal for walking, and there are plenty of trails weaving through the pines. The island's rugged coast is indented with several tempting coves.

La Maddalena and Caprera are just two of the seven main islands that form the Parco Nazionale dell'Arcipelago di La Maddalena. These islands, along with the park's 40 granite islets, and several small islands to the south, form the high points of an underwater valley that once joined Sardinia and Corsica. Over the centuries, the *maestrale* (northwesterly wind) has moulded the granite into natural sculp-tures. If you don't have your own mega-yacht, there are some boat cruises that allow you to explore the archipelago, while providing lunch and plenty of opportuni-ties for some glorious swimming.

To read about:
Living Luxe on Lake Como see page 288
Luxury Stays see page 300

Right **Yacht moored,** Mortorio Island, Costa Smeralda, Sardinia

Italy on the Silver Screen

From Spaghetti Westerns to acclaimed contemporary dramas, countless celluloid classics have been filmed in Italy's sunny cities and on its hills and coastlines. Combining spectacular scenery with visionary directors, iconic stars and that trademark Italian pathos, Italy's films have helped to shape cinema, and offer a unique window into the nation's psyche.

ITALY-WIDE / ARTS

Spaghetti Westerns

Emerging in the mid-1960s, Italian-style Westerns had no shortage of high-noon showdowns featuring flinty characters and Ennio Morricone's whistled tunes. Top of the directorial bill was Sergio Leone, whose Western debut *Per un Pugno di Dollari* (A Fistful of Dollars; 1964) helped launch a young Clint Eastwood's movie career. After Leone and Eastwood teamed up again in *Il Buono, il Brutto, il Cattivo* (The Good, the Bad, and the Ugly; 1966), it was Henry Fonda's turn in Leone's *C'era una Volta il West* (Once Upon a Time in the West; 1968), a story about a revenge-seeking widow.

Romance all'Italiana

In Michael Radford's *Il Postino* (The Postman; 1994), exiled poet Pablo Neruda brings poetry and passion to the drowsy Italian isle of Salina and a misfit postman, played with heartbreaking subtlety by Massimo Troisi. Another classic is Giuseppe Tornatore's Oscar-winning *Nuovo Cinema Paradiso* (Cinema Paradiso; 1988), a bittersweet tale about a director who returns to Sicily and rediscovers his true loves: the girl next door and the movies. In Silvio Sordini's *Pane e Tulipani* (Bread and Tulips; 2000), a housewife left behind at a tour-bus pit stop runs away to Venice, where she befriends an anarchist florist, an eccentric masseuse and a suicidal Icelandic waiter – and gets pursued by an amateur detective.

Neorealist Grit

Out of the smouldering ruins of WWII emerged unflinching tales of woe, including Roberto Rossellini's *Roma, Città Aperta* (Rome: Open City; 1945), a story of love, betrayal and resistance in Nazi-occupied Rome. In Vittorio De Sica's Academy-awarded *Ladri di Biciclette* (The Bicycle Thieves; 1948), a doomed father attempts to provide for his son without resorting to crime in war-ravaged Rome, while Pier Paolo Pasolini's *Mamma Roma* (1962) revolves around an ageing prostitute trying to make an honest living for herself and her deadbeat son. More recently, Gianfranco Rosi's Oscar-nominated documentary *Fuocoammare* (Fire at Sea; 2016) has drawn comparisons to the neorealist movement in its confronting, moving exploration of the European refugee crisis as played out on the island of Lampedusa.

Shock & Horror

Sunny Italy's darkest dramas deliver style and suspense. In Michelangelo Antonioni's *Blow-Up* (1966) a swinging-'60s fashion photographer spies dark deeds unfolding in a photo of an elusive Vanessa Redgrave. Gruesome deeds unfold at a ballet school in Dario Argento's *Suspiria* (1977), while in Mario Monicelli's *Un Borghese Piccolo Piccolo* (An Average Little Man; 1977), an ordinary man goes to extraordinary lengths for revenge. The latter stars Roman acting

Right Il Postino film poster, Salina

great Alberto Soldi in a standout example of a comedian nailing a serious role.

Crueller and bloodier than their American counterparts, Italian zombie films enjoy international cult status. One of the best is director Lucio Fulci's *Zombi 2* (aka *Zombie Flesh Eaters;* 1979). Fulci's other gore classics include *City of the Living Dead* (1980), *The Beyond* (1981) and *The House by the Cemetery* (1981).

Tragicomedies

Italy's top comedians pinpoint the exact spot where pathos intersects with the funny bone. A group of ageing pranksters turn on one another in Mario Monicelli's *Amici Miei* (My Friends; 1975), a satire reflecting Italy's own postwar midlife crisis. Midlife crisis also underscores Paolo Sorrentino's Oscar-winning *La Grande Bellezza* (The Great Beauty; 2013), a Fellini-style tale that evolves around Jep Gambardella, an ageing, hedonistic bachelor haunted by lost love and memories of the past. Contemporary woes feed Massimiliano Bruno's biting *Viva l'Italia* (2012), its cast of corrupt politicians and nepotists cutting close to the nation's bone. Italy is slapped equally hard by Matteo Garrone's *Reality* (2012), winner of the Grand Prix at the 2012 Cannes Film Festival. Darkest of all, however, remains actor-director Roberto Benigni's Oscar-winning *La Vita è Bella* (Life is Beautiful; 1997), in which a father tries to protect his son from the brutalities of a Jewish concentration camp by pretending it's all a game.

Crime & Punishment

Italy's acclaimed contemporary dramas combine the truthfulness of classic neorealism, the taut suspense of Italian

Above **Villa Vignamaggio,** filming location for Much Ado About Nothing

thrillers and the psychological revelations of Fellini. Among the best is Matteo Garrone's brutal Camorra exposé *Gomorra* (2008). Paolo Sorrentino's *Il Divo* (2008) explores the life of former prime minister Giulio Andreotti, from his migraines to his alleged mafia ties. The entanglement of organised crime and Rome's political class is at the heart of Stefano Sollima's neo-noir *Suburra* (2015), while mafiosi also appear in the deeply poignant *Cesare Deve Morire* (Caesar Must Die; 2012). Directed by octogenarian brothers Paolo and Vittorio Tavianian, this award-winning documentary tells the story of maximum-security prisoners preparing to stage Shakespeare's *Julius Caesar*. Italy's political and social ills drive Gabriele Mainetti's acclaimed film *Lo Chiamavano Jeeg Robot* (They Call Me Jeeg; 2015), which gives Hollywood's superhero genre a gritty local twist.

Filmed in Tuscany

Tuscany has long been a popular location for shooting international films. *A Room with a View* (1985) is a hugely popular period drama that was set in Florence, which also had a 2007 UK ITV adaptation by Andrew Davies. Kenneth Branagh shot his adaptation of Shakespeare's comedy *Much Ado about Nothing* (1993) in Chianti, with stars Emma Thompson and Keanu Reeves. *The English Patient* (1996) includes scenes that were shot in a monastery outside Pienza but is predominantly remembered for its lyrically beautiful sequence when Kip (Naveen Andrews) takes Hana (Juliette Binoche) into Arezzo's Cappella Bacci and hoists her aloft on ropes so that she can see Piero della Francesa's frescoes in the

light of a flare. Other films that feature the stunning Tuscan countryside include: *Stealing Beauty* (1996), *Tea with Mussolini* (1999), *Gladiator* (2000), *Hannibal* (2001), *Quantum of Solace* (2008) and *Inferno* (2016), among many more.

To read about:
Il Postino's Salina see page 142
The Godfather's Corleone see page 184

On Location – Ciao Roma!

Rome's Cinecittà is Europe's largest film studio complex and the historic hub of the Italian film industry. Aside from homegrown productions, the complex has served as a shooting location for numerous Hollywood films, including *Ben-Hur* (1959) and *Cleopatra* (1963), as well as the recent small-screen hit *The Young Pope* (2016). Rome is Italy's most prominent filming location, where Bernardo Bertolucci uses the Terme di Caracalla in the oedipal *La Luna* (1979), Gregory Peck gives Audrey Hepburn a fright at the Bocca della Verità in William Wyler's *Roman Holiday* (1953) and Anita Ekberg cools off in the Trevi Fountain in Federico Fellini's *La Dolce Vita* (1960). Fellini's love affair with the Eternal City culminated in his silver-screen tribute, *Roma* (1972). More recent tributes include Woody Allen's romantic comedy *To Rome with Love* (2012) and Italian director Paolo Sorrentino's sumptuous, decadent *La Grande Bellezza* (2013).

Lake Garda: Lemon Houses & Olive Oil

Surrounded by three distinct regions – Lombardy, Trentino Alto-Adige and the Veneto – the cultural diversity of Lake Garda (Lago di Garda) attracts 7% of all tourists to Italy. But many visitors miss the attractions of two of the area's local food industries: the long-defunct lemon industry and the renowned (and current) olive-oil industry.

NORTHERN ITALY / FOOD & DRINK

Lemons

It's thought that monks from Genoa brought lemons to Gargnano when they arrived at the monastery of St Francis in the 13th century. Lake Garda's temperate climate provided good conditions for a fruit normally grown further south, and by the 18th century hundreds of *limonaie* (lemon houses) were being built. These kept the frosts off the trees by laying sheets of glass over a wooden latticework supported by tall stone pillars. Hundreds of thousands of lemons were exported annually to Germany and Russia, providing a crucial local income. But by the second half of the 19th century the industry fell into terminal decline due to disease and the discovery of artificial citric acid.

Today, terraces of weathered stone pillars are evidence of this lost industry. You can visit restored lemon houses at Limonaia del Castèl in Limone sul Garda on the west bank of the lake and at Torri del Benaco's Castello Scaligero on the east bank.

Olive Oil

Lake Garda's microclimate resembles the Mediterranean's, ensuring ideal olive-growing conditions. The lake's banks produce a tiny 1% of Italy's olive oil, but the product is renowned for being light, soft and sweet. Some 15 varieties of olives are grown here; the local black fruit produces subtler tasting oil, while the green olives are spicier – the oil makers' skill lies in achieving the perfect blend. Lake Garda's lighter oils work well with fish, the medium blends are delicious drizzled over mozzarella, and the stronger, spicier varieties are superb with grilled meats and soup. Locals advise not to use the best oils for salads, arguing if you're adding vinegar it ruins the taste.

Among the places where you can tour the olive groves and purchase the oil are Frantoio San Felice del Benaco and Comincioli in the Valtenesi and the Consorzio Olivicoltori di Malcesine in Malcesine.

To read about:
Olive Harvest see page 131
Lake Como see page 288

Driving the Amalfi Coast Road

SOUTHERN ITALY / JOURNEYS

Snaking around impossible corners, over deep ravines and through tunnels gouged from sheer rock, this road puts driving skills to the supreme test, but the views are assuredly sublime.

Officially known as the SS163 and colloquially as the 'Blue Ribbon' (or 'Nastro Azzurro'), the Amalfi Coast Road stretches for just 50km. It was commissioned by Bourbon king Ferdinand II and completed in 1853, and it hugs the Amalfi Coast's entire length, dramatically linking all the coastal towns that lie along the way. For a long time after Amalfi saw the last of its original glory days, which lasted from the 9th to the 12th centuries, the area was poor and its isolated villages were frequently subject to foreign invasion and natural disasters. But this isolation later had a positive side, when it became a drawcard for many visitors in the early 1900s and paved the way for tourism in the area today.

The Amalfi Coast ranks among Italy's finest and most unique destinations, favoured by jet setters, celebrities and ordinary people alike. Everyone finds the coastal road rewarding on many different levels, with those precipitous peaks harbouring a hidden network of ancient paths. Cliffs terraced with scented lemon groves sheer down into sparkling seas, whitewashed villas cling precariously to unforgiving slopes, and sea and sky merge into one vast, blue horizon.

The coastal road is an awe-inspiring feat of civil engineering, and consequently a severe test of driving skill and courage. Knuckles are frequently whiter than sheets as foolhardy drivers pit themselves against the supernatural ability of local bus drivers. Of course, if they find driving too nerve-wracking, many travellers simply opt out and take the bus, but either way someone has to negotiate the numerous switchbacks and plunging drops to

Top **Sorrento**
Bottom **Positano**

the sea, frequently with only waist-high barriers between living the high life and oblivion.

But relax: there are far fewer accidents than you'd think.

The Journey

Start at Sorrento, gateway to the Sirens' domain, negotiate the coastal road's notorious traffic and eventually you'll find yourself pulling into Sant'Agata sui due Golfi, where you can admire the spectacular views of the Bay of Naples on one side and the Gulf of Salerno on the other. Although the town is small, it is home to a sophisticated culinary scene and many options for a memorable lunch, such as elegantly served baby-sirloin rolls filled with raisins at two-Michelin-starred Ristorante Don Alfonso.

Further down the road, exquisitely photogenic Positano is also exquisitely expensive but its preternatural beauty and hillsides crusted with ornate, period architecture are otherworldly, or as John Steinbeck put it: 'Positano bites deep. It is a dream place that isn't quite real when you are there and becomes beckoningly real after you have gone.'

Once you've had your fill, push on half an hour to pretty little Amalfi for its sun-filled piazzas and small beach. Walking from one end of the town to the other takes little more than 20 minutes.

Should you be fortunate enough to extend your drive over a longer period, the Amalfi Coast boasts some seriously stylish accommodation, from sumptuous restored *palazzi* to superb B&Bs. But if you're not overnighting at a roadside town, there'll be time for just one more stop in

The Armchair Experience

Gran Turismo 4 (2004) Hone your driving before tackling the real thing; this racing game features the road alongside lovingly rendered clifftop views.

The Talented Mr Ripley (Patricia Highsmith) This 1955 novel and its film adaptation (1999), starring Matt Damon, take place in 'Mongibello', an imaginary town modelled on Positano.

Avanti! (1972) Billy Wilder's comedy-drama stars Jack Lemmon and Juliet Mills, and was filmed in classic coastal locations including Sorrento and Capri.

Amalfi: Rewards of the Goddesses (2009) This Japanese thriller, about a mother's search for her kidnapped daughter, makes full use of the coast, coming on at times more like a tourism promo than a feature film.

your day: Atrani, just around the headland, a charming knot of whitewashed alleys and arches surrounding a homely piazza and fashionable beach.

To read about:
Targa Florio see page 248
Amalfi Coast Luxuries see page 286

Little Luxuries on the Amalfi Coast

SOUTHERN ITALY/ FOOD & DRINK

The Amalfi Coast has long been famed for its grand beauty and glamour but there is a lot of enjoyment to be found in the smaller details as well. Whether you take in a beautiful sunset, sip on exquisite limoncello or become captain of your own yacht, these experiences will create your own slice of local luxury in this glorious corner of the world.

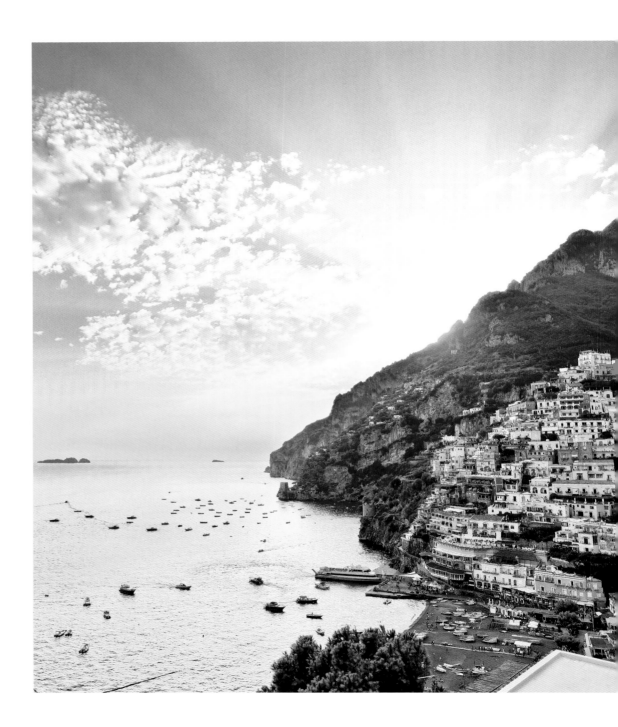

Watch the Sun Set on Positano

Positano is one of the most beautiful towns anywhere in Italy. Arranged around a beach of soft, volcanic sand and the tiled dome of the Church of Santa Maria Assunta are high terraces of terracotta-roofed buildings; these contrast in pink, yellow and brilliant white against the impossibly blue sky and sea. The Sirens in Homer's *Odyssey* lured sailors to their doom on a rocky island by singing a song of seduction, and according to local tradition, that island lies just off the Amalfi Coast.

The Hotel Le Sirenuse is named after these mythical creatures, and its terrace offers what is generally agreed to be the most sublime view of Positano. It also serves the best drinks in town, a good tip to know for that hour when the sun sets and the lights start to twinkle. Were the Sirens really in Positano, they need not have sung for Odysseus – they could just have raised a glass of perfectly chilled prosecco from this terrace, and he would have made a beeline for the treacherous rocks below.

Learn the Secrets of Limoncello

In the terraced groves outside Praiano, Valentino Esposito picks lemons from a tree. Most are the size of two fists, and weigh heavily on the slender branches. He espouses their uses with meat, fish, ice cream and water but the highlight is *limoncello,* the region's traditional and much-loved lemon liqueur, usually served as an after-dinner *digestivo*. Esposito's *limoncello* is so well regarded that chefs Jamie Oliver and Gennaro Contaldo are long-term admirers, and he sometimes hosts picnics for them in his lemon groves.

Back at his small artisan factory, Il Gusto della Costa, Esposito brews some lemon coffee: dark espresso with two thin slices of peel in the pot. Meanwhile, two assistants pour vibrant yellow liquid into glass bottles. Esposito explains how pith makes the liqueur bitter and so the peel should have no pith on it at all. The peel is infused in alcohol for three or four days before a syrup of cold water and sugar is added. Four ingredients and a naturally bright hue. A sip of the stuff is a revelation. It is thick, sweet, potent and full of the fresh, zingy flavour of the Amalfi Coast's most famous fruit. *Limoncello* fans take note: the greener the tinge, the better the drop.

Limoncello is remarkably easy to make. Just make sure you use good unwaxed lemons, even if they are not the sun-kissed variety from Capri. If you read Italian, you'll find a good recipe at www.limoncellodiprocida.it (and they also ship...).

Leap Into the Mediterranean

The waters off Amalfi Town are filled with boats, ranging from modest dinghies to massive super-yachts. Some coves along the coast become floating cities at the weekend, with scores of vessels moored together and parties in full swing. Yet the greatest thrill to be had on the Amalfi Coast is to head out on the open sea. Every town along the coast has a sign reading '*noleggio barche*' (boat hire), indicating that anyone with a few euros to spare can become the captain of his or her own vessel.

Speeding away from the quay, the vastness of the Tyrrhenian Sea and sky opens up ahead. When the sun has heated the varnished wooden deck to the point where it feels like an egg broken on the side would fry in an instant, the time comes. Line up along the side, toes clinging to the edge: three, two, one...with a yell, leap into the warm air and plunge into the sea. For a submerged moment, all around is blissfully cool and quiet. Then bob up again, salty and cool, and scramble back on board to do it all over again.

To read about:
Yachting on the Costa Smeralda see page 274
Palazzi see page 300

Living Luxe on Lake Como

NORTHERN ITALY / LANDSCAPES

Travellers traversing the Alps into Italy descend from the mountains to be greeted by a Mediterranean burst of colour: gardens filled with rose-red camellias and hot-pink oleanders surrounding the cerulean blue of Lake Como. It's impossible not to be seduced. Fishing boats bob in tiny harbours, fighetti (dudes) race their Riva yachts across the lake, and belle époque villas admire their own reflections in the water.

Formed at the end of the last ice age, and a popular holiday spot since Roman times, the Italian lakes have an enduring, beguiling beauty. Of them, Lake Como, which sits in the shadow of the snow-covered Rhaetian Alps and is hemmed in on both sides by steep, forested hills, is the most beautiful. It is littered with historic villages, including exquisite Laglio, Bellagio and Varenna; and, at the southwestern tip, Como, a handsome town, once the centre of the silk trade.

Like the prow of a ship, sitting at the crux of the inverted Y that is the lake, sits Bellagio, the two southern arms of the lake washing off to the port and starboard side. If you wander out of the old town to Punta Spartivento you can gaze north all the way up to the snowy Alps.

For a touch of glamour, consider taking a tour in one of Barindelli's cigarette boats. These leather-seated beauties swoop around Bellagio's headland offering you a peerless view of Villa Serbelloni, built by the Marquis of Stanga in 1508.

West, across the water in Tremezzo, you'll spy flower-fringed Villa Carlotta, named for the Prussian princess who was given it as a wedding gift by her mother in 1847. Inside, its salons are strung with paintings and sculptures by Antonio Canova, while outside its extravagant gardens brim with one of the finest collections of azzaleas and rhododendrons in Europe.

From here you can take a slow ferry to Lenno, where at weekends you can walk the 1km lakeside path to Villa Balbianello amid vegetation so florid as to seem Southeast Asian. This spectacularly sited villa, built by Cardinal Angelo Durini in 1787, has an impressive cinematic pedigree: this is where scenes from the 2006 James Bond *Casino Royale* and the three *Star Wars* prequels were shot. The sculpted gardens, which seem to drip off the high promontory like a melting *gelato*, are the perfect place for romantic couples to spend a day.

Further south still in the villages of Laglio, Cernobbio and Moltrasio 18th- and 19th-century villas line the lake shore, home to Russian oligarchs, global fashion dynasties and Hollywood movie stars such as George Clooney (outside whose home, Villa Oleandra, it is a fineable offence to linger). Drop by Harry's Bar in Cernobbio for a first rate *spritz* with a fine view over the lake or book a front-row table on the romantic terrace at Gatto Nero and enjoy far-reaching views of the lake below.

Finally, you'll find yourself in patrician Como with its 12th-century city walls and beautiful people who wander from shop to cafe, sweeping past the luxurious villas and the loveliness of its lakeshore with admirable insouciance. The town is best for an aimless wander, a quick ride up the Brunate funicular and a walk along Passeggiata Lino Gelpi, which leads along the wisteria-lined shore to the Lido di Villa Olmo where you can plunge into open-air pools and soak up the mountain views.

To read about:

Cioccolato
Per Favore

TURIN / FOOD & DRINK

There is far more to Italian cioccolato (chocolate) than devouring fairy-dust specks of palate-piercing dark chocolate in creamy stracciatella gelato or popping gold-wrapped Ferrero Rocher. Tracing its story is an enriching, tantalising journey through Aztec ritual, royal protocol and artisan tradition. Key stop: Turin (Torino), a deliciously stylish city in Piedmont, Northern Italy, long considered the country's chocolate capital.

Above **Ferrero Rocher**

In 1502, on his penultimate voyage to the Americas, pioneering Genoese explorer Christopher Columbus – Cristoforo Colombo to fellow Italians – returned to Europe, Jack and the Beanstalk-style, with a stash of unknown cocoa beans in hand. But royals at the Spanish court spurned the dull-looking beans for glitzier, gold and silver New World treasures and it was not for several more decades that Europe would embrace chocolate.

Enter Modica, a gravity-defying medieval hilltop town on the island of Sicily with baroque cathedral, monumental churches and cult-status chocolate. The cacao arrived from Mexico in the 1580s with Sicily's Spanish overlords. The conquistadors also brought with them the Aztecs' ancient tribal recipe for *xocóatl,* a buttery chocolatey paste – subsequently watered down and drunk – made by grinding raw cocoa beans against a stone slab. Just as the Aztecs flavoured *xocóatl* to make the bitter brew more palatable, so Modica's contemporary chocolate makers add chilli, cinnamon and orange peel to the utterly unique chocolate bars they craft using the same cold-pressed method. Unlike conventional chocolate, Modica chocolate is not conched or tempered, resulting in its notably gritty, unrefined texture. Antica Dolceria Bonajuto, a sixth-generation artisanal chocolatier in Modica with an 1880 pedigree, is one of the world's few chocolatiers that crafts dark chocolate in this way.

Cocoa arrived on mainland Italy with the marriage of Catherine Michelle of Spain to Charles Emmanuel I, Duke of Savoy, in 1585. Again, it was only drunk at first. In 1678 the first commercial chocolate house serving fashionable tea cups of *cioccolato caldo* (hot chocolate) opened in Turin, city of the Savoy court, and by the mid-18th century Turin chocolatiers were producing some 350kg of chocolate a day.

But the real game-changer came in 1778. A Frenchman in Turin called Doret invented a hydraulic machine to grind cocoa beans and mix the resultant butter with vanilla and sugar to create sweet, bite-sized pralines – the world's first solid chocolate form. Englishman Joseph Fry (1728–87) subsequently refined the process to create chocolate bars, but for aficionados of Italian chocolate, Turin is still *cioccolato* queen. Strolling its tree-lined boulevards, peppered with art nouveau cafes tucked beneath arcades and wood-panelled confectioner shops heavy with the scent of freshly roasted cocoa and coffee beans, is a gourmet treat. At Caffè Al Bicerin tall glasses of *bicerin* – a bittersweet mix of homemade chocolate, coffee and cream – have been served beneath gilded chandeliers since 1763. Fuelling the likes of Dumas, Puccini, Nietzsche and Calvino, along with Savoy royalty and Turin's workers, the price didn't rise for a century to ensure no one missed out on the signature drink.

Italy also gave the world the original Nutella. During the Napoleonic Wars (1803–15) the price of cocoa beans rocketed, prompting Turin chocolate-makers to substitute some of the gold-dust beans with their own sweet hazelnuts (the world's most expensive) that grew in abundance in the nearby Langhe hills of southern Piedmont. The combo was an instant hit. At Turin's traditional Mardi Gras carnival in 1865, local chocolate maker Caffarel distributed handfuls of *gianduiotto* – miniature pyramids of toasted hazelnut cream, coated in chocolate and wrapped in gold foil (the world's first individually wrapped chocolates). During WWII rationing, Alba confectioner Pietro Ferrero again utilised the region's indigenous hazelnut booty to create *pasta gianduja*, a chocolate-hazelnut loaf eaten in slices as an affordable chocolate alternative. Within a few years, it had been superseded by a spreadable *supercrema* and in 1964 the latter was popped in a glass jar and renamed Nutella.

Nineteenth-century industrialisation cemented Turin's status as chocolate capital of Italy: Turin-born Venchi (founded 1878) became a household name with its *nougatines* (caramelised hazelnuts enrobed in dark chocolate); Peyrano (founded 1914) created *Dolci Momenti a Torino* (Sweet Moments in Turin); Pepino invented ice cream dipped in chocolate on a stick in 1937; Ferrero fathered Kinder eggs in the 1960s and its iconic hazelnut-filled *rocher* in 1982.

The Piedmont region currently produces 40% (or 77,000 tons a year) of all Italian chocolate, although it's Turin's third-wave master chocolatiers – smaller producers for whom expert craft and bespoke quality are paramount – who pose the ultimate temptation: Domori crafts single-origin chocolate (with tasting notes and pairings) from aromatic Criollo cocoa beans grown on its own plantations in Venezuela; Guido Gobino's bean-to-bar artisanal *gianduiotto* is the silkiest in town. *Buono degustazione!*

To read about:

Italian Wine see page 70
Tiramisu see page 268

A Night at the Opera

ITALY-WIDE / MUSIC

Whether it's track pants and Verdi at the stadium or tuxedos and Puccini at La Scala, Italy's opera legacy remains a source of national pride. Home to four of the world's great opera houses and to the biggest open-air lyrical music event in the world, Italy is the veritable home of the art form.

Right **Puccini's** *Tosca*

Not only did Italy invent opera, it gave the world some of its greatest composers and compositions. Gioachino Rossini (1792–1868) transformed Pierre Beaumarchais' *Le Barbier de Séville* (The Barber of Seville) into one of the greatest comedic operas, Giuseppe Verdi (1813–1901) produced the epic *Aida,* while Giacomo Puccini (1858–1924) delivered staples such as *Tosca, Madama Butterfly* and *Turandot.*

The opera season traditionally runs from mid-October to March but summer seasons in Rome and Verona take advantage of balmy nights with some spectacular outdoor events. Verona's Arena Opera festival sees 14,000 music lovers fill the Roman Arena and light their candles at sunset. It's a goosebump-inducing effect, even before the performance starts.

The word *diva* was invented for legendary sopranos such as Parma's Renata Tebaldi and Italy's adopted Greek icon Maria Callas, whose rivalry peaked when *Time* quoted Callas saying that comparing her voice to Tebaldi's was like comparing Champagne and Coca-Cola. Both were fixtures at La Scala, along with the wildly popular Italian tenor Enrico Caruso, to whom others are still compared. Tenor Luciano Pavarotti remains beloved for attracting broader public attention to opera, while best-selling, blind tenor Andrea Bocelli became a controversial crossover sensation with what critics claim are over-produced arias.

Opera fans at any venue, outdoors or otherwise, can be just as ruthless as their counterparts at the football. Performers dread the sound of *fischi* (mocking whistles), which possess a mysterious power to blast singers right off stage. In December 2006, a substitute in street clothes

Dolce Vita / 293

Armchair Opera

To experience opera without leaving your living room, check out the Opera Platform (www.theopera platform.eu), a free service that streams performances from Turin's acclaimed Teatro Regio. If you're interested in hearing more, Rossini's *Le Barbier de Séville,* Verdi's epic *Aida,* and Puccini's *Tosca, Madama Butterfly* and *Turandot* are some of the Italian greats, along with the following performers.

Luciano Pavarotti The beloved tenor with mass crossover appeal.

Fiorenze Cedolins Performed a requiem for the late Pope John Paul II and scored encores in Puccini's iconic *La Bohème.*

Francesco Meli A celebrated tenor and regular fixture at many of the world's great opera houses.

Salvatore Licitra Famed for stepping in for Pavarotti in his final show at New York's Metropolitan Opera, the 43-year-old died tragically after a motorcycle accident in 2011.

had to step in for Sicilian-French star tenor Roberto Alagna when his off-night aria met with vocal disapproval at Milan's legendary La Scala.

To read about:
La Scala see page 202
Italy on Screen see page 276

Fine Dining Italian-Style

ITALY-WIDE / FOOD & DRINK

Gastronomy is one of Italy's raisons d'être. Brimming with superlative produce, finely tuned culinary know-how and centuries of recipes shared between generations, the country is a gargantuan kitchen where it takes real effort to eat badly – Italian home cooking, trattoria (bistro) fare, even fast food are all insanely delicious and memorable. So here's why it's still worth it to splurge on a fine meal.

The history of the Italian *cucina* (kitchen) is a veritable rollercoaster ride of affluence and poverty resulting in the creation of a cuisine that is one of the most regional in the world: only in Italy do you eat risotto and polenta, couscous and strudel, tripe and bloody blue T-bone steak, over 200 pasta types and more than 500 different cheeses – each a perfect reflection of its geographic origin – in their own special part of the country. It is this extraordinary grass-roots commitment that fuels the work of Italy's most prized, fine-dining *ristorante* (restaurants) as chefs take local, traditional dishes to an entirely new, gastronomic level. Creativity and regional pride are their mantra.

Clever, occasionally wild, interpretations of ancient staples and recipes is one brilliant aspect of Italian fine dining. In a reclaimed 19th-century warehouse in Florence in Tuscany, capital city of one of the most gourmet regions on Italian Earth, talented young chef Simone Cipriani re-invents ancient Tuscan recipes such as *pappa al pomodoro* (tomato and bread soup) to dazzling effect in his loft-style restaurant called Essenziale. If you're lucky, it is the chef himself – a serious game-changer on the gastronomic scene – who brings the dish to your table and treats you to a detailed explanation: the tale behind his remarkable Fior d'Evo dessert, notably with kale (another of his desserts includes artichokes), is unforgettable. Moving south to Rome, Colombian-born chef Roy Caceres at Metamorfosi morphs Italian classics into playful works of art: the Michelin-starred chef's signature Uovo 65° carbonara *antipasto* is an eclectic deconstruction of Rome's traditional pasta dish and a

much-welcome breath of fresh air for any-one who has already dined in the staunch-ly conservative capital for a few days. In Pompeii, President – another of Italy's best-priced Michelin-starred restaurants – serves whimsical re-interpretations of Campanian cuisine.

A fervent veneration of an exceptional, usually seasonal, local product (hazelnuts in Piedmont, black truffles in Umbria etc) is another thing Italy's beloved fine-dining chefs do awfully well. Table reservations open the first day of the month for the following four months at Enrico Crippa's triple Michelin-starred restaurant, Piazza Duomo, in Alba, a small town in the vine-striped Langhe hills in Piedmont, North-ern Italy. Foodies flock here from all over the world in autumn and winter to revel in the extraordinary aroma, taste and experi-ence of much-revered local white truffles. The striking, fleshy-pink dining room is the epitome of elegance and gracious living. Start with a salad containing 21, 31, 41 or 51 different seasonal ingredients – lots of leaves, watercress, beetroot, Mordigallina Flower and primrose among them, all lov-ingly grown in the restaurant greenhouse and served, it should be added, with a pair of tweezers allowing diners to delicately pick out and slowly revel in the unique taste of each rarified leaf.

Extraordinary, effortlessly romantic settings are another big attraction of Italy's fine-dines: Renaissance cloisters, vintage chapels, garden-graced *palazzi*, all with sensational views. In Rome, Michelin-starred rooftop restaurant Aroma has 'marry-me' vistas over the Colosseum; La Veranda offers fine-dining beneath 15th-century Pinturicchio frescoes; and Antonello Colonna Open lounges beneath

a soaring glass ceiling on a star-topped mezzanine in Palazzo degli Esposizioni. In Venice, on the banks of the Giudecca Ca-nal, Riviera marries feather-light gnocchi and lagoon crab with heartbreaking views of Venetian domes and hot-pink sunsets. *Buon appetito!*

To read about:
Truffles see page 102
Aperitivo Time see page 182

A Walk in the Park

ITALY-WIDE / PARKS & GARDENS

For every resplendent Italian villa there is at least one similarly beguiling garden. Italians practically invented the modern notion of gardening, designing their multi-functional green spaces with an eye for art and aesthetics as much as plant production and horticulture. It's a line that begins with the Romans and can be traced through the Renaissance to the majestic, often flamboyant, sanctuaries that embellish the peninsula today.

Right **Vatican Gardens**, Rome

Since 1997, Italy's finest gardens have been sheltered under the umbrella of the Grandi Giardini Italiani, a network of over 120 leafy domains, most of which are open to the public. The organisation's collection of gardens is hugely varied. Some are botanical, packed with exotic plants and managed by local universities; others are connected to palatial villas; several, including sculpture-filled Negombo on the Neapolitan island of Ischia, are de facto art gardens. A few enclaves are more unusual and esoteric. The Parco di Monza just north of Milan is not only the largest walled park in Europe, it also hosts the annual Italian Grand Prix motor race. The Castello di San Pelagio near Padua is an aviation museum where a winding maze and an aromatic rose garden are juxtaposed against a smattering of vintage fighter planes and helicopters.

In a country dripping in history there are plenty of gardens that evoke memories of the past. A large portion of Rome's Vatican City is given over to the papal gardens, the oldest in Italy, originally conceived by Pope Nicholas III in the late 13th century but re-landscaped and improved by Pope Julius II two hundred years later. Open for guided tours since 2002, the 23-hectare grounds take up more than half the tiny city-state's land area. They are dotted with fountains and archaeological remains, and doused with a tangible atmosphere of peace and spirituality.

While Italy's enthusiasm for gardening dates back to the Romans, the style and aesthetics that characterise its green spaces today were solidified during the Renaissance. Starting in the early 1500s, architects Niccolo Tribolo and Pirro Ligorio began landscaping the grounds of opulent mansions such as the Villa d'Este in Tivoli and the Medici Villas in Florence with the aim of creating gardens that weren't just small crop-growing farms but also spirit-enlightening places of beauty and nature. Down came walls and barriers; up went fountains, classical statues and geometrically laid out hedges and trees.

Italy's Renaissance gardens soon became the blueprint against which all others were measured, as architecturally accomplished as the villas and palaces with which they were associated. Leading examples included the gardens of Villa Garzoni near Lucca in Tuscany with their symmetrical staircases and elegant balustrades; the historic grounds of the Villa Borghese Cavazza cocooned on an island in Lake Garda; and the so-called 'sacred wood' of Bomarzo in Lazio where fantastical animal sculptures have been known to inspire poets and artists, Salvador Dalí among them.

A central ethos of the Grandi Giardini Italiani is the accessibility of its gardens to the general public. As well as listing regular opening hours, the association also sponsors numerous garden-hosting events. Some, such as an annual children's Easter-egg hunt, take place simultaneously in over two dozen gardens. Others, including flower shows, historical tours, music concerts and art expos, are more specific and spontaneous. What makes them all so special is the venues in which they play out – foliage-filled realms full of artistry and creativity that are as grand and monumental as anything Michelangelo produced.

Tivoli Gardens

If St Peter's Basilica is the pinnacle of Italian church-building then, just outside Rome, Tivoli's Villa d'Este marks the apex of Italian gardening. A steeply terraced garden complex endowed with serene fountains, landscaped grottoes and classical sculptures was fashioned in the 1550s by Cardinal Ippolito II who raided the erstwhile villa of Roman emperor Hadrian for much of his decor. The Tivoli remains one of Italy's oldest and most iconic gardens and is an early example of an Italian Renaissance garden, an expansive green space that re-examined the gardens of classical Rome. It provided plenty of inspiration for composer Franz Liszt who stayed at Tivoli between 1865 and 1886 and immortalised it in his 1877 piano composition *The Fountains of the Villa d'Este*.

To read about:
The Vatican see page 92
Villa Gardens see page 300

Clockwise from top left **Parco di Monza**, Milan; **Medici Villas**, Florence; **Villa Borghese Cavazza**, Isola del Garda; **Villa d'Este**, Tivoli

A Palazzo Here, a Villa There

ITALY-WIDE / PALACES & VILLAS

From Florence's blockbuster Palazzo Pitti, designed by iconic architect Brunelleschi for a wealthy banker in the 15th century, to Andrea Palladio's classically arcaded Villa di Masèr in the Veneto countryside, Italy is peppered with sensational palaces and villas, built for the royal and wealthy during the Renaissance. With the right address in hand, romantics can kip the night in luxury.

Heart of the Roman Empire and birthplace of the Renaissance, Italy is a place where grandiose history looms large. It slips quietly beneath your skin, gnaws at your soul, is impossible to resist with its bottomless chest of fabulous stories and unfaltering romance – which is why staying in a historic *palazzo* (palace) or villa (no ghosts involved, promise) is considered to be the only proper way to do Italy.

The earliest *palazzi* graced the Romanesque and Gothic periods in the 10th and 12th centuries. But it was with the Renaissance, from the 15th century, that *palazzi* took off as noble families, rich from new trade opportunities, had palatial mansions built in towns and cities to reflect their newfound wealth. Many commissioned summer villas, from modest to sublimely decadent, in the surrounding countryside.

Palazzo accommodation transcends budget. In Florence, kick back like a down-and-out king on the cinematic loggia terrace of 16th-century Palazzo Guadagni –

an artfully revamped Renaissance palace hotel – and swoon over bird's-eye views of lively Piazza Santa Spirito: Zeffirelli shot scenes of *Tea with Mussolini* (1999) here. Or check into Hotel Scoti, squirrelled away in a *palazzo* between designer fashion shops on the city's smartest shopping strip and rub shoulders with blue-blooded nobles on the sweeping staircase. In Genoa, stay in rarefied splendour at Palazzo Morali, a B&B embellished with gold-leafed four-poster beds, gilt-framed mirrors and Genovese art. All three addresses are – happy sigh – decidedly budget in price.

Or blow the budget. Luxurious *palazzo* hotels are plentiful in Venice where guests at the Gritti Palace (1525) on the Grand Canal don't leave their balconies to go sightseeing: the landmark doge's *palazzo* is an opulent orgy of Rubelli-silk-damask-lined-rooms, antique fainting couches, stucco ceilings, hand-painted vanities and bathrooms sheathed in rare marble.

At nearby Palazzo Abadessa (1540), staff fluff pillows, ply guests with prosecco, arrange gondolas to the opera, plot irresistible marriage proposals and serve breakfast in an enchanting, tree-shaded, lily-perfumed garden.

Should you not be overnighting, a cocktail or dinner can be the perfect taster of noble lifestyle. In Rome consider Michelin-starred Enoteca La Torre inside Villa Laetitia and Zuma, the fashionista rooftop bar in the family palazzo of luxury fashion brand Fendi. Does *la vita* (life) get any more *bella* (beautiful)?

To read about:

Italian Art see page 58
Italian Architecture see page 64

Right The Gritti Palace, a Luxury Collection Hotel, Venice

The Versailles of Italy: Reggia di Caserta

SOUTHERN ITALY / PALACES

The one compelling reason to stop at the otherwise nondescript town of Caserta, 30km north of Naples, is to gasp at the colossal, World Heritage–listed Reggia di Caserta, which began life in 1752 after Charles VII ordered a palace to rival Versailles. Bigger than its French rival, it was reputedly the largest building in 18th-century Europe.

With its 1200 rooms, 1790 windows, 34 staircases and 250m-long facade, and film credits including *Mission: Impossible 3* and the interior shots of Queen Amidala's palace in *Star Wars Episode 1: The Phantom Menace* and *Star Wars Episode 2: Attack of the Clones*, this former royal residence is Italy's monumental swansong to the baroque.

Vanvitelli's immense staircase leads up to the royal apartments, lavishly decorated with frescoes, art, tapestries, period furniture and crystal. The restored back rooms off the Sala di Astrea house an extraordinary collection of historic wooden models of the Reggia, along with architectural drawings and early sketches of the building by Luigi Vanvitelli and his son, Carlo.

The apartments are also home to the Mostra Terrea Motus, an underrated collection of international modern art commissioned after the region's devastating earthquake in 1980. Among the contributors are US heavyweights Cy Twombly and Robert Mapplethorpe, as well as local luminaries Mimmo Paladino and Jannis Kounellis.

To clear your head afterwards, explore the elegant landscaped park, which stretches for some 3km to a waterfall and a fountain of Diana. Within the park is the famous Giardino Inglese (English Garden), a romantic oasis of intricate pathways, exotic flora, pools and cascades.

To read about:
La Bella Figura see page 200
Grandi Giardini see page 296

VENICE

The Most Serene One

Venice is sheer madness. That this floating city of marble palaces and glassy canals was ever built above a wave-tossed lagoon is audacious, but that it became a maritime and artistic force to reckon with is testament to the undying romance and tenacity of the Venetians themselves. Laughing brazenly in the face of the acqua alta that threatens to eventually sink it, La Serenissima (the Most Serene One) has all the mystic and fairy-tale allure of the next Atlantis.

The fact that Venice is slowly slipping into the lagoon has done nothing to hold back the tides of art that it has given to the world over centuries. Artists, poets, writers, composers and Hollywood filmmakers have for centuries been in its thrall: from Shakespeare to Lord Byron, Proust to Monet. Stand on the Ponte dei Sospiri (Bridge of Sighs) as the light of evening creeps across the crumbling, pastel-hued facades of ornate palazzi and the songs of gondoliers reverberate into the blue dusk, and in a pinch-yourself moment you can picture yourself in a Canaletto painting.

Nudging past the crowds on Piazza San Marco, you'll blink in disbelief at Palazzo San Marco's riot of Byzantine domes glittering in 24-carat gold leaf, and the lacy pink Gothic Palazzo Ducale, once the doge's residence. Across the canal, the Dorsoduro district's show-stopping Galleria dell'Accademia is a romp through the Venetian school of Renaissance painting, with Bellini, Titian, Tintoretto and Veronese masterpieces. Edging north to the San Polo and Santa Croce neighbour-hoods reveals more art treasures: Scuola Grande's uplifting Tintoretto ceiling and Italian-brick Gothic church I Frari, hiding Titian's *Assunta* (Assumption) altarpiece. Further north still, Cannaregio and the Ghetto provide an insight into Jewish life in their recently revamped Museo Ebraico and synagogues. Turkish merchants and Slavic labourers once did trade in Castello, on Venice's eastern fringes, where you can now dine like a doge and drink like a sailor.

Nowhere in Italy does *la dolce vita* better than Venice. Dodge the masses and this is a festive, ravishing feast of a city, whether you're partying at masked balls at Carnevale, gazing up at coloured Murano chandeliers, gorging on spice-route flavours in *osterie* (casual taverns), haggling for lagoon crab at Rialto's 600-year-old fish market, drinking a *spritz* (prosecco and Aperol) with *cicheti* (bar snacks) as day fades into watercolour sunset, or dancing a tango at a piazza-side cafe. Eccentric to the last, Venice is there for the embracing. For now, anyway.

Right Piazza San Marco

CARNEVALE SEASON

VENICE / FESTIVALS

Masqueraders party in the streets of Venice for the two weeks preceding Shrove Tuesday. A Cannaregio Canal flotilla marks the outbreak of festivities, which feature processions and masked balls. Ball tickets can run up to about €800, but there's no shortage of less expensive diversions, from costume competitions in Piazza San Marco to public parties in every campo (square).

To read about:

Saints, Feasts & Festivals see page 168
Vogalonga see page 310

LIFE ON WATER

VENICE / CULTURE

In Italo Calvino's Invisible Cities, Venetian explorer Marco Polo describes the cities he's seen to Kublai Khan – only everywhere he describes is actually Venice. From the moment you arrive, you'll understand why. No one comes to Venice and fails to be struck by the uniqueness of this city of marble palaces floating in the midst of its fragile lagoon.

From their beloved morning *spritz* to the odd things they eat, the byzantine way they do business and their talent for non-linear navigation, Venetians are a product of the lagoon within which they live. Like all lagoons, it is a continually evolving environment although through careful interventions, it is the only one in the world to have maintained its equilibrium for more than 1000 years, the only survivor of a system of estuarine lagoons that in Roman times extended from Ravenna to Trieste. In fact, the world *laguna* (lagoon) is Venetian.

To really understand Venice, you have to see the city as Venetians do. Early birds can make a start with Getty photographer Marco Secchi, who hosts photography walks and workshops through the quieter corners of the city, showing you how to train your eye to make the most of the extraordinary light and how to capture the beguiling mirage-like effect of the city's endless reflections in teal-coloured canals.

Venetian author Tiziano Scarpa reveals the strange psychological impact living in an insular medieval city in the midst of a lagoon has on its residents. His best-selling book *Venice is a Fish* (2008) offers a psycho-geographic tour of Venice's labyrinthine layout, which requires you to think through the soles of your feet, and explains why the Venetian space-time continuum is shaped more by the moon and tides than it is by the 24-hour clock.

But nothing connects you with Venice's shape-shifting character more than stepping up on the stern of a *coda di gambero* (shrimp-tailed boat) and taking a lesson in *voga alla Veneta* (Venetian-style stand-up rowing) with regatta winners at Row

Venice. For thousands of years this was the only way to navigate the shallow bowl of the lagoon with its ribbed, sandy channels, tall grasses and marshes. Standing up and facing forward gives a good view over reeds and water, while placing the oar to one side facilitates manoeuvrability within the intricate canal system.

It's a peculiar experience – the 4m-long oar is heavy and cumbersome to start with before you get the hang of the rhythmic rocking motion of leaning in to the *prèmer* (push), angling the oar downwards, and pulling back for the *stalìr* (return stroke). It feels a bit like weight-lifting while surfing. The rewards though are worthwhile. Gliding down the glassy green canals you suddenly find yourself moving within a view that other travellers only get to glance across – it's like entering another dimension.

Offering the same magic without the pirouetting skill of a gondolier, kayaking is perhaps the most fun of all Venice's watery pursuits. Well-planned tours take you into the warren of Venice's canals alongside police boats, fire boats and floating funeral hearses, or out to remote islands in the broad garden of the lagoon.

Continue the gondolier-theme by lunching alongside them at Osteria Ruga di Jaffa, a casual tavern with artsy wall lamps, hiding in plain sight on the busy Ruga Giuffa. You should be able to spot it by the gondoliers packing out the tables at lunchtime; they come to feast on the massive serves of pasta and delicious homemade bread.

Head to Rio di San Trovaso to spy gondolas being made in a wood-brick cabin that may look like a stray ski chalet, but is one of Venice's handful of working *squeri*

Mazzorbo's Micro-Vineyard

Wine has been produced in Venice and its lagoon for centuries, and now Gianluca and Desiderio Bisol, one of Prosecco's leading producers, have heavily invested in replanting a micro-vineyard in the lagoon, on the near-deserted island of Mazzorbo. They have chosen an all-but-forgotten native grape, Dorona, and while the yields are very small, the wine, named Venissa, is quite incredible, especially considering the vineyard is almost a 'non-terroir', with sandy, salty soil right at sea level.

The grapes are vinified in Tuscany, at Montalcino, but visitors here are treated to a tasting in the ancient wine tenuta (estate) and a tour of the vineyard (www.venissa.it). You can stay overnight in their small hotel, and dine in a Michelin-starred restaurant overlooking the vines.

(shipyards), complete with refinished gondolas drying in the yard. When the door's open, you can peek inside in exchange for a donation left in the basket by the door. To avoid startling gondola-builders working with sharp tools, no flash photography is allowed.

On the bank nearby, drop in to legendary Cantinone Gia' Schiavi, a lively bacaro known to all Venetians as the Bottegon – 'the storeroom'. Opened 120 years ago, the bar has been overseen for more than 50 years by one Sandra de Respinis, arguably Venice's queen of *cicheti*. Her speciality is rough slices of crusty bread

topped off with a cornucopia of different ingredients, and Sandra has created more than 70 different recipes, creating each one like an alchemist. She makes at least 500 *cicheti* a day, including such bites as delicious aged provolone cheese with pickled wild fennel leaves, tuna tartare sprinkled with cocoa powder or creamy Gorgonzola and crunchy apple drizzled with balsamic vinegar. Regulars gamely pass along orders to timid newcomers, who might otherwise miss out on delights such as smoked swordfish *cicheti* with top-notch house Soave or *pallottoline* (mini-bottles of beer) with generous *sopressa* panini. Chaos cheerfully prevails as Accademia art historians and tourists rub shoulders with San Trovaso gondola builders without spilling a drop.

Venice's most popular, non-competitive regatta, the annual Vogalonga, held in May, is a vital reminder of Venice's reliance on the lagoon. Established in 1975 as a protest against the damage caused to the foundations of the city by the waves from the wake of motorboats, it is the only day of the year when motorised traffic is banned from the Grand Canal and parts of the 30km lagoon circuit.

Unlike Carnevale, this is a real celebration of *vera venezianità* (true Venetianness) when residents are more important than tourists and the deep connection between the lagoon and the city is evident to see.

To read about:
Yachting on the Costa Smeralda see page 274
Palazzi see page 300

Right Vogalonga regatta, Grand Canal

Index

Image Credits

Behind the Scenes

Associate Product Director Kirsten Rawlings
Series Designer Campbell McKenzie
Senior Product Editor Kate Chapman
Cartographic Designer Wayne Murphy
Product Editor Alison Ridgway
Book Designer Mazzy Prinsep
Senior Cartographer Diana Von Holdt

Written by Bonnie Alberts, Sarah Barrell, Oliver Berry, Alison Bing, Abigail Blasi, Cristian Bonetto, John Brunton, Alex Butler, Kerry Christiani, Gregor Clark, Dan Cruickshank, Francesco da Mosto, Matthew Fort, Paula Hardy, Abigail Hole, James Martin, Annemarie McCarthy, Stephen Mc-Clarence, Kate Morgan, Tim Parks, Olivia Pozzan, Brendan Sainsbury, Simon Sellars, Oliver Smith, Marcel Theroux, Orla Thomas, Alex Von Tunzelmann, Tony Wheeler, Nicola Williams, Lonely Planet Travel News (www.lonelyplanet.com/news)

Thanks to Will Allen, Robin Barton, Bridget Blair, Meri Blazevski, Cheree Broughton, Hannah Cartmel, Barbara Di Castro, Grace Dobell, Sasha Drew, Evan Godt, Shona Gray, James Hardy, Victoria Harrison, Noirin Hegarty, Liz Heynes, Simon Hoskins, Indra Kilfoyle, Alison Lyall, Katherine Marsh, Jean-Pierre Masclef, Anne Mason, Fin McCarthy, Jenna Myers, Catherine Naghten, Darren O'Connell, Lauren O'Connell, Anthony Phelan, Piers Pickard, Martine Power, Rachel Rawling, Kathryn Rowan, Wibowo Rusli, Diana Saengkham, Vicky Smith, Lyahna Spencer, Kate Sullivan, Anna Tyler, Tracy Whitmey, Juan Winata, Chris Zeiher

Published by Lonely Planet Global Limited
CRN 554153

1st edition – April 2018
ISBN 9781787013315

© Lonely Planet 2018
Photographs © as indicated 2018
Printed in Malaysia
10 9 8 7 6 5 4 3 2 1

LONELY PLANET OFFICES

Australia
The Malt Store, Level 3, 551 Swanston Street, Carlton, VIC 3053
Phone 03 8379 8000

United Kingdom
240 Blackfriars Road, London SE1 8NW
Phone 020 3771 5100

USA
124 Linden St, Oakland, CA 94607
Phone 510 250 6400

Ireland
Digital Depot, Roe Lane (off Thomas St), Digital Hub, Dublin 8, D08 TCV4

STAY IN TOUCH lonelyplanet.com/contact